The Illustrator 8
Wow!
Book

Sharon Steuer

The Illustrator 8 Wow! Book

Sharon Steuer

Peachpit Press
1249 Eighth Street
Berkeley, CA 94710
510/524-2178
510/524-2221 (fax)

Peachpit Press is a division of Addison Wesley Longman.

ISBN 0-201-35399-7
0 9 8 7 6 5 4 3 2 1

Printed and bound in the United States of America.

Revision Production Credits

Author & Curator: Sharon Steuer

Book Designer: Barbara Sudick

Preface, Chapter 1 & Intros Revision Co-author: Robin AF Olson

Revisions Tech Editor: Sandy Alves

Contributing Writers: Sandy Alves, Mordy Golding, Sandee Cohen

Wow! CD-ROM Coordinator: Diane Hinze Kanzler

Wow! CD-ROM Mastering: Victor Gavenda

Wow! Testers: Lisa Jackmore, Richard Marchessault, Adam Z Lein

Assistant to the Author: Peg Maskell Korn

Revisions Copyeditors: Gail Nelson, Karen Unger

Revised Index: Peg Maskell Korn

Cover Art-direction: Barbara Sudick

Front Cover Illustration: Nancy Stahl

Back Cover Illustrations: Ivan Torres, Sharon Steuer, Lisa Jackmore

Kibbitzer: Sandee Cohen

Caterer: Jeff Jacoby

Comedy Relief: Puma and Bear

Important: Read me first!

This book has been designed to help you harness the enormous power of Adobe Illustrator by providing you with hundreds of pages of useful production techniques, timesaving tips and beautiful art generously shared by *Illustrator Wow!* artists nationwide. Whether you're a recent convert to Illustrator, or one of the thousands of Illustrator experts who haven't had the time to learn the newer features, this book is for you. All techniques were kept deliberately short to allow you to squeeze in a lesson or two between clients, and to encourage the use of this book within the confines of a supervised classroom.

In order to keep the content in this book tantalizing to everyone—from novice to expert—I've assumed a reasonable level of competence with basic Mac and Windows concepts such as opening and saving files, launching applications, copying objects to the clipboard, and doing mouse operations. I've also assumed that you've completed the tutorials on the Adobe Illustrator CDs, and understand the basic functionality of the tools.

I'd love to tell you that you can learn Adobe Illustrator by flipping through the pages of this book, but the reality is, there is no substitute for practice. The good news is, the more you work with Illustrator, the more features you'll be able to integrate into your creative process.

Use this book as a reference, a guide for special techniques, or just a source of inspiration. After you've read this book, read it again, and you'll undoubtedly learn something you missed the first time. As I hope you'll discover, the more experienced you become with Adobe Illustrator, the easier it will be to assimilate all the new information and inspiration you'll find in this book. Happy Illustrating!

Sharon Steuer

Sharon Steuer

How to use this book...

Before you do anything else, read the *Wow! Glossary* on the pull-out quick reference card at the back of the book. The *Glossary* provides definitions for the terms used throughout *The Illustrator 8 Wow! Book* (such as: ⌘ = the Command key for Mac/the Control key for Windows, or what "toggle" means).

WELCOME TO *WOW!* FOR WINDOWS AND MAC

If you already use Adobe Photoshop 4 or later, you'll see many interface similarities to Illustrator 8. Adobe intends this version of Illustrator to create, in part, a common look and feel across Photoshop, PageMaker and Illustrator. The change should make the time you spend on learning each program much shorter (especially if you're a newcomer to all three products). Your productivity should also increase across the board once you adjust to the new shortcuts and methodologies (see "Shortcuts and keystrokes" following, and page 3).

Setting up your palettes

In terms of following along with the lessons in this book, you'll probably want to disable the "Type Area Select" option (see the red Tip on page 133). Next, I recommend you view swatches as sorted by name: hold down Option (Alt) and choose "Name" from the Swatches pop-up menu to list all Swatch views by name (see at right).

By default, Illustrator sometimes has the habit of filling palettes with excess styles; to customize the default styles loaded into new documents, see the "Startup" Tip on page 26. To clear out an existing palette of unwanted, unused styles, first click on the All Swatches icon, then choose "Select All Unused" from the Swatches pop-up, and immediately click the Trash icon to remove these unwanted extras—sometimes you'll have to repeat the select-and-delete procedure to ensure the palette is cleared (please see the "Caution" Tip on page 48).

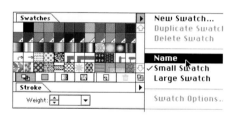

With the All Swatches icon selected and the Option (Alt) key pressed, choosing "Name" from the Swatches pop-up

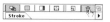

Choosing Select All Unused from the Swatches pop-up; then immediately clicking the Trash icon to safely remove unused swatches

Shortcuts and keystrokes

To simplify the reading of this book, keyboard shortcuts are given almost exclusively in Macintosh terminology—if you're on Windows, simply substitute **Ctrl** (Control) for ⌘, and **Alt** for Option. On the *Wow!* disk you'll find "Adam Z's Shortcuts Kit," which, along with the "Shortcuts" listing found in the Help menu, can be printed and kept tucked into the book.

For details on recent improvements to Illustrator tool and menu navigation (such as single key tool access and Tab to hide palettes), please refer to *Chapter 1.*

HOW THIS BOOK IS ORGANIZED...

You'll find six kinds of information woven throughout this book—all of it up-to-date for Illustrator 8: **Basics**, **Tips**, **Exercises**, **Techniques**, **Galleries** and **References**.

1 Basics. *Chapter 1: Illustrator Basics* and *Chapter 2: The Zen of Illustrator* qualify as full-blown chapters on basics and are packed with information that distills and supplements your Adobe Illustrator manuals and disks. Every chapter starts with a general overview of the basics. Although these sections have been designed so that advanced users of Illustrator can move quickly through them, I strongly suggest that the rest of you read them very carefully. Please keep in mind that this book serves as a supplement to, not a substitute for, your Adobe Illustrator *User Guides* and CD-ROM.

2 Tips. Look to the information in the gray and red boxes for hands-on tips that can help you work more efficiently. Usually you can find tips alongside related textual information, but if you are in too impatient a mood to read a section in depth, you might just want to flip through, looking for tips that are of interest to you. The red arrows ➞, red outlines and red text found in tips (and sometimes with artwork) have been added to emphasize or further explain a concept or technique.

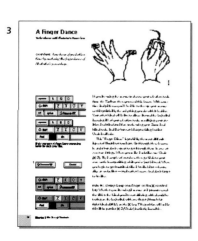

Tip boxes

Look for these gray boxes to find Tips about Adobe Illustrator.

Red Tip boxes

The red Tip boxes contain warnings or other essential information.

3 Exercises. (Not for the faint of heart.) I have included intermediate-level, step-by-step exercises to help you make the transition to Illustrator technician extraordinaire. *Chapter 2: The Zen of Illustrator* and the *Zen Lessons* on the *Wow!* disk are dedicated to helping you master the mechanics, and the soul, of Illustrator. Take these lessons in small doses, in order, and at a relaxed pace.

4 Techniques. In these sections, you'll find step-by-step techniques gathered from almost a hundred *Illustrator Wow!* artists. Most *Wow!* techniques focus on one aspect of how an image was created, though I'll often refer you to different *Wow!* chapters (or to a specific page where a technique is introduced) to give you the opportunity to explore a briefly-covered feature in more depth. Feel free to start with almost any chapter, but, since each technique builds on those previously explained, try to follow the techniques within each chapter sequentially. Some chapters conclude with an **Advanced Technique**, which assumes that you have assimilated all of the techniques found throughout the chapter. *Chapter 8: Masks & Special Effects* is an entire chapter dedicated to advanced tips, tricks and techniques.

5 Galleries. The gallery pages consist of images related to techniques demonstrated nearby. Each gallery piece is accompanied by a description of how the artist created that image, and may include steps showing the progression of a technique detailed elsewhere. *Chapter 9: Illustrator & Other Programs* consists almost entirely of gallery pages to give you the flavor of Illustrator's flexibility.

6 References. *Technical Notes, Resources, Publications* and *Artists* appendixes, and a *General Index* can be found in the back of this book. In addition, I will occasionally direct you to the *User Guide* when referring to specific information already well-documented in the *Adobe Illustrator User Guide*.

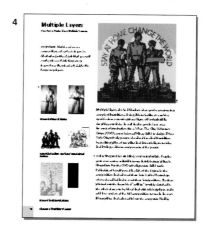

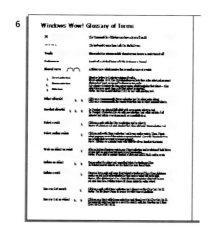

Contents

3

Lines, Fills & Colors

8

Masks & Special Effects
Advanced Techniques Chapter

9

Illustrator & Other Programs

10

Web, Multimedia & Animation

Dedication

To everyone who helped make this update possible: Robin, Diane, Sandy, Gail, Barbara and Peg. To Sandee Cohen for being the best underpaid consultant in the business, and for helping me to see how Illustrator brushes would change my life. To Puma and Bear for helping me to maintain some degree of humor. To my wonderful, loving family and friends who make everything worthwhile. And as always, a most special dedication to Jeff Jacoby, my love and husband, for his unwavering love and belief in me.

—Sharon Steuer

To Sharon Steuer, for giving me this opportunity—again! and for her endless patience. To my family; Joseph and Judith Feminella, my brother Daniel, his son Ryan, Anne, and the entire Olson Clan. To my truly precious friends; Chuck Farnham, Lynda Weinman, Jeff Foster, Chuck Carter, Matt Brown, Dr. Leslie Freedman, Sandy Schneible, Rich Siegel, Stacy Kagiwada, Jeff Robinson, John Ryan, Tracey Dinkins, Dave Wilson, Paul Street, Shelby Streit, Becky Larsen (get better soon!) and Bob P., my twin. To my kitties; Squeegee & Stanley. To Sam Moore, for being my tech and life support system. Thank you all.

—Robin AF Olson

What's New in Illustrator 8?

by Robin AF Olson (edited by Sharon Steuer)

There's a lot of ground to cover, so with this edition of *The Illustrator 8 Wow! Book* we're going to begin with an overview of this upgrade, along with pointers on where to find more in-depth information. You'll also find some Tips about problem areas in the program and what you can do to avoid them.

ADOBE'S LISTENING

Adobe has heard our pleas for adjustments to Illustrator and has implemented over 300 such user requests, ranging from keyboard shortcuts to tool modifications. In addition to the request-based updates, a number of new tools enhance performance and expand your ability to create more elegant and expressive artwork.

Regardless of the version of Illustrator you're upgrading from, some time spent with Tool Tips enabled will help you with the shortcuts (This is on by default; you can disable it in General Preferences).

SPEED DEMON?

Adobe has implemented many speed enhancements across the board. Program opening, screen redraws, printing and saving times have all been reduced, *but* you'll need more RAM then ever to run version 8 — 20 MB at least, and some argue 64 MB is realistic when you're working with some of the new tools or rasterizing objects within the program.

THE ONE WITH THE MOST PALETTES...

There are now over a dozen palettes you may choose to display on your desktop. Taking into consideration the ability to tear off tool sets (mini-palettes) from the Toolbox, you'll really be able to crowd the screen. Thankfully, since you can dock palettes together, you can manage

Some favorites return

Requested one-handed shortcuts for Lock/Unlock and Hide/Show have returned—although they're not exactly the same as in past versions:

- ⌘-2 locks an object.
- ⌘-Option-2 unlocks all objects.
- ⌘-Shift-Option-2 locks all unselected objects.
- ⌘-3 hides an object.
- ⌘-Option-3 shows all objects.
- ⌘-Shift-Option-3 hides all unselected objects.
- ⌘-Shift-W toggles Hide Template and Show Template.

Document and Page Set-up have returned as separate dialog boxes! You can now choose them separately, as the need arises.

- ⌘-Option-P opens Document Set-up.
- ⌘-Shift-P opens Page Set-up.

If you prefer, you can still access Page Set-up from within the Document Set-up dialog box.

Shortcut Shenanigans

Be careful! If you're accustomed to working in Illustrator 7, ⌘-U is *not* the way to Unlock All—it's now the way to toggle Smart Guides on and off! Unlock objects with ⌘-Option-2.

In previous versions of Illustrator, when using the pull-down menu to access Pathfinders, you'd also get an icon next to the name of the filter depicting what those filters do. The newly arrived Pathfinder palette, displays only a simple button icon indicating that filter's function. This can be confusing. With Tool Tips enabled, when you drag your cursor near the filter button, you'll see a description of what that filter does before you apply it to any objects. If you prefer, you can also use the custom Pathfinder *Wow! Actions* included on the *Wow!* disk.

Illustrator on your screen

Illustrator images on your computer screen display at approximately 72 to 96 pixels per inch (ppi) depending on your platform and your monitor. Preference: Anti-Alias Type fixed the jaggy type resulting from this, but that didn't help paths or objects look better. Preference: Anti-Aliased Artwork replaces this preference. Although paths and type appear more accurately, enabling it may slow down screen redraws on large files. Toggle it on or off as by choosing File: Preferences: General: Anti-Aliased Artwork.

screen real estate even if there are almost too many palettes to choose from (see "Working with palettes" in *Chapter 1*). Highlights of the new palettes include:

The Actions palette

Actions, borrowed from Photoshop, enable you to record, edit and replay specific events. For example, say you'd like to to create a drop shadow on a type object, then send the shadow to a new layer. If you have to create this effect more than once or in different documents, create an action, save it, then apply the action to objects as the need arises. You can also create menu and function key access to areas of the program that don't currently have keyboard shortcuts assigned to them, giving you the ability to customize how Illustrator works. You'll save time using Actions, but keep in mind you can't use it for batch processing and it can take some time to learn. Find some custom *Wow! Actions* on the *Wow!* disk, as well as others in the Illustrator Extras folder on the Adobe Illustrator 8.0 Application CD-ROM.

The Pathfinder palette

The filters contained within the Pathfinder palette aren't new to this version of Illustrator, but the fact that there's a palette for the filters, instead of access only via a pull-down menu is new. To open the Pathfinder palette, simply choose Window: Show Pathfinder. See *Chapter 6* for more information.

The Navigator palette

If you work in Photoshop 4.0 or later, you'll be familiar with the Navigator palette. If it's not already on your desktop, open it by choosing Window: Show Navigator.

Navigator displays a proxy of your entire document, all contained within its palette area. When your cursor is over the palette, a hand icon appears. As you click and drag the hand over the display, the view area of your document changes along with it. You can also use the palette to zoom in and out of your document by clicking on the small and large mountain icons. Clicking on the smaller mountain will decrease the magnification of your document; the larger mountain icon will increase the magnification. Use the slider to adjust view percentages as you work. This is a very helpful tool for working on documents with large dimensions, but can be troublesome on *large files.* For more about the Navigator palette, or more on how to disable it when you're working on a large files, see "Navigator palette" in *Chapter 1.*

Links palette

This is a completely new feature designed to keep track of placed and embedded images, as well as provide a place to update or replace them quickly. You'll be able to view rotation and scale information of each image and determine if any linked files have broken links. You'll find the Links palette by choosing Window: Show Links. For more on the Links palette, see *Chapter 1.*

Templates return via the Layers palette!

Creating templates is much easier than in previous versions of the program. To create a Template layer, simply select the layer that contains the art to use as a template. Select Template from the Layers palette pop-up menu or double-click the layer in the Layers palette and choose Template. Not only can you create a Template layer easily, you can also choose to dim raster art on the layer. For more details on templates and layers, see *Chapter 4.*

ENHANCED CREATIVITY TOOLS
Live blends

You can now create a blend with a command (Object: Blends: Make), a keyboard shortcut (⌘-Option-B) or by using the Blend tool. After you make your blend, you can reshape or move any of the key objects and the blend will reshape or reblend itself automatically. Blend between multiple objects in one command and even blend between grouped objects (see figures at right), compound paths (such as text objects you've converted to outlines)

STEUER (blend consultant: Eric Hess)

Groups of objects blended into each other (pumpkins into pumpkins, shadows into shadows) using the Align to Path orientation, Specified Distance, and the "spines" edited into **S** *curves (for more about blends see* Chapter 5 *and the "Blends folder" on the* Wow! *disk)*

A selection of custom brushes created by Lisa Jackmore— all on the Wow! *disk*

or with gradients. You can reverse the order of objects in a blend, as well as use Replace Spine (a "spine" is the path that lies between key objects in a blend), which copies blend objects onto any selected path. Access the Blend tool from the Toolbox or by pressing "W." For more on live blends, see *Chapter 5*.

BRUSHES & THE BRUSH PALETTE

Brushes are one of the most exciting new features in Illustrator 8. There are two ways to create with a brush— by drawing directly with the Paintbrush (press "B"), and by applying a brush to an existing path. You can apply, remove or replace brushes after applying them to a path, or even Expand an applied brush into editable artwork. To use any Brush, first open the Brush palette by choosing Window: Show Brushes. Choose a brush style by selecting from the choices in the Brush palette, a Brush Library, or create your own brush (see pages 54–55 and 68–69 on the basics of how to make custom brushes). You can also modify existing brushes by double-clicking the Brush you want to modify in the Brush palette.

Once you copy a brush from one document to another, it is stored in that document's Brush palette. Adobe provides Brush libraries to get you started. To use them, choose Window: Brush Libraries. You'll also find a number of custom *Wow!* brushes on the *Wow!* disk along with Illustrator Extras on the Illustrator Application CD. See the lessons in *Chapter 6* for help designing your own brushes.

The Calligraphy Brush

You'll now find Calligraphy brush, along with the other brushes, in the Brush palette. It's much more natural to use, and the Preferences dialog allows you to create a wider range of stroke style. The most important change in the Calligraphy brush is that it now creates a single path (instead of an object with too many points) for every stroke you make. You can edit these paths in the same way you edit any path. You can also set the

Calligraphy brush to work with pressure-sensitive tablets. For help creating your own custom Calligraphy brush, see pages 68–70.

The Art Brush

Create a small illustration you'd like to paint with—as an example, let's say a palm tree leaf. Now imagine painting each leaf onto an illustration of a palm tree branch. With each stroke, a single leaf appears that follows the contour of the path you create. As a path curves and varies, the leaf Brush adjusts along with the path. You can reshape the path itself and the brush style will follow each refinement. Within Brush options you can also vary the tint to reflect the path color and scale or size of the brush. See pages 126–127 for a lesson on making custom Art brushes, and pages 71 and 129 for galleries using "natural media" Art brushes.

The Scatter Brush

The Scatter brush paints with one object at varied sizes, shapes and positions along a path. This is great for scattering leaves onto trees or stars in the sky. Simply create one leaf or star, then use the Scatter brush options to determine how they repeat and change size and position as they are painted in your illustration. You can set the Scatter brush to respond to pressure-sensitive tablets. See pages 126–127 for help making Scatter brushes, and pages 178–179 on how to use Scatter brushes as an image library.

The Pattern Brush

The Pattern brush replaces Path Patterns and more! One simple way you can use Pattern brushes is to create a border on a document without having to cut and paste sections of a design together. A big improvement over Path Patterns is that once you've applied a Pattern brush, you can easily edit its path and the pattern will readjust. One of the *Wow!* ways described for using this feature is to create custom brushes that allow mapmakers to create

JACKMORE

STEUER

Top is Lisa Jackmore's "Still Life" using the Calligraphy Brush from page 70; remaining figures are: Art Brush palm trees, Scatter Brush stars and Pattern Brush grass from page 126–127 all by Steuer

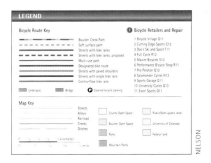

David Nelson's map legend (on pages 178–179) with custom pattern and art brushes

Ivan Torres's fish illustration created with gradient mesh (from pages 130–132)

Adam Z Lein's bison created with Photo Crosshatch (from page 118)

Printing Gradient Mesh objects

Gradient Mesh objects rely on PostScript Level 3's printing technology (PS3). Printing files to PostScript Level 2 printers will result in the Gradient Mesh objects being converted to a 150-dpi JPEG! If you're using an older printer, use the Export command, rasterize the art at the desired resolution, or open the file in Photoshop 5.02 (or later) to rasterize it there.

railroad lines more simply than previously (see pages 54–55) and complex multicolored dashed lines that just weren't possible before (pages 178–179). Also see pages 126–127 for an example of how to use Pattern brushes to generate natural-looking foliage.

The Gradient Mesh tool

This is an exciting first—the Gradient Mesh tool! Simply put, the Gradient Mesh tool transforms an object into a mesh object, a single object on which a mesh (similar to a grid) is created. On this mesh you can apply colors that can flow in different directions from one into another, in the same smooth way watercolors blend together or in more intense, abrupt color shifts, as you desire.

The mesh can consist of a few intersecting lines, or many. You can add, delete or edit the mesh in the same way you work with any anchor points in Illustrator. Access the Gradient Mesh tool from the Toolbox (or by pressing "U"). For detailed help (including lessons) with the Gradient Mesh tool, see *Chapter 6*.

The Photo Crosshatch Filter

The Photo Crosshatch filter transforms rasterized (not vector) images into something that looks like it was created with pen and ink. It's a rather nifty filter, and there are many choices once you're inside the filters' options. Actually, there are so many possibilities (and sadly, *no preview!*) that it will probably be confusing at first.

To rasterize a vector object for use with the Photo Crosshatch filter, select the object, then choose Object: Rasterize and select the color model, resolution and other options. Deselect Create Mask. Once the object is rasterized, choose Filter: Pen and Ink: Photo Crosshatch. See *Chapter 6* for examples of Photo Crosshatch.

MAKING THE BASICS A BIT EASIER
Bounding Box

The Bounding Box is visible as a rectangle with handles that appear around any object or group of objects selected with the solid Selection tool. By dragging any of the handles, you can quickly scale objects and even use ⌘-D to Transform Again once you've scaled with the Bounding Box. You can still move and duplicate objects just as you normally would using the Selection tool. It's on by default; to disable the Bounding Box Preference, choose File: Preferences: General: Bounding Box.

Smart Guides

Guides are no longer just for simple lining up of vertical and horizontal objects. They can now highlight or label paths, anchor points, intersections of paths, even path handles and more. They help you line up objects on different angles to each other and basically eliminate the need for single-use guides.

Initially, it's a bit overwhelming to leave all the Smart Guides on, all of the time. To toggle Smart Guides on or off quickly, choose ⌘-U. You can fine-tune which guides you have on by choosing File: Preferences: Smart Guides.

The Free Transform Tool

The Free Transformation tool allows you to resize, reflect, rotate and shear without having to switch to other tools. Access the Free Transform tool from the Toolbox (or press "E"). The benefit of using this tool is to make adjustments as you work. If you need to be more precise in your transformations, you can still make numeric transformations. See *Chapter 1* for more details.
Note: *The tool icons for the Free Transform tool are easy to confuse with the Selection tool (see Tip at right).*

The Pencil Tool

The Pencil tool has seen some welcome improvements that make it work much more as an actual pencil would. Fidelity and Smoothness options (see Tip in *Chapter 1* for details) further refine the quality of Pencil tool paths. One of the most important features is the ability to edit paths quickly as you create them, whether you use the Pencil tool by itself or in conjunction with the Smooth

Working with Smart Guides

Here are a few Smart Guide preferences. Understanding how to incorporate Smart Guides into your workflow is the key to unlocking their power. (See *Chapter 1* for more on Smart Guides.)

- **Text Label Hints** identify types of points, paths and angles of alignment as you pass your cursor over them.
- **Transform Tools** provide hints about objects you are scaling (uniformly), rotating or shearing (angle from origin).
- **Object Highlighting** highlights any visible object, locked or unlocked, as the cursor passes near it.
- **Construction Guides** are the temporary guidelines that appear as you use Smart Guides.

Confusing Tool Icons—Beware!

The icon for the Free Transform tool can look identical to the Selection tool icon! This can be *very confusing*, especially if you're in the Free Transform tool and mistakenly think you can select an object because of the tools' similarities. To select, hold down the ⌘ key to access a real Selection tool so you can select the objects, then let go and transform. (Below are icons for: the Selection tool, Free Transform, then...*either one!*)

Registration Color

If you want a color to print on all the plates in your job, including the spot color plate, you can use Registration Color, found in the Swatches palette. Registration Color is typically used for crop and trim marks. By default, it's set to C=100, M=100, Y=100 and K=100, but you can change the color by opening Swatch options and adjusting the color sliders.

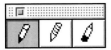

Pencil, Smooth and Erase tools shown in a Tearoff palette

A secret surprise

In the Brushes palette, choose a Calligraphy brush. Double-click the brush to open the Brush options. Set the options to Angle 5, Roundness 26 and Diameter 56, then click the preview window for a surprise.

Note: *5/26/56 is someone's birthday at Adobe. Whose birthday is it? Our lips are sealed. — Robin AF Olson*

and Erase tools. Access the Pencil tool from the Toolbox (or press "N"). For a lesson on using the Pencil tool, see pages 82–83.

The Erase Tool

Use the Erase tool to remove a section of a path by dragging the tool over the portion of the path you wish to edit. The Erase tool adds new anchor points to the edited path—very handy indeed! Access the Erase tool tool from the Toolbox or cycle through the Pencil, Erase and Smooth tool by pressing Shift-N. For more information, see *Chapter 1*.

The Smooth Tool

This tool is a real timesaver. It smooths out paths while trying keep the original shape of the path intact. It also reduces the number of anchor points in the path, depending on how much smoothing you do. You can access the Smooth tool from the Toolbox or press Shift-N until it shows up in the Toolbox. For more information, see Tips on pages 83 and 179.

ADDED FUNCTIONALITY
Eyedropper and Paint Bucket Tools

The Eyedropper tool now copies text formatting between text blocks including font, leading, color, size, kerning, tracking and more. The Paint Bucket tool applies text formatting to text blocks or text strings. To set what the Eyedropper samples and the Paint Bucket applies, double-click either tool to open the Options dialog box (see *Chapter 7*).

Illustrator Basics

1

This chapter is packed with tips and techniques chosen to help you use Adobe Illustrator with optimal ease and efficiency. Whether you're a veteran of Illustrator or a relative newcomer, you're likely to find information here that will greatly increase your productivity and help you get up to speed on the latest features. Remember, this chapter is an addendum to, not a replacement for, Adobe Illustrator's *User Guide* or tutorials.

COMPUTER & SYSTEM REQUIREMENTS

Creating artwork on the computer is wonderful and exciting. Blissfully, our computer art tools, including Adobe Illustrator, have seen great improvements in the past few years. Unfortunately, one of the sad facts about demands for better and more powerful software is that the more powerful upgrades might not run on older computers. For example, the minimum requirement for using Illustrator on the Macintosh is a PowerPC processor. Owners of 040 non-PowerPC computers will have to upgrade their hardware with at least 32 MB of installed RAM and 20 MB of RAM made available to Illustrator. This is over twice the RAM required in past versions of the program. For rasterizing in Illustrator, allotting more than 20MB is more realistic. Illustrator users will now need the Mac OS 7.5 or later and 35 MB free to install the program. You'll also need more hard disk space than you might think; Illustrator files containing live blends, brushes, placed raster images or gradient mesh can get quite large! You'll also need a CD-ROM drive for installation.

Don't start yet!

Before you begin this book, make sure you read both the "How to Use This Book" section in the front of the book, and the pullout *Glossary* at the back of the book. If you are on Windows, pay special attention to these sections for help translating the Mac keyboard labels used here into the appropriate counterparts for Windows.

Additional recommendations

The minimum requirements to run Illustrator are just that: *minimum*. Anything you add will increase performance and efficiency.
- 64 MB of RAM (or more)
- CD-ROM drive
- Extra hard drive space
- Video card or extra VRAM (for 24-bit color)
- A 17" monitor or larger (better yet, two monitors)

Plug-ins

Newer versions of Illustrator may not work with all third-party plug-ins (such as Extensis VectorTools).

Understanding Smart Guides

There are a multitude of Smart Guide preferences. Here's what each one does:

- Text Label Hints provide information about an object when the cursor passes over it—helpful for identifying a specific object within complicated artwork.
- Construction Guides are the temporary guidelines that help you align between objects and anchor points.
- Transform Tools help with transformations.
- Object Highlighting enables the anchor point, centerpoint and path of a deselected object to appear as your cursor passes within a specified tolerance from the object. This can be very useful for aligning objects. For best results, select an object's anchor point or centerpoint to align with.

Note: *Smart Guides will slow you down when working on very large files. Also, you can't align using Smart Guides if View: Snap To Grid is enabled.*

PC owners will need a Pentium processor, a Windows 95, 98, or NT 4.0 Workstation or Server operating system and 32 MB of installed RAM. To install Illustrator, you'll need a minimum 35 MB of free space on your hard drive and a CD-ROM drive.

MAKING YOUR MOVES EASIER

Whether you're a beginning or veteran Illustrator user, take a minute to look over this section to make sure you're aware of some of the alternate ways in which you can select tools and access features. Between Tool Tips and context-sensitive menus, you won't always have to mouse over to the toolbox or use the pull-down menus.

Single key tool-selection and navigation

Need to access a tool? Press a key. Press "T" to choose the Type tool, "P" for the Pen tool, and so on. Choose any tool in the toolbox by pressing its single-key equivalent. To access hidden tools that are part of the same tool set, press the Shift key before pressing the single key until the desired tool appears. For example, to access the Star tool, press Shift-L until the Star tool is selected.

To learn the single-key equivalent for all your tools, hold the cursor over any tool in the toolbox, and its single-key shortcut will appear—as long as you have Show Tool Tips enabled in General Preferences (⌘-K). Tool Tips will also display descriptive captions for all icons and certain functions and is well worth leaving enabled while you accustom yourself to these shortcuts.

Note: *Single-key navigation won't work inside a text block.*

Context-sensitive menus

If you're not already familiar with Context-sensitive menus, you might find them a great timesaver. Windows users merely click the right mouse button. If you're on a Mac, hold down the Control key while you click and hold the mouse button. In both cases a menu pops up, specific to the tool or objects you are working with, providing you with an alternative to the regular pull-down menus.

Tear-off palettes

The Illustrator toolbox now lets you to *tear off* subsets of tools so you can move the entire set to another location; click on a tool with a pop-up menu, drag the cursor to the arrow end of the pop-up and release the mouse.

WORKING WITH POSTSCRIPT OBJECTS
Anchor points, lines and Bézier* curves

Adobe uses its own language, PostScript, to describe mathematically each of the objects you create in Illustrator. Instead of using pixels to draw shapes, Illustrator creates objects made up of points, called "anchor points." They are connected by curved or straight outlines called "paths," and are visible if you work in Artwork viewing mode (View: Artwork). The PostScript language describes information about the location and size of each path, as well as its dozen or so attributes, such as its fill color, and its stroke weight and color. Because you are creating objects, you'll be able to change the order in which they stack. You'll also be able to group objects together so you can select them as if they were one object, and even ungroup them later, if you wish.

If you took geometry, you probably remember that the shortest distance between two points is a straight line. In Illustrator, this rule translates into each line being defined by two anchor points you create by clicking with the Pen tool.

In mathematically describing rectangles and circles, Illustrator computes the center, length of the sides or radius, based on the total width and height you specify. For more complex shapes involving freeform curves, Adobe Illustrator allows you to use the Pen tool to create Bézier curves, defined by nonprinting anchor points (which literally anchor the path at that point), and direction points (which define the angle and depth of the curve). To make these direction points easier to see and manipulate, Illustrator connects each direction point to its anchor point with a nonprinting direction line, also called a "handle." The direction points and handles are

In a jam? There's help available

Adobe provides many ways to help you learn Illustrator and troubleshoot problems.

Find help and keyboard shortcuts under the Help menu (Mac or Windows), along with instant access to Adobe Online, under the File menu or by pressing the Venus icon on top of the toolbox.

Resizing and line weight

If you double-click the Scale tool, you can resize your selection with or without altering line weights (see page 13):

- To scale a selection while also scaling line weights, make sure to enable Scale Stroke Weight.
- To scale a selection while maintaining your line weights, disable "Scale Stroke Weight."
- To decrease line weights (50%) without scaling objects, first scale the selection (200%) with Scale Stroke Weight disabled. Then scale (50%) with Scale Stroke Weight enabled. Reverse to increase line weights.

STEUER

How to allocate RAM (for Mac)

Just because your computer has a lot of RAM (memory) that doesn't mean Illustrator has enough *allocated* to it (Adobe allocates a pre-set minimum amount of RAM to run the program). To improve the speed of many of Illustrator's functions or allow it to perform a function, you'll want to increase the memory allocation. *Single-click* the Illustrator application icon when the program isn't running, and press ⌘-I (for Info) to open the Get Info dialog box. Then adjust the Minimum and Preferred sizes. Remember to reserve enough RAM for your computer to run the system, and any other applications you'll want open simultaneously.

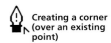Starting an object

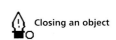Adding a point

Closing an object

Creating a corner (over an existing point)

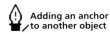Adding an anchor to another object

Basic cursor object options for the Pen tool, "P"

visible when you're creating a path with the Pen tool or editing the path with the Direct-selection tool. While all of this might sound complicated, and could involve some initial awkwardness, manipulating Bézier curves can prove quite intuitive.

More about Bézier curves

If you're new to Bézier curves, you should go through the Adobe training materials. For some Bézier fine-tuning, I have included several "Zen" practice lessons in the Training folder on the *Wow!* disk.

Many graphics programs include Béziers, so learning to master the Pen tool, though perhaps challenging at first, is very important. Friskets in Painter, paths in Photoshop, and the outline and extrusion curves of many 3D programs all have at their base a Bézier curve.

The key to learning Béziers is to take your initial lessons in short doses and stop if you get frustrated. Designer Kathleen Tinkel describes Bézier direction lines as "following the gesture of the curve." This artistic view should help you to create fluid Bézier curves.

And finally, some rules about Bézier curves

- The length and angle of the handles "anticipate" the curves that will follow.
- The length of the handles is equal to approximately one-third the length of the curve, if it were straightened.
- Place anchor points on either side of an arch, not in between.
- The fewer the anchor points, the smoother the curve will look and the faster it will print.
- Adjust a curve's height and angle by dragging the direction points, or grab the curve itself to adjust its height.

WATCH YOUR CURSOR!

Illustrator's cursors change to indicate not only what tool you have selected, but also which function you are about to perform. If you watch your cursor, you will avoid the most common Illustrator mistakes.

If you choose the Pen tool:

- **Before you start,** your cursor displays as the Pen tool with "×" indicating that you're starting a new object.

- **Once you've begun your object,** your cursor changes to a regular Pen. This indicates that you're about to add to an existing object.

- **If your cursor gets close to an existing anchor point,** it will change to a Pen with "−" indicating that you're about to delete the last anchor point! If you click-drag on top of that anchor point, you'll redraw that curve. If you hold the Option key while you click-drag on top of the point, you'll pull out a new direction line, creating a corner (like the petals of a flower). If you click on top of the point, you'll collapse the outgoing direction line, allowing you to attach a straight line to the curve.

- **If your cursor gets close to an end anchor point of an object,** it will change to a Pen with "o" to indicate that you're about to "close" the path. If you do close the path, then your cursor will change back to a Pen with "×" to indicate that you're beginning a new object.

- **If you use the Direct-selection tool to adjust the object as you go,** make sure that you look at your cursor when you're ready to continue your object. If it's still a regular Pen, then continue to place the next point, adding to your object. If the Pen tool has "×" (indicating that you are about to start a new object), then you must redraw your last point. As you approach this last anchor point, your cursor will change to a Pen with "/"—click and drag over this last point to redraw the last curve. To form a corner on the point as you draw, hold down your Option key to click-drag out a new direction line.

Bézier-editing tools
The group of tools you can use to edit Illustrator paths are called Bézier-editing tools. To access them, click and

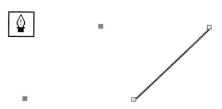

Clicking with the Pen tool to create anchor points for straight lines

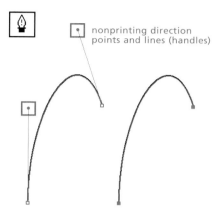

nonprinting direction points and lines (handles)

Click-dragging with the Pen tool to create anchor points and pulling out direction lines for curves

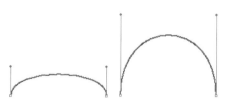

When direction handles are short, curves are shallow; when handles are long, curves are deep

The length and angle of the handles determine the gesture of the curves

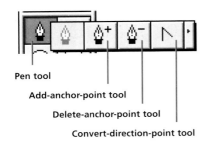

Pen tool

Add-anchor-point tool

Delete-anchor-point tool

Convert-direction-point tool

The hollow Snap-to arrow

As long as Snap To ☒ Snap to point Point is enabled (View window), you can grab objects from any path or point and drag until they snap to a guide or another anchor point. Watch for the cursor to change to a hollow arrow.

Correcting common mistakes

Avoid these common mistakes:

- If you try to deselect by clicking outside your object while you still have the Pen tool chosen, you'll scatter extra points throughout your image, causing possible problems later. If you're aware that you clicked by mistake, Undo. To remove stray points, choose Edit: Select Stray Points and then delete.
- If you try to delete an object that you selected with the Direct-selection tool, you'll delete only the selected point or path. What remains of the object will now be fully selected. Delete again to remove the remaining portions of your object.

hold the Pen, Pencil or Scissors tool and drag to select one of the other tools. (To learn about *filters* that edit, see details on Pathfinder filters, *Chapter 6.*)

- **The Pen tool and Auto Add/Delete** can perform many functions. Auto Add/Delete, when enabled (General Preferences), allows the Pen tool to change automatically to the Add-anchor-point tool when the tool is over a selected path segment, or to the Delete-anchor-point tool when over an anchor point. To temporarily disable the Auto Add/Delete function of the Pen tool, hold down the Shift key. If you don't want the path to constrain to an angle, release the Shift key prior to releasing the mouse.

- **The Convert-direction-point tool,** found hidden with the Pen tool (Shift-P), lets you convert an anchor point on a path from a smooth curve to a corner point by clicking on the anchor point. To convert it from a corner-point to a smooth curve, click-drag on the anchor point counterclockwise to pull out a new direction line (or twirl the point until it straightens out the curve). To convert from a smooth curve to a hinged curve (two curves hinged at a point), grab the direction point and Option-drag it to the new position. With the Pen tool selected, you can temporarily access the Convert-direction-point tool by holding down the Option key.

- **The Add-anchor-point tool** accessible from the Pen pop-up menu or by pressing +, adds an anchor point to a path at the location where you click.

- **The Delete-anchor-point tool** accessible from the Pen pop-up menu or by pressing –, deletes an anchor point when you click *directly* on the point.
  Note: *If you select the Add/Delete-anchor-point tools by pressing + or –, to get the Pen tool you must press Shift-P.*

- **The Pencil tool** reshapes a path. Select a path and draw on or close to the path to reshape.

- **The Smooth tool** merely smooths points on a path, keeping the original shape of the path intact.

- **The Erase tool** removes sections of a path. Select a path; by dragging along the path you can erase or remove portions of it. You must drag along the path; drawing perpendicular to the path will result in unexpected effects. This tool adds a pair of anchor points to the remaining path, on either side of the erased section of the path.

- **The Scissors tool** cuts a path where you click by adding two disconnected, selected anchor points exactly on top of each other. To select just one of the points, deselect the object, then click with the Direct-selection tool on the spot where you cut to select the upper anchor point, and drag it to the side to see the two points better.

- **The Knife tool** slices through all unlocked visible objects and closed paths. Simply drag the Knife tool across the object you want to slice, then select the object(s) you want to move or delete (also see "Slice" Tip on page 15).

Geometric objects

The Ellipse, Rectangle, Polygon, Spiral and Star tools create objects called "geometric primitives." These objects are mathematically-described symmetrical paths grouped with a nonprinting anchor point, which indicates the center. Use the centers of the geometric objects to snap-align them with each other or with other objects and guides. You can create these geometric objects numerically or manually. Access the Polygon, Star and Spiral tools as hidden tools from the Ellipse tool in the Toolbox. (See *Chapter 2* for exercises in creating and manipulating geometric objects, and see Tip, next page.)

- **To create a geometric object with numeric input,** select the desired geometric tool and click on the artboard to establish the upper left corner of your object. Enter the desired dimensions in the dialog box, and click

Fidelity & Smoothness Options

The Pencil, Smooth, and Brush tools have new options you'll need to understand to guide you in creating a far greater range of types of paths, from very realistic to more shapely and elegant ones, without the constant need to adjust anchor points (see pages 80–81 for a technique using the Pencil tool).

- **Smoothness:** Drawing freehand while holding a mouse or even a digital pen can be less than elegant. The smoothness option varies the percentage of smoothness you'll see as you create and edit paths. Use a lower percentage of smoothness for more realistic lines and brush strokes and a higher percentage for less realistic but more elegant lines.

- **Fidelity:** Increases or decreases the distance between anchor points on the path created or edited. The smaller the number, the more points that will make up the path and vice versa.

Note: *Closing Pencil and Brush tool paths is a bit awkward. Hold down the Option key when you're ready to close the path. This will bring up the "o" mark indicating the closure of the object. Release the option key just before you close and the path will close itself. Set the tool preferences to low numbers to make closing easier.*

Serious fun with shapes

The Polygon, Spiral and Star, from the Oval (Ellipse), or by typing "L" are deceptively powerful tools. Used in conjunction with the following key combinations, they are likely to become indispensable:

- **Spacebar-drag** allows you to reposition your object.
- **Shift** constrains the object's proportions.
- **Up-arrow** (↑) increases points on a star, sides on a polygon and coils on a spiral.
- **Down-arrow** (↓) removes points from a star, sides from a polygon, and coils from a spiral.
- **Option** increases the angle of the points of the star.
- **Command-drag** changes the inside and outside radius of a star, or increases or decreases the decay in a spiral.
- **Option-click** to create the object numerically.
- **Various combinations of the above:** Try experimenting with all the keys separately and in combination with the other keys. Actually, playing with the modifier keys as you draw is the only way to understand fully these fun and powerful tools.
- For full details, see "GeoTools by Scott McCollom.pdf" on the *Wow!* disk ("Plug-ins" folder).

OK. To create the object numerically from the object's center, Option-click the artboard.

- **To create a geometric shape manually,** select the desired geometric tool, and click-drag to form the object from one corner to the other. To create the object from the center, hold down the Option key and drag from the center outward (keep the Option key down until you release the mouse button to ensure that it draws from the center). Access the Rounded Rectangle tool hidden within the Rectangle tool. Once you have drawn the geometric objects, you can edit them exactly as you do other paths.

GROUPING & SELECTING OBJECTS
To group or not to group…

Many object-oriented programs (that is, programs that create objects, such as Illustrator and CorelDraw) provide you with a grouping function so you can act upon multiple objects as if they were one. In Illustrator, though, you don't have to group objects or parts of objects to act on them as a unit; you merely have to select them. But since grouping objects together places all the objects on the same layer, you don't want to group objects unless you actually need to (for more information on layers and reordering objects, see *Chapter 4*).

So when do you want to group objects? Group objects when you need to select them *repeatedly* as a unit. Take an illustration of a bicycle as an example. Use the Group function (⌘-G) to group the spokes of a wheel, next group the two wheels of the bicycle, then group the wheels with the frame (⌘-Shift-G ungroups). We will continue referring to this bicycle below.

Selecting within groups
- **With the Direct-selection tool.** Click on a point or path with the Direct-selection tool to select that point or portion of the path. If you click on a spoke of a wheel, you'll select the portion of the spoke's path you clicked on.

- **With the Selection tool.** Click on an object with the Selection tool to select the largest group containing that object. In our example, it would be the entire bicycle.

- **With the Group-selection tool.** Use the Group-selection tool to select subgroupings progressively. First, click with the Group-selection tool to select the entire spoke path. The second click selects the entire wheel, the third, both wheels, and the fourth, the entire bicycle.
  Note: *Once you've selected objects with the Group-selection tool, if you want to grab and move them you must change to one of the other selection tools. If you click again with the Group-selection tool, you'll be selecting the next group up!*

- **See the "Finger Dance" lessons in *Chapter 2*.** This section includes a variety of selection exercises.

Joining & Averaging

Two of Illustrator's most useful functions are Average and Join (both found under the Object: Path menu). Use ⌘-J or the Context-sensitive menu to join a single pair of open endpoints. This function will operate differently depending on the objects.

- **If the two open endpoints are exactly on top of each other,** then Join opens a dialog box asking if the join should be smooth (a curved Bézier anchor with direction handles) or a corner (an anchor point with no handles). Both points will fuse into one point.

- **If the two open endpoints are *not* exactly on top of each other,** then Join will create a straight line joining the two points. If you attempt to join two points to fuse as one but you don't get the dialog box, then you have merely added an adjoining straight line! Undo and see "Averaging & Joining" below.

- **If you select an open path** (in this case, you don't need to select the endpoints), then Join closes the path.

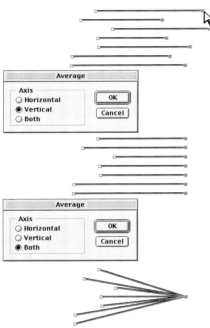

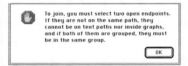

Using the Average command to align selected endpoints vertically, then choosing Both

- **If the two open endpoints are on different objects,** then Join connects the two paths into one.

Averaging, in essence, allows you to align selected *points*. (To align *objects*, use the Align palette.) To average, use the Direct-selection tool to marquee-select or Shift-select any number of points belonging to any number of objects. Then use ⌘-Option-J or the Context-sensitive menu to average, aligning the selected points horizontally, vertically or along both axes.

Averaging & Joining in one step. Hold down Option and choose Object: Path: Join, or ⌘-Shift-Option-J. The join forms a corner if joining to a line, or a hinged curve if joining to a curve.

WORKING WITH PALETTES

Illustrator's palettes are accessible via the Window menu. Each palette is unique, but many share common features:

- **Dock tabbed palettes to save desktop space.**
Reduce the space that palettes require by docking palettes together into smaller groups. Grab the palette tab and drag it to another palette to dock it. You can also drag a tab to the *bottom* of a palette to stack palettes vertically.

- **You can make most palettes smaller or larger.**
If there's a sizing icon in the lower right corner, click and drag it to shrink or expand the palette (the Gradient palette won't expand if it's docked with other palettes). Some palettes also have a pop-up menu offering additional Options. Click the square on the top right bar of the palette to shrink all palettes docked together down to just title bars. Click the right square again, and the palette will re-expand. Double-click the title bar to cycle through expanded and collapsed states of the palettes.

- **You must select your object(s) first; then you can make changes to the style.** With your objects selected,

Joining warning

If you get an error message that you can't join points, do the following—in addition to the conditions in the warning:

> To join, you must select two open endpoints. If they are not on the same path, they cannot be on text paths nor inside graphs, and if both of them are grouped, they must be in the same group.
>
> OK

- Make sure you've selected only *two* points (no third stray point selected by mistake?).
- Make sure you've selected *endpoints*, not midpoints.

Teeny tiny palettes

Double-click the tab name, or the space to the right of the tab, to cycle through expanded and collapsed views of that palette.

you can select any box in the palette containing text (click on the label or in the box) and type. If you're typing something that has limited choices (such as a font or type style), Illustrator will attempt to complete your word; just keep typing until your choice is visible. If you're typing into a text field, use the Tab key to move to other text fields within the palette.

IMPORTANT: *When you're finished typing into palette text fields, you must press Return (or Enter). This action signals to Illustrator that you are ready to enter text somewhere else or resume your illustration.*

- **You can edit selective characteristics on multiple objects.** With palettes, you can set one specific style for all selected objects without affecting any other characteristics. For example, your selection might contain multiple objects, one with no stroke, and the rest with outlines of different colors and weights. If, in the Stroke palette, you set the stroke weight to 1 (point) and leave the other choices unchanged, this will set the stroke weight of all objects that have strokes to 1 (point), but it won't add strokes to unstroked objects and won't affect the colors of any strokes. You can use the same technique to change assorted text blocks to the same typeface while maintaining differences in type sizes and other formatting.

- **The many ways to fill or stroke an object**
Focus on a selected object's fill or stroke by clicking on the Fill or Stroke icon near the bottom of the Toolbox, or toggle between them by pressing the "X" key (if you want to set the stroke or fill to None, just use the "/" key). Set the color you want by: 1) adjusting the sliders in the Color palette, 2) clicking on a swatch in the Swatches palette, 3) sampling colors in the color ramp at the bottom of the Color palette, or 4) using the Eyedropper tool to sample from other objects in your file. In addition, you can drag a color swatch from any palette to a selected object or to the Fill/Stroke icon in the Toolbox itself.

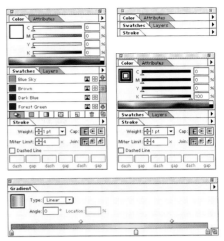

Modes of expansion for docked palettes; lower figure is Gradient palette, alone and expanded

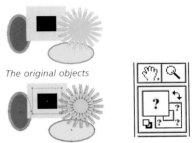

The original objects

Objects selected, and the bottom of the toolbox indicating that differing styles are selected

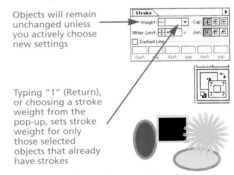

Objects will remain unchanged unless you actively choose new settings

Typing "1" (Return), or choosing a stroke weight from the pop-up, sets stroke weight for only those selected objects that already have strokes

The objects after setting a stroke weight of 1

Palette be gone!

Press Tab to hide the palettes and toolbox, then Tab to toggle them into view again. If you'd rather keep the toolbox and hide the other palettes, just use Shift-Tab.

To use the current unit of measurement, type the number, then Tab to the next text field, or press Return. To use another unit of measurement, *follow* the number with "in" or " (inch), "pt" (point), "p" (pica), or "mm" (millimeter) and Return. To resume typing into an *image* text block, press Shift-Return. (*Tip from Sandee Cohen:* Type *calculations* in text fields!)

Easy default styling

Select an object styled the way you want your next object to be. Illustrator automatically resets the default to style the next object identically. A real timesaver! **Note:** *This doesn't work for type.*

If you can't see a new style...

If you're trying to make style changes, but nothing seems to change on the screen, make sure:

• your objects are selected.
• you are in Preview and not Art-work mode.

Moving complex images

If the Transform palette fails, create a proxy rectangle closely surrounding the objects you wish to move. Move the proxy in one motion to the desired location, and delete. To apply the move, select your objects, double-click the Selection arrow and click OK.

TRANSFORMATIONS

Moving, scaling, rotating, reflecting and shearing are all operations that transform selected objects. Always begin by selecting what you wish to transform. If you're not happy with the transformation you've just applied, use Undo before applying a new transformation—or you'll end up applying the new transformation on top of the previous one.

In Illustrator, you can perform all transformations manually (see *Chapter 2* for exercises), through a dialog box for numeric accuracy or with the Free Transform tool. In addition, you can also select more than one object and choose Object: Transform: Transform Each. This applies the transformation to each individual object.

Illustrator also remembers the last transformation you performed, storing those numbers in the appropriate dialog box until you enter a new transform value or restart the program. For example, if you previously scaled an image numerically and chose not to scale the line weights, the next time you scale, manually or numerically, your line weights will not scale.

The Bounding Box

A new addition to Illustrator is the Bounding Box, not to be confused with the Free Transform tool (which allows you to perform additional functions; see discussion of the Free Transform tool opposite). The Bounding Box appears around selected objects when you are using the solid Selection tool, and can be useful for quick moving, scaling or duplicating objects. With the Bounding Box you can easily scale several objects at once. Select the objects click on a corner of the Bounding Box and drag. To constrain proportionally while scaling, hold down the Shift key and drag a corner. By default the Bounding Box is on. Turn it off by deselecting Use Bounding Box in General Preferences. To reset the Bounding Box after performing a transformation so it's once again square to the page, choose Object: Transform: Reset Bounding Box.

Moving

In addition to grabbing and dragging objects manually, you can specify a new location numerically: Double-click the Selection arrow in the Toolbox or use the Context-sensitive menu to bring up the Move dialog box (select the Preview option). For help determining the distance you wish to move, click-drag with the Measure tool the distance you wish to calculate. Then *immediately* open the Move dialog box to see the measured distance loaded automatically, and click OK (or press Return).

The Free Transform Tool

In some ways, the Free Transform tool is an all-in-one way to transform objects. In addition to performing transformations such as rotate, scale and shear, you can also create perspective (see Tip at right). Keep in mind that the Free Transform tool makes its transformations from a fixed centerpoint or bounding box point, just as the Transformation palette does—you cannot move the centerpoint from which your transformations are made using the Free Transform tool. To move the center point of objects use the individual transformation tools.

You'll need a number of keyboard combinations to take advantage of the functions of the Free Transform tool. Making the effort to learn them will be a great time-saver for any future transformations you need to make quickly and without specific amounts.

Individual transformation tools

For scaling, rotation, reflection and shearing of objects with adjustable centerpoints, you can click (to manually specify the center about which the transformation will occur), then grab your object to transform it. (For practice with manual transformations, see *Chapter 2.*)

From the dialog box you can specify distance, degree of rotation, number of steps or scale percentage. You can also decide whether to scale lines, make a copy of the object, or transform patterns that fill the objects. (For more about transforming patterns, see Tip on page 74).

An exception to the rule!

Usually, you should scale an image before placing it in a page layout program. An exception to the rule if your file contains brushes— you may want to scale the final placed image after you have placed it into a page layout program.

Transform again

Illustrator remembers the last transformation you performed— from simple moves to rotating a *copy* of an object. Press ⌘-D (or Context-sensitive menu Transform Again) to repeat the effect.

Free Transform variations

With the Free Transform tool selected you can apply the following transformations to your selected objects.

- **Rotate**–click outside the bounding box and drag.
- **Scale**–click on a corner of the bounding box and drag. Option-drag to scale from the center and Shift-drag to scale proportionally.
- **Distort**–click on a corner handle of the bounding box and ⌘-drag.
- **Shear**–click on a side handle of the bounding box and ⌘-drag the handle.
- **Perspective**–click on a corner handle of the bounding box and ⌘-Option-Shift-drag.

Scaling objects to an exact size

- *The transformation palette way:* Type the new width or height in the palette and press Return.
- *The proxy way:* Create a proxy rectangle the size of your image, then from the upper left corner of the proxy, Option-click to create another rectangle in the target dimensions. Then with your proxy selected, click with the Scale tool in the upper left and grab-drag the lower right to match the target. (Hold down Shift to scale in only one dimension.) Delete these rectangles, select your objects, double-click the Scale tool and apply the settings.

Transform palette modifiers

To modify your transformations when you press Return, hold down Option to transform a *copy*; ⌘ to maintain proportions; ⌘-Option to maintain proportions of a copy. (See top Tip on page 12 for numeric entry options.)

Click a point in the Transform palette to select a reference point.

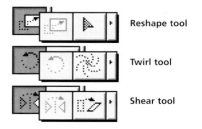

Reshape tool

Twirl tool

Shear tool

Here's how the transformation will affect the selected objects:

- **Double-click on a transformation tool** to access the dialog box. This allows you to transform the objects numerically, originating from an object's center.

- **Option-click on your image with the transformation tool** to access the dialog box to transform your objects numerically, originating from where you clicked.

- **Click-drag on your image with a transformation tool** to transform the selected objects, originating from the center of the group of selected objects.

The Transform palette

From this palette you can determine numeric transformations that specify an object's width, height, location on the document and how much to rotate or shear it. You can also access a palette pop-up menu which offers options to Flip Horizontal and Vertical, as well as Transform Object, Pattern or Both and enable Scale Stroke Weight. The Transformation palette that ships with Illustrator is a bit odd: you *can* Transform Again (⌘-D) once you've applied a transformation, but the information in the palette is not retained. To maintain your numeric input, apply transformations through the transform tool's dialog box, discussed above.

More transformation tools—Reshape, Twirl & Shear

The Reshape tool is quite different from the other transformation tools. Start by Direct-selecting the paths you wish to reshape. Next, choose the Reshape tool from the Scale tool pop-up (or press Shift-S until it appears). With this tool, marquee or Shift-select all points you wish to affect, then drag the points to reshape.

Using the Twirl tool (from within the Rotate tool, or press Shift-R), click-drag or Option-click to transform selected objects (for details, see "GeoTools by Scott

McCollom.pdf" on the *Wow!* disk).

You will find the Shear tool hidden within the Reflect tool (Shift-O).

WORKING SMART
Saving strategies

Probably the most important advice I can give you is to save (⌘-S) every few minutes or so. Whenever you make a substantial change to your image, use File: Save As and give your image a new name.

It's much more time-efficient to save incremental versions of your image than it is to reconstruct an earlier version all over again. Back up your work at least once a day before you shut down. Just think to yourself, "If this computer never starts up again, what will I need?" Develop a backup system using disks, Zip or Jaz drives, SyQuests, DATs (digital audio tapes), opticals or CDs so you can archive all of your work. I suggest using a program such as Dantz's Retrospect, so you can automatically add new and changed files to your archives.

I believe in archiving virtually everything and have finally developed a file-naming system that actually helps me keep track of my working process—simplifying my recovery of a working version if necessary. My system involves three components. First, start with a meaningful description of your current image ("hearts compound") and second, add a numerical notation of the version ("1.0"). Keep your numbering system consecutive regardless of the label throughout the entire project. Keep the number in a sequence decimally when you make an incremental change to your image ("1.1, 1.2, 1.3..."). Change to the next numeric sequence when you make a substantive change ("2.0"). Don't start numbers at 1.0 for each phase of the project or you'll be unable to figure out which came first: "Sky 1.0" or "Heart 1.0." Instead, if labels are "Sky 1.0" and "Heart 4.0," then the creation order is self-explanatory. Lastly, add a suffix to indicate its file type (.ai for Illustrator, .psd for Photoshop, .eps for Encapsulated PostScript file). Also, make sure that you

The selected area indicated in red

Direct-selected and dragged wing objects

HESS

For Eric Hess's "Soaring Hearts Futons" logo, he roughly Direct-selected, then with Reshape he marqueed as indicated above, and dragged)

A more precise slice

Use any selected *path* to slice through all visible unlocked objects—choose Object: Path: Slice.

To change your object...

To make changes to a path, click on the path with the Direct-selection tool. Then make adjustments by selecting and dragging anchor points, direction points or the curve itself. If you select an object but don't see direction handles:

- Deselect it, then try again.
- If you're in Preview mode, be sure to click on the *path itself* or switch to Artwork mode. Or, deselect the Use Area Select option in General Preferences.
- Show Edges is selected.

Note: *Only* curves *have handles!*

keep all files in a named and dated folder that distinguishes them from other projects. For saving in other formats, see "Image Formats" later in this chapter.

Multiple Undos

Most programs give you one chance to undo your last move. Illustrator allows up to 200 levels of undo, but will only hold the user-specified number of undos in a low-memory situation. When it needs to purge levels of undo to regain memory, Illustrator will remove all levels beyond what you've selected as your minimum. In File: Preferences: Units & Undo you can set the number of levels of undo to a number less than 200. This number will be the most levels saved in low-memory situations. I suggest 20 to 30 levels is usually adequate and keeps you aware that you should still save frequently.

Even after you save a file, your Undos (and Redos) are still available, making it possible to save the current version, undo it to a previous stage and then save it, or continue working from an earlier state. Having 20 to 30 undos available in each of multiple documents should come close to the experience of having infinite undos! (Be aware, though, that some actions, such as Preference settings, might not be undoable).

CHANGING YOUR VIEWS
Preview and Artwork

To control the speed of your screen redraw, learn to make use of the various Preview and Artwork modes. Choose from the View menu or press ⌘-Y to go from Artwork to Preview and ⌘-Y again to return to Artwork. To use Preview Selection, press ⌘-Shift-Y, which leaves everything in Artwork mode except the object(s) currently selected. From the View menu, you can also hide and show grids and guides, edges and page tilings (see *Chapter 4* for details on Preview and Artwork modes for layers).

ZOOMING IN & OUT

Illustrator provides many ways to zoom in and out:

- **With the Zoom tool.** Click to zoom *in* one level of magnification; hold down the Option key and click to zoom *out* one level. Or click-drag to define an area, and Illustrator will attempt to fill the current window with the area that you defined.

- **From the View menu.** Choose Zoom In/Out, Actual Size or Fit in Window (see "Zippy zooming" on page 19).

- **Using the shortcut commands for Zoom.** With any tool selected, use ⌘-hyphen (think "minus to zoom out") and ⌘-+ (think "plus to zoom in").

- **Through Context-sensitive menus**. With nothing selected, hold down your Control key (Mac) or Right mouse button (Windows) to access a pop-up menu so you can zoom in and out, change views, undo, and show or hide guides, rulers and grids.

- **Navigator palette**. With the Navigator palette you can quickly zoom in or out and change the viewing area with the help of the palette thumbnail (see Tip at right).

New Window

Before Illustrator allowed editing in Preview, New Window was an essential feature. Although Illustrator now allows editing in Preview, New Window (Window: New Window) is still extremely useful. This allows you to display different aspects of your current image simultaneously. You can separately zoom each window in or out, resize them, have edges hidden or visible, or hide or lock different *layers* in Preview or Artwork (see "Hide Edges/ Show Edges" below, and see *Chapter 4* for more on layers). Most window configurations are saved with the file.

New View

New View (View: New View) allows you to save your current window viewpoint, remembering also your zoom

The Navigator palette & views

With the arrival of the Navigator palette (always in Preview mode) there are new ways to zoom in and out of your documents:

- Double-click the mountain icons along the bottom edge of the palette window to increase or decrease the amount of zoom in 200% increments.

- Hold the ⌘ key and drag to marquee the area (in the palette thumbnail display) you want to zoom into or out from.

- Enable View Artboard Only to keep your view limited to the artboard area. This is helpful if you are working on a large document with objects on the pasteboard that are distracting from the focus on the artboard.

Change the color of the border around the thumbnail in the Navigator palette via View Options from the palette pop-up menu. **Note:** *Navigator slows down large files. If Illustrator is running sluggishly, quit Illustrator, move the Navigator file out of the Plug-ins folder and relaunch Illustrator.*

Where did the window go?

If you have many file windows open, simply select the file you want to bring to the front from the bottom of the Window menu.

Customize your grids in Illustrator. Select a grid style and color.

- Show grids by pressing ⌘-' (apostrophe), View: Show Grid or using the Context-sensitive menu.
- Toggle Snap To Grid on and off from the View menu, or by pressing ⌘-Shift-' (apostrophe).
- Set the division and subdivision for your grid in Preferences: Guides & Grid and choose either dotted divisions or lines and the color of those lines.
- To toggle the grid display in front or in back of your artwork, enable or disable the Grids In Back checkbox (Preferences: Grid & Guides).
- Tilt the grid on an angle by choosing File: Preferences: General, and in Tool Behavior change the Constrain angle. **Note:** *Changing the Constrain angle also affects the angle at which you can draw and move objects are drawn and moved—see pages 56–57, where the Constrain angle is adjusted for creating isometrics.*

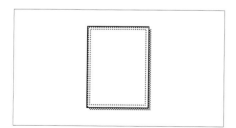

A zoomed-out view of a new document

level and which layers are hidden, locked or in Preview mode. Custom views are added to the bottom of the View menu to easily recall a saved view (see *Chapter 4* for more info on views). Views are not editable—if you need to make a change to a view, you'll have to make a New View.

Hide Edges / Show Edges

If looking at all those anchor points and colored paths distracts you from figuring out what you need to do with selected objects in your current window, choose View: Hide Edges (⌘-H or Context-sensitive menu), and ⌘-H again to Show Edges (see Tip opposite).

Window controls

As in Photoshop, you'll see three small icons at the very bottom of the toolbox. One is always selected; this is the default in which Illustrator will display your file window. Choose from (starting at the far left) Standard Screen Mode (desktop showing around the edges of your file), Full Screen Mode with Menu Bar (file window visible, but confined to the center of the screen with no desktop showing; you can access your menu bar) and Full Screen Mode (same as above, but you cannot access your menu bar). Toggle among the views by pressing the "F" key.

SETTING UP YOUR PAGE

The truth is, controlling your page and printing options is more difficult than it ought to be. You will find page information and specifications distributed among various menu options.

Double-click the Hand tool to fit your image to the current window. A box with a solid black outline representing the size of your Artboard defines the parameters of your final document size. A dotted line indicates the margins of the printer that is currently selected.

Document & Page Setup

In this version of Illustrator Document Setup and Page Setup separate once again. Press ⌘-Option-P to select

Document Setup and ⌘-Shift-P to select Page Setup. You can also continue to access Page Setup from within the Document Setup dialog box.

Use Document Setup to set the size and orientation of the artboard, adjust output resolution and more.

Use Page Setup if you want to change the selected printer and page orientation. Select your printer from the Paper pop-up menu, and choose portrait or landscape orientation.

For Mac, change the Reduce or Enlarge option to scale your image in relation to Page Setup. This is a terrific way to scale something quickly to see how it looks when printed out smaller or larger. A 4" line of a 4-pt weight, printed at 25% reduction (the maximum you can reduce), will print as a 1", 1-pt line. However, because Page Setup only scales your image in relation to the current printing setup, it will not affect the size of the image when placed into another program or another document. Use View: Hide Page Tiling to hide the dotted lines. Use the Page tool to click-drag the dotted-line page parameters around the Artboard; only objects within the dotted line will print to your printer.

The Artboard

Think of the Artboard as the final image size. To change Artboard size, choose File: Document Setup. To match the artboard to your current printer, enable Use Page Setup and choose from one of the pop-up presets, or set the size—now twice the maximum size of previous versions, up to 227" x 227" (which switches your paper size to "Custom"). Why might you want your Artboard to be a different size from that of your current printer? Commonly, you might want to create a large image that you'll eventually print to an imagesetter, but it first needs to be proofed on your laser printer. If this is the case, choose Page Setup to reduce the image size to fit your current printer. Another option is to tile your image onto pages you can physically paste together to simulate the larger page size.

Zippy zooming

Current magnification is displayed in the bottom left corner of your document. Access a list of percentages from 3.13% to 6400% (Control-click the mouse button), or simply select the text and enter a percentage. Other options for zooming are the Zoom tool to magnify or Option-Zoom tool to reduce, the View menu (Zoom In/Out) or the Navigator palette.

Don't forget about your edges!

If you like Photoshop's Hide Edges command, be forewarned: Once you hide your edges (⌘-H), all subsequent selected shapes will also have invisible handles and paths, which can cause confusion if you forget you issued the command! If you can't select something, check to see if you need to toggle to Show Edges.

How many Undos are left?

The status line in the lower left corner of your image window is actually a pop-up menu that lets you choose to display Current Tool, Date and Time, Free Memory or Number of Undos.

For an Easter egg surprise, hold down Option while clicking the status line. — Robin AF Olson

To set units of measurement for rulers, palettes and some dialog boxes or filters, choose File: Document Setup (⌘-Option-P). To set units for *new* documents, change units in General Preferences.

Note: *Mac users, press ⌘-Control-U to cycle through the different units of measurement.*

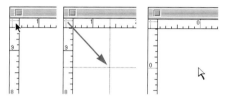

Grabbing and dragging the ruler corner to re-center the ruler origin (zero point)

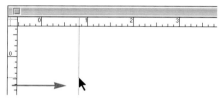

Clicking inside the ruler and dragging into your image to create a vertical or horizontal guide

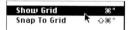

Too many guides?

If you get to a point where there are just too many guides on the page in your document, get rid of them in one easy move. Simply choose View: Clear Guides. This will only work on guides that are on visible unlocked layers. Hiding or locking layers retains any guides you have created.

Rulers, Ruler Guides, Grids and Smart Guides

From the View menu, toggle Illustrator's Show/Hide Rulers (⌘-R), or use the Context-sensitive menu (as long as nothing in your document is selected). The rulers are set to the unit of measurement in Document Setup.

In previous versions of Illustrator, the ruler origin was in the lower right corner of the image. Now the ruler origin (where 0,0 is) is in the *lower left* corner of your image. To change the ruler origin, grab the *upper left* corner (where the vertical and horizontal rulers meet) and drag the crosshair to the desired location. The zeros of the rulers will reset to the point where you release your mouse (to rezero the ruler, *double-click* the upper left corner). But beware—resetting your ruler origin will realign all new patterns and affect alignment of Paste In Front/Back between documents (see *Chapter 4* for more on Paste In Front/Back).

To create simple vertical or horizontal ruler guides, click-drag from one of the rulers into your image. A guide appears where you release your mouse. You can define guide color and style in General Preferences. Guides automatically lock after you create them, so the easiest way to move a locked guide is ⌘-Shift-drag the guide. To release a guide quickly, ⌘-Shift-double-click it. You can lock and unlock guides with the Context-sensitive menu (⌘-Option-;). You should note that locking or unlocking guides affects every open document. (For help turning objects into custom guides, see pages 96–98 and 164.)

A recent addition to Illustrator is Smart Guides. (See the Tip on page 2 for details on Smart Guides.) Keep in mind that seeing Smart Guides flash on and off your screen as you work can be somewhat unnerving (⌘-U toggles Smart Guides on and off), but with practice and understanding of each option, you'll be able to refine how to incorporate them into your workflow.

Illustrator also has automatic grids. To view grids, either type ⌘-', select View: Show Grid, or use the Context-sensitive menu. You can adjust the color, style of line (dots or solid) and size of the grid's subdivisions from

File: Preferences: Guides & Grid.

As with guides, you can also enable a snap-to grid function. Toggle Snap To Grid on and off by choosing View: Snap To Grid. See "Glorious grids" on page 18 for more on grids.

IMPORTANT: *If you adjust the x and y axes in File: Preferences: General: Constrain Angle, it will affect the drawn objects and transformations of your grid, as they will follow the adjusted angle when you create a new object. This is great, however, if you're doing a complicated layout requiring alignment of objects at an angle.*

COLOR IN ILLUSTRATOR

Consumer-level monitors, which display color in red, green and blue lights (RGB), cannot yet match four-color CMYK (cyan, magenta, yellow, black) inks printed onto paper. Therefore, you must retrofit the current technology with partial solutions, starting with calibrating your monitor.

Some programs (such as the Gamma utility installed with Photoshop) provide you with some degree of control over the way your monitor displays colors. In addition, Illustrator ships with a CMS (Color Management System) that for some will help keep the colors on screen closer to the color you output. ColorSync (Mac) and Kodak Digital Science Color Management (Windows) are the two main systems (please see the *User Guide* for information on installing and using these systems and others following).

In addition to this software calibration, methods of hardware calibration are available that actually adjust the beams of the cathode-ray tube emitting the RGB lights. Generally, the larger the monitor, the more likelihood that colors will vary in different areas of the screen. Monitor color is also affected by the length of time your monitor is on and the ambient light in your workroom.

In order to produce an accurate proof (if a printing press is your target), Illustrator would need to support printing profiles for both composite (your printer) and

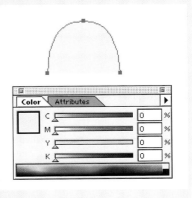

Converting RGB to CMYK

Although computers can make conversions from CMYK to RGB (and vice versa) seem as simple as a menu command, such conversions often result in muddy colors. If you plan on rasterizing, convert your file in Photoshop, where you'll have greater control over ink density, UCR and GCR separations and more. Consult your service bureau and printer for detailed directions based on your job specifications.

Out of Gamut Warning Caution

If you plan to print in CMYK and see an Out of Gamut Warning in the Color palette, take this as a caution that the current color is out of the range of printable colors. Either switch your color mode to CMYK from the Color pop-up, or click on the Closest Approximation box next to the gamut warning for an RGB or HSB color approximation. Switching to CMYK mode will allow you to see the actual values of the plates.

New levels of PostScript

Adobe's PostScript 3 language is full of new features that improve printing time, deliver truer colors and provide Web-Ready printing. For details on PS3, refer to Adobe's "white paper" on PS3 from the web at www.adobe.com

separation (the final printing device) ICC(M) printers. Currently, Illustrator only supports one ICC(M) profile for printing. Thus Illustrator lacks the ability to emulate the separation printer on the composite printer. When creating art for placement into QuarkXPress or PageMaker, you'll also discover that no application-level color management module currently supports the EPS file format. All this means is that it's okay to use Illustrator for proofing directly from Illustrator to your printer, but don't rely on its color management for accurate press proofs. Always consult with your prepress house and run a proof prior to printing an entire job.

Working in RGB, CMYK and HSB (Oh my!)

Illustrator gives you the flexibility of being able to work and print out of RGB, CMYK and HSB. This is a mixed blessing, in that print cannot accurately capture vibrant RGB colors and muddy printed colors can result. If you work in print, just work in CMYK!

The best aspect about being able to work in RGB is that these colors are great for creating artwork for on-screen display and for identifying particular spot colors, such as day-glo colors, to your printer. See *Chapter 10* for more on working in RGB.

Multiple color models—all in one document!

Unlike Photoshop, which requires you to select a color model before you can begin working on your document, Illustrator allows you to work in multiple color models at the same time. Especially if you work in print (I just can't say this enough), be very careful to always check your objects to make certain they are in the appropriate (and similar) color model before you output your work. Do this by choosing File: Document Info: Objects and look for RGB Objects and CMYK Objects.

Color systems, styles and the Web palette

In addition to mixing color in RGB, HSB and CMYK, you can also select colors from other color matching systems or the new 216-color "web-safe" palette. You can access Focoltone, Dicolor, Toyo, Trumatch, and Pantone libraries or the Web palette by choosing Window: Swatch Libraries, then locate the specific color system you wish to work with. Keep in mind that you now open color libraries as separate uneditable palettes. The default for the Swatches palette is to open with swatches—*not* view by name. Use the palette pop-up menu to change the view to Names if this is what you prefer.

In previous versions of Illustrator, styles and colors in any open document were automatically listed and accessible to all other open documents. In order to access styles in another document, you must choose Window: Swatch Libraries: Other Library, then choose the Illustrator file from which you wish to access the styles. This opens a new palette with that document's swatches. To store a swatch from an open library into your current document, just use the swatch or drag the swatch from its library palette to your Swatches palette.

IMAGE FORMATS
Earlier Illustrator formats
FreeHand, Canvas, CorelDraw and a number of 3D programs allow you to save images in older Illustrator formats, or you might have a document created in an earlier version of Illustrator. To open any file saved in an earlier version, drag it onto an Illustrator alias or open the older formatted file from within Illustrator by choosing File: Open (⌘-O) and selecting the document you want to open. If it's a file you plan to work on or open again, use Save As to save a copy in the current Illustrator format.

EPS (Encapsulated PostScript)
EPS is a universal format, meaning that a wide variety of programs support importing and exporting images in EPS format for printing to PostScript printers. In most programs, when saving an image in EPS format, you can choose to include a Preview (the Preview is an on-screen PICT or TIFF representation of your image; an EPS

CMY Color Model   RGB Color Model

CMY (Cyan, Magenta, Yellow) **subtractive** colors get darker when mixed; RGB (Red, Green, Blue) **additive** colored lights combine to make white

Trapping issues
Continuous-tone, antialiased bitmapped images naturally form "traps" to hide misregistration of CMYK inks, but hard, crisp PostScript edges are a registration nightmare. Some products, such as Island Graphics' IslandTrapper, used for this book, can globally trap pages. If you know the exact size and resolution of your final image, you can rasterize Illustrator files (or specific objects) into bitmaps by using Object: Rasterize, or rasterize in Photoshop (see *Chapter 9*).

If you don't wish to rasterize:

- Construct your images so that overlapping shapes having common inks form natural traps (see page 64).
- Set individual colors to Overprint in the Attributes palette.
- Globally set blacks to overprint (Filter: Colors: Overprint Black).
- See the *User Guide* for details on setting traps in *solid* objects using Object: Pathfinder: Trap.
- For trapping patterns and gradients, see Tip on page 64.

The Links palette keeps a running (and updatable) list of all images in your document, whether they are linked or embedded. The key features of this palette are:

- You can quickly find out if you are missing a link (stop sign icon on the link layer) or need to update a link (exclamation icon).
- You can replace a link, update a link, go to a link or edit a link with the press of a button.
- You can change a linked image into an embedded image through the pop-up menu.
- You can find out information about the link (file name, location, size, kind, date modified and transformations made) by double-clicking on a link layer to open the Link information dialog box (not all information is available for all formats).

Note: *Until the Links palette provides information on the color mode (RGB, CMYK, bitmapped or Grayscale), be careful to check your links manually! (See "Links" Tip in "What's New" preface.)*

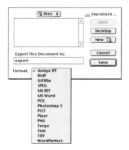

image placed in another program without a Preview will print properly, but can't be viewed). To import an EPS image into Illustrator, choose File: Place (see *Chapters 4* and *9* for examples and more about EPS).

Other image formats

Illustrator supports a wealth of file formats (such as JPEG, TIFF, PICT, PCX, Pixar and Photoshop). If you choose to place these formats, you can choose whether these files will remain *linked* (see Tip "Links are manageable" at left) or will become *embedded* image objects (see *Chapter 9* for specifics on embedding, and *Chapter 10* for details on web-related formats). If you choose Open, most of these become embedded. See the Adobe *User Guide* and *Read Me* files for listings of supported formats that shipped with this version. Check Adobe's website (www.adobe.com) for the latest information on supported formats as well as additional file format plug-ins. You can also open and edit PDF (Acrobat format) documents and even "raw" PostScript files directly from within Illustrator. (For more on file format issues, see *Chapter 9*.)

POSTSCRIPT PRINTING & EXPORTING

When you're ready to print your image (to a laser or inkjet printer, imagesetter or film recorder), you should use a PostScript printing device. Adobe owns and licenses the PostScript language, making PostScript printers somewhat more expensive than non-PostScript printers. Some companies produce PostScript-compatible printers or provide PostScript emulation. Although Illustrator images sometimes print just fine to these printers, at other times you might run into problems. In general, the newer the PostScript device, the faster and less problematic your printing will be. PostScript Level 2 and Level 3 printers provide better printing clarity and even some special effects, such as Illustrator's new integration of PostScript Level 3's "smooth shading" technology (which should greatly enhance gradients and reduce banding problems). Lastly, the more memory you install in your printer, the quicker your text and images will print. For crucial jobs, you must develop good relations with your service bureau, and get into the habit of running test prints to identify possible problems. (Also see the Tip "Proofing your prints," next page.)

Correcting and avoiding printing problems

If you have trouble printing, first of all make sure your placed images are linked properly and the fonts needed to print the document are loaded. Second, check for any complex objects in the document. Save As a Copy, remove the complex object(s) and try to print. If that doesn't work, make sure File: Document Setup and Separation Setup have the correct settings for your output device. Also see Tip on page 132 for issues regarding printing gradient mesh objects.

More about controlling the size of your files

The major factors that can increase your file size are the inclusion of image objects, path pattern, brushes and ink pen objects, complex patterns, a large number of blends and gradients (especially gradient mesh objects and gradient-to-gradient blends), and linked bitmapped images. Although linked bitmaps can be large, the same image embedded as an image object is significantly larger. If your Illustrator file contains linked images, and you need to save the entire file in EPS (for placement and printing in other programs), you have the option Include Placed Images. Most service bureaus highly recommend this option, as it will embed placed images in your Illustrator file and make printing from page layout programs and film recorders much more predictable (be sure to see top Tip "Proofing your prints," next page). However, since including placed images will further increase the file size, wait until you've completed an image and are ready to place it into another program before you save a copy with placed images embedded. Whether or not you choose to embed linked images, you *must* collect all of the files that have been linked into your Illustrator

Saving time and space

Note: *Before you attempt to minimize the size of your file, make certain that you're working on a copy.* To minimize the size of your file, first remove all your unused colors and patterns. Open the appropriate palette, click the All Swatches icon, choose Select All Unused from the Swatches pop-up menu, then click the Trash icon to delete. (You may have to repeat the select and delete process to remove *all* the excess colors.) You should minimize the time it takes to print an Illustrator file, even if it's been placed into another program, such as QuarkXPress or PageMaker (see *Chapter 9* for details on exporting). If you've scaled or rotated an Illustrator image once it's been placed into another program, note the numeric percentages of scaling and the degrees of rotation. Next, reopen the file in Illustrator, perform the identical scale or rotation, then place this pretransformed version back into the other program, making sure to rezero the scaling and rotation for this already transformed image.

Note: *Be certain to scale line weight, objects and pattern tiles when you perform these transformations in Illustrator (see page 14).*

Proofing your prints

Get into the habit of proofing all your images to a laser printer to gauge whether your image will take a long time to print. The higher your printing resolution, the longer your PostScript image will take to print. Based on your laser test, if you know that your image will require hours to print, you might be able to arrange for your service bureau to print your image overnight or on a weekend to save extra charges.

Using Startup documents

In your Plug-ins folder (in the Adobe Illustrator folder) is a file called "Adobe Illustrator Startup"; this file loads information into Illustrator such as which colors, patterns, brushes and gradients will be automatically loaded when you start a new document. To create a *custom* startup file, make a duplicate of the original and move the original to a safe place (out of the plug-ins folder). Open the copy from within Illustrator and add or subtract styles from this document and save—the next time you launch Illustrator, this startup file will determine the set of styles available to new files. For more details see the *User Guide*. (**Hint:** You can make different startup files for each project!)

documents and transport them along with your Illustrator file. Illustrator makes your task easier if you choose File: Document Info: Linked Images, which outputs a text file of all images in your document. Press Save to create a text file that you can file for future reference or give to your service bureau as a record of the images included in your files.

Printing speed

A related but even more crucial factor to take into consideration when creating an image is understanding what elements make an image take longer to print. Special effects such as transforming or masking placed images, using complex patterns or a slew of patterns, gradients, live blends, brushes, path pattern or ink pen effects are the worst culprits for increasing file size, and thus printing time.

Although in most cases you'll want to perform any scaling of your final image in Illustrator before placing it into a page layout program (make certain to enable the Scale Stroke Weight option), if your image contains brushes, it may not scale properly within Illustrator (see top Tip on page 13).

If you're going to place bitmaps into your Adobe Illustrator file, you'll greatly reduce your printing time if you perform all scaling and transformations of the bitmaps *before* placing them in Illustrator. Another reason to scale your bitmapped images before placing them in Illustrator is to ensure that the pixel-per-inch (ppi) resolution of the images is 1.5 to 2 times the size of the line screen at which the final image will print. For instance, if your illustration will be printed at 2" x 2" in a 150-line screen, then the resolution of your bitmapped image should not exceed 300 ppi at 2" x 2". Talk to your service bureau and print shop for advice about your specific job before you make decisions about what resolution your bitmap images should be.

A LAST WORD ON ACTIONS

Actions are a set of commands or a series of events that you can record and save as sets in the Action palette. Once it's recorded, you can play back an action in the same order in which you recorded it, to automate a job you do repeatedly (a production task or special effect).

Select the action in the Action palette and play it by clicking the Play button at the bottom of the palette, choosing Play from the pop-up menu, or assigning the Action to a keyboard F-key (function key) so you can play the action with a keystroke. You can select an action set, a single action or a command within an action to play. To exclude a command from playing within an action, click the checkbox to the left of the command. In order to play some types of actions you may have to first select an object or some text. Load action sets using the pop-up menu. (Find sets of premade Actions on the Adobe Illustrator Application CD in the Illustrator Extras folder as well as *Wow! Actions* on the *Wow!* disk.)

Since you must actions record and save within an action set, begin a new action by clicking the Create New Set button or choosing New Set from the pop-up. Name the action set and click OK. With the new set selected, click the Create New Action button, name the action and click Record. Illustrator records your commands and steps until you click Stop. To resume recording, click on the last step, choose Begin and continue adding to the action. When you've finished recording, you'll need to save the action file by selecting the action set and choosing Save Actions from the pop-up menu.

Keep in mind when recording that not all commands or tools are recordable. For example, the Pen tool itself is not recordable, but you can add the paths the Pen tool creates to an action by selecting a path and choosing Insert Selected Paths again from the pop-up menu. For a more complete list of what is recordable, see Tip at right. Recording actions take some practice, so don't get discouraged, Always save a backup file, and refer to the *User Guide* for more details on Actions.

Action—what's recordable

Tools: Ellipse, Polygon, Star, Spiral, Rectangle, Rotate, Scale, Shear and Reflect.

File menu: New, Open, Close, Save, Save As, Save a Copy, Revert, Place and Export.

Edit: Cut, Copy, Paste, Paste In Front, Paste In Back, Clear, Select All, Deselect All and the Select pop-up menu items.

Object: Transform Again, Move, Scale, Rotate, Shear, Reflect, Transform Each, Arrange pop-up items, Group, Ungroup, Lock, Unlock All, Hide Selection, Show All, Expand, Rasterize, Blends, Mask, Compound Path and Crop Marks.

Type: Character, Paragraph, MM Design, Tab Ruler, Block, Wrap, Fit Headline, Create Outlines, Find/Change, Find Font, Change Case, Rows & Columns, Type Orientation and Glyph Options.

Filters: Colors, Create, Distort and Stylize.

Guide-related views.

Window: Transform, Align, Pathfinder, Color, Gradient, Stroke, Swatches, Brushes, Layers, Attributes and Actions.

Bounding Box transformations.

Selecting objects in an action

When recording an action, use the Attributes palette (Show Note) to name an object, and Select Object (Action pop-up) to type in the object's name (note) to select it.

The Zen of Illustrator

2

Zen: *"Seeking enlightenment through introspection and intuition rather than scripture."**

You're comfortable with the basic operations of your computer. You've conquered the Adobe Illustrator *Tutorial*. You've committed enough hours to Illustrator to be familiar with how each tool in the palette (theoretically) functions. You even understand how to make Bézier curves. Now what? How do you take all this knowledge and turn it into a mastery of the medium?

As with learning any new artistic medium (such as engraving, watercolor or airbrush), learning to manipulate the tools is just the beginning. Thinking and seeing in that medium is what really makes those tools part of your creative arsenal. Before you can determine the best way to construct an image, you have to be able to envision at least some of the possibilities. The first key to mastering Illustrator is to understand that Illustrator's greatest strength comes not from its myriad tools and functions but from its extreme flexibility in terms of how you construct images. The first part of this chapter, therefore, introduces you to a variety of approaches and techniques for creating and transforming objects.

Once you've got yourself "thinking in Illustrator," you can begin to *visualize* how to achieve the final results. What is the simplest and most elegant way to construct an image? Which tools will you use? Then, once you've begun, allow yourself the flexibility to change course and try something else. Be willing to say to yourself: How else can I get the results that I want?

* Adapted from *Webster's New World Dictionary of the English Language*

The second key to mastering Illustrator (or any new medium) is perfecting your hand/eye coordination. In Illustrator, this translates into being proficient enough with the "power-keys" to gain instant access to the tools and functions through the keyboard. With both eyes on the monitor, one hand on the mouse, and the other hand on the keyboard, an experienced Illustrator user can create and manipulate objects in a fraction of the time required otherwise. The second part of this chapter helps you to learn the "finger dance" necessary to become a truly adept power-user.

The ability to harness the full power of Illustrator's basic tools and functions will ultimately make you a true master of Adobe Illustrator. Treat this chapter like meditation. Take it in small doses if necessary. Be mindful that the purpose of these exercises is to open up your mind to possibilities, not to force memorization. When you can conceptualize a number of different ways to create an image, then the hundreds of hints, tips, tricks, and techniques found elsewhere in this book can serve as a jumping-off point for further exploration. If you take the time to explore and absorb this chapter, you should begin to experience what I call the "Zen of Illustrator." This magical program, at first cryptic and counterintuitive, can help you achieve creative results not possible in any other medium.

Building Houses
Sequential Object Construction Exercises

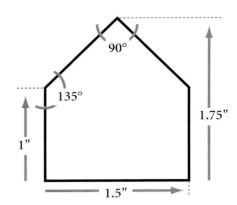

Overview: *Explore different approaches to constructing the same object with Illustrator's basic construction tools.*

1

2

Dragging out a guide from the Ruler, and choosing Window: Show Info to open the Info palette if it's not open before you begin

3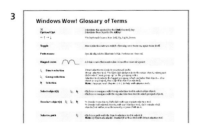

4

> ⇧ Shift   ⇧ Shift
>
> Option   Alt

Hint: *Hold down the Shift key to constrain movement to horizontal/vertical direction. For more modifier key help, see the end of this chapter for the "Finger Dance" lesson.*

This sequence of exercises explores different ways to construct the same simple object, a house. The purpose of these exercises is to introduce you to the flexibility of Illustrator's object construction, so don't worry if some exercises seem less efficient than others. In File: Preferences: Units & Undo, set Inches for Ruler units (so you can use the numbers provided and the measurements above). And read through the recommendations below for preparing your working environment.

1 Work in Artwork mode. Doing so keeps you from being distracted by fills or line weights and lets you see the centers of geometric objects (marked by "×").

2 Use Show Rulers and Show Info. Choose Show Rulers from the View menu (⌘-R) so you can "pull out" guides. Use the Info palette to view numeric data as you work (I arrived at these numbers just this way!), or ignore the numeric data and just draw the houses by eye.

3 Read through the *Wow! Glossary*. Please make sure to read *How to use this book* and the *Glossary* pull-out card.

4 Use "modifier" keys. These exercises use Shift and Option (Alt) keys, which you must hold down until *after* you release your mouse button. If you make a mistake, choose Undo (⌘-Z) and try again. Some functions are also accessible from the Context-sensitive menu.

Exercise #1:

Use Add-anchor-point tool

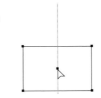

1

1 Create a rectangle and a vertical guide. Create a wide rectangle (1.5" x 1") and drag out a vertical guide that snaps to the center.

2

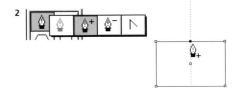

2 Add an anchor point on the top. Use the Add-anchor-point tool to add a point on the top segment over the center guide.

3

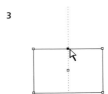

3 Drag the new point up. Use the Direct-selection tool to grab the new point and drag it up into position (.75" for a total height of 1.75").

Exercise #2:

Make an extra point

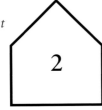

1

1 Create a rectangle, delete the top path and place a center point. Create a wide rectangle (1.5" x 1"). With the Direct-selection tool, select the top path and delete it. With the Pen tool, place a point on top of the rectangle center point.

2

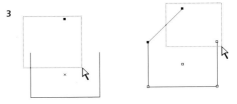

2 Move the point up. Double-click on the Selection tool in the Toolbox to open the Move dialog box and enter a 1.25" vertical distance to move the point up.

3

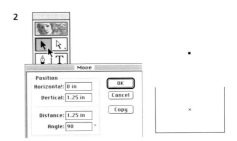

3 Select and join the point to each side. Use the Direct-selection tool to select the left two points and join (⌘-J) them to the top point. Repeat with the right two points.

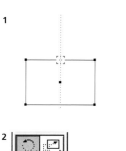

1

2

3

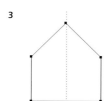

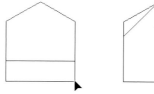

3

Exercise #3:
Rotate and unite

3

1 Create two rectangles, one centered on the other. Create a wide rectangle (1.5" x 1") and drag out a vertical guide snapping it to the center. With the Option key down, click with the Rectangle tool (Option-click) on the center guide (on the top segment). Enter 1.05" x 1.05".

2 Rotate one rectangle. Double-click the Rotate tool to rotate the new rectangle around its center and enter 45°.

3 Select and unite the rectangles. Marquee-select both objects and click Pathfinder: Unite (the first Pathfinder icon, or use the *Wow! Action* from the *Wow!* disk).

Exercise #4:
Make a six-sided polygon

4

1 Create a six-sided polygon. With the Polygon tool selected, click once and enter 6 sides and a .866" Radius. Then double-click the Rotate tool and enter 30°.

2 Delete the bottom point. With the Delete-anchor-point tool, click on the bottom point to delete it.

3 Move the two bottom points down, then the two middle points. Use the Direct-selection tool to select the bottom two points. Then grab one of the points and Shift-drag in a vertical line (down .423"). Lastly, Direct-select, grab and Shift-drag the middle two points down vertically into position (down .275").

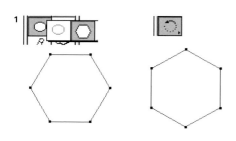

Exercise #5:

Use Add Anchor Points filter in a three-sided polygon

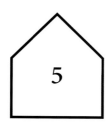

1 Create a three-sided polygon. With the Polygon tool selected, click once and enter 3 sides and a 1.299" Radius.

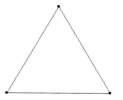

2 Use the Add Anchor Points filter. With the polygon still selected, choose Object: Path: Add Anchor Points (or use the *Wow! Action* from the *Wow!* disk).

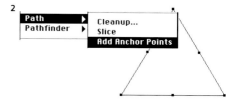

3 Average the left two points, then Average the right two points. Direct-select the left two points and Average them along the vertical axis (Context-sensitive: Average, or Object: Path: Average, or ⌘-Option-J), then repeat for the right two points.

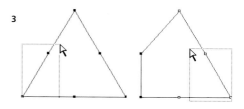

4 Delete the bottom point. With the Delete-anchor-point tool, click on the bottom point to delete it.

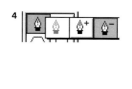

5 Move the top point down. Use the Direct-selection tool to select the top point, then double-click on the Selection tool itself in the Toolbox to open the Move dialog box and enter a −.186" vertical distance.

6 Slide in the sides towards the center. Use the Direct-selection tool to click on the right side of the house and drag it towards the center until the roofline looks smooth (hold down your Shift key to constrain the drag horizontally). Repeat for the left side of the house. Alternatively, select the right side and use the ← key on your keyboard to nudge the right side towards the center until the roofline looks smooth. Then, click on the left side to select it, and use the → key to nudge it towards the center. (If necessary, change your Cursor-key setting in Preferences: Keyboard Increments.)

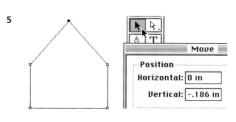
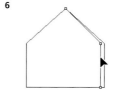

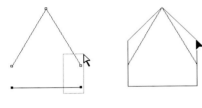

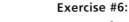

Exercise #6:
Cut a path and Paste In Front

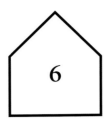

1 Cut, paste, then move the bottom of a triangle. With the Polygon tool selected, click once and enter 3 sides and a .866" Radius. With the Direct-selection tool, select and cut the bottom path to the Clipboard (⌘-X). Choose Edit: Paste In Front (⌘-F), then grab the bottom path and drag it into position (down .423").

2 Create the sides and move middle points into place. Direct-select the two right points and join them (⌘-J), then repeat for the left two points. Finally, select the two middle points, and grab one to drag *both* up (.275").

Exercise #7:
Join two objects

1 Make two objects. Click once with the Polygon tool, enter 3 sides and a .866" Radius. Zoom in on the lower left corner and, with the Rectangle tool, click exactly on the lower left anchor point. Set the rectangle to 1.5" x 1".

2 Delete the middle lines and join the corners. Direct-select marquee the middle bisecting lines and delete. Select the upper-left corner points and Average-Join (hold down Option while choosing Object: Path: Join, or ⌘-Shift-Option-J) to average and join simultaneously. Select and Average-Join the upper right points.

3 Drag the top point down. Grab the top point, hold the Shift key and drag it into position (down .55").

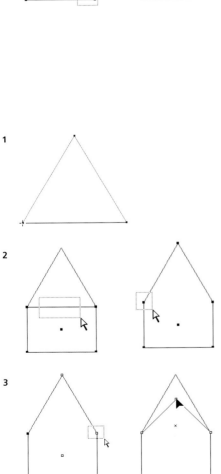

Exercise #8:

Use Add Anchor Points filter, then Average-Join

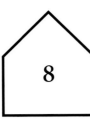

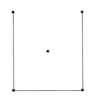
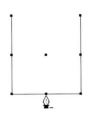

1 Make a tall rectangle, delete top path, add anchor points, remove bottom point. Create a tall rectangle (1.5" x 1.75") and delete the top path. Choose Add Anchor Points (Object: Path) and use the Delete-anchor-point tool to remove the bottom point.

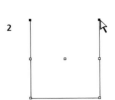

2 Select and Average-Join the top points and move middles into position. Direct-select the top two points and Average-Join (see Exercise #7, step 2). Then Direct-select the middle points, grab one, and with the Shift key, drag them both into position (up .125").

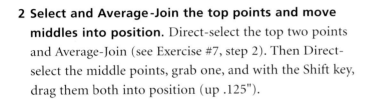

Exercise #9:

Reflect a Pen profile

1 Create a house profile. Drag out a vertical guide, then reset the ruler origin on the guide. To draw the profile, use the Pen tool to click on the guide at the ruler zero point, and Shift (to constrain your lines to 45° angles) and click to place the corner (.75" down and .75" to the left) and the bottom (1" down).

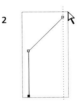

2 Reflect a copy of the profile. Select all three points of the house profile, and with the Reflect tool, Option-click on the guide line. Enter an angle of 90° and click Copy.

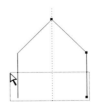

3 Join the two profiles. Direct-select and Join (⌘-J) the bottom two points. Then Direct-select the top two points and Average-Join (see Exercise #7, step 2).

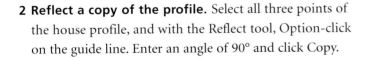

A Classic Icon

Five Ways to Re-create Simple Shapes

Overview: *Finding different ways to construct the same iconic image.*

1

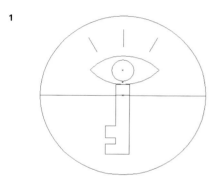

The Artwork view of the original logo

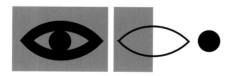

The original logo, constructed from a stroked line and a solid circle

You can construct even the simplest of iconic images in myriad ways. Patricia McShane and Erik Adigard of the M.A.D. graphics firm designed this classic logo for the *Computers Freedom & Privacy* annual conference, which addresses the effects of computer and telecommunications technologies on societal and personal freedom and privacy. This simple iconic representation of an eye is a perfect example of how you can explore different ways to solve the same graphics problem.

1 First, construct your logo in the way that seems most logical to you. Everybody's mind works differently, and the most obvious solutions to you might seem innovative to the next person. Follow your instincts as to how to construct each image. But if design changes require you to rethink your approach (for instance, what if the client wanted a radial fill instead of the black stroke?), then try something slightly, or even completely, different.

Viewed in Artwork mode, the original *Computers Freedom & Privacy* logo is clean and elegant with a minimum number of anchor points and lines. The M.A.D. team constructed the eye from a stroked line (made with the Pen tool) and a filled, black circle.

2 Make the outer eye shape. Create the solid black, almond-shaped object any way you wish: Try drawing it with the Pen tool like M.A.D. did, or maybe convert an oval into the correct shape by clicking on the middle points with the Convert-direction-point tool in the Pen tool pop-up (or cycle to this tool by pressing "P").

3 Try using solid objects. Starting with your base object, construct the eye with overlapping solid objects. Scale a version of the outline for the green inset and place a black circle on the top.

4 Try making a compound object. Use the objects that you created in the previous version to make a compound object that allows the inner part of the eye to be cut out. Select the outer black outline and the inner green inset and choose Object: Compound Paths: Make (⌘-8).

5 Try making the eye from a symbol font. Included on the *Wow!* disk is a sample international symbols font from Image Club called "Mini Pics International." The character "W" is an eye very close to our icon. First, load your Mini Pics font (see your operating system manual for loading fonts). Choose the Mini Pics font from the Character palette (⌘-T), then click with the Type tool and type the character W. Next, click on a Selection tool (this selects your type as an object) and press ⌘-Shift-O or, choose Type: Create Outlines. This command converts the letter into a compound object different from the one you made in version 4 (above), with three objects cut out of the outline. Since the eye you're trying to make doesn't have a dark solid center, use the Direct-selection tool to select and delete the center compound object. Then try to match the original eye by adjusting the remaining compound paths with the Direct-selection and Scale tools.

Converting and transforming this symbol font may be a convoluted way to create such a simple shape, but the technique is certain to come in handy.

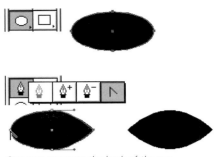

One way to create the back of the eye

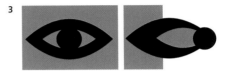

Constructing the logo with three solid objects

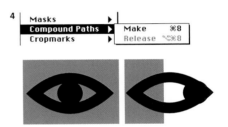

Constructing the logo from an outer compound object and an inner solid circle

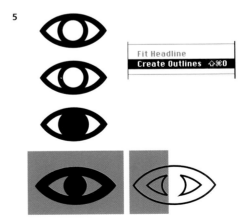

The same logo constructed from a text object converted to an outline, then scaled

Zen Scaling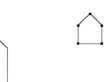

Note: *Use the Shift key to constrain proportions.* **Zen Scaling** *practice is also on the* **Wow!** *disk.*

1 Scaling proportionally towards the top Click at the top, grab lower-right (LR), drag up

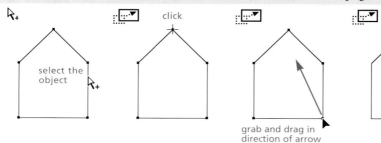

select the object

click

grab and drag in direction of arrow

2 Scaling horizontally towards the center Click at the top, grab LR, drag inwards

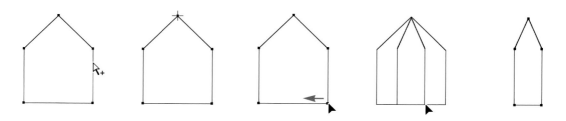

3 Scaling vertically towards the top Click at the top, grab LR, drag straight up

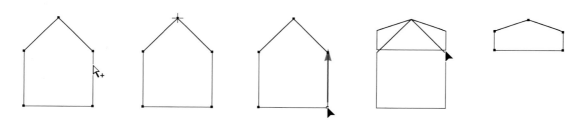

4 Scaling vertically and flipping the object Click at the top, grab LR, drag straight up

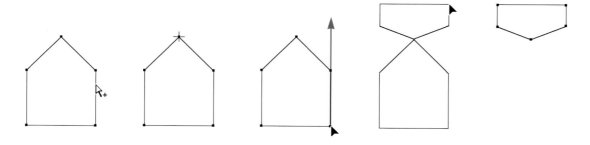

Zen Scaling *(continued)*

Note: *Use the Shift key to constrain proportions.* **Zen Scaling** *practice is also on the* **Wow!** *disk.*

5 Scaling proportionally towards lower-left (LL) Click LL, grab upper-right, drag to LL

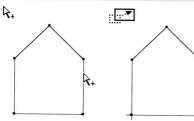  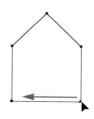 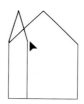 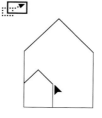

6 Scaling horizontally to the left side Click LL, grab lower-right (LR), drag to left

   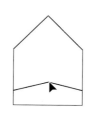 

7 Scaling vertically towards the bottom Click center bottom, grab top, drag down

8 Scaling proportionally towards the center Click the center, grab corner, drag to center

 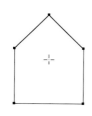 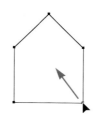 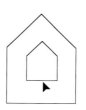

Or, to scale about the center, use the Scale tool to click-drag outside the object towards the center

Zen Rotation ↻

Note: *Use the Shift key to constrain movement.* **Zen Rotation** *practice is also on the* **Wow!** *disk.*

1 Rotating around the center Click in the center, then grab lower-right (LR) and drag

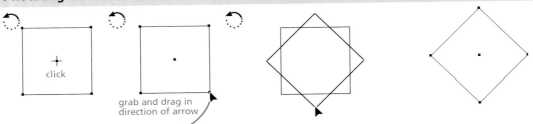

click

grab and drag in
direction of arrow

Or, to rotate about the center, use the Rotate tool to click-drag outside the object towards the center

2 Rotating from a corner Click in the upper left corner, then grab LR and drag

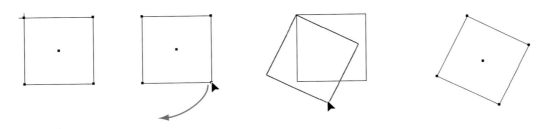

3 Rotating from outside Click above the left corner, then grab LR and drag

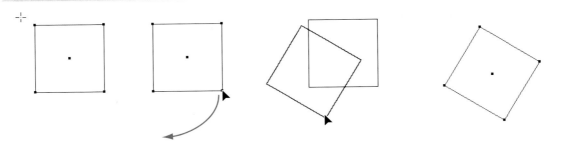

4 Rotating part of a path Marquee points with the Direct-selection tool, then use Rotate tool

Marquee the forearm with Direct-selection tool   *With the Rotate tool, click on the elbow, grab the fingers and drag it around*

Creating a Simple Object Using the Basic Tools

Key: *Click where you see a RED cross, grab with the GRAY arrow and drag towards BLACK arrow.*

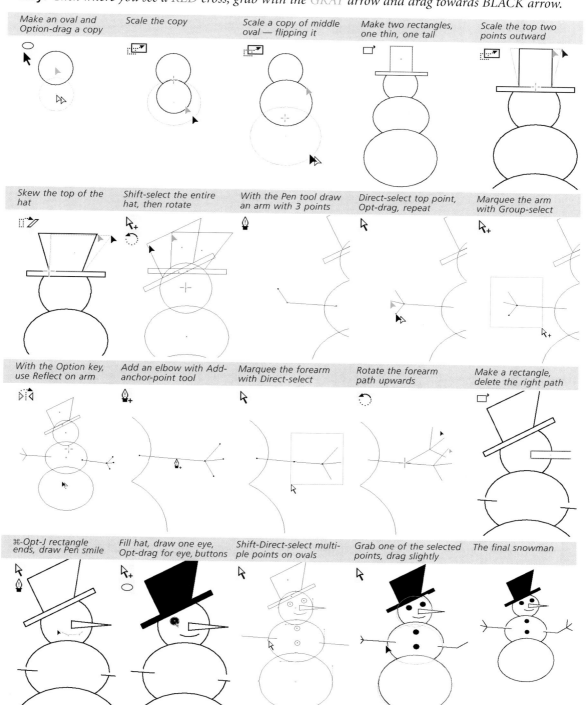

Make an oval and Option-drag a copy

Scale the copy

Scale a copy of middle oval — flipping it

Make two rectangles, one thin, one tall

Scale the top two points outward

Skew the top of the hat

Shift-select the entire hat, then rotate

With the Pen tool draw an arm with 3 points

Direct-select top point, Opt-drag, repeat

Marquee the arm with Group-select

With the Option key, use Reflect on arm

Add an elbow with Add-anchor-point tool

Marquee the forearm with Direct-select

Rotate the forearm path upwards

Make a rectangle, delete the right path

⌘-Opt-J rectangle ends, draw Pen smile

Fill hat, draw one eye, Opt-drag for eye, buttons

Shift-Direct-select multiple points on ovals

Grab one of the selected points, drag slightly

The final snowman

A Finger Dance

Turbo-charge with Illustrator's Power-keys

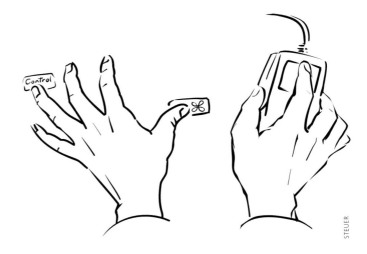

Overview: *Save hours of production time by mastering the finger dance of Illustrator's power-keys.*

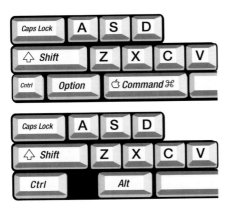

Find a summary of Finger Dance power-keys on the pull-out quick reference card.

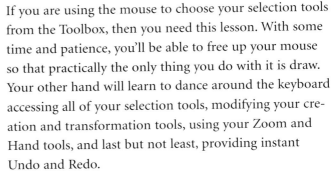

If you are using the mouse to choose your selection tools from the Toolbox, then you need this lesson. With some time and patience, you'll be able to free up your mouse so that practically the only thing you do with it is draw. Your other hand will learn to dance around the keyboard accessing all of your selection tools, modifying your creation and transformation tools, using your Zoom and Hand tools, and last but not least, providing instant Undo and Redo.

This "Finger Dance" is probably the most difficult aspect of Illustrator to master. Go through these lessons in order, but don't expect to get through them in one or even two sittings. When you make a mistake, use Undo (⌘-Z). Try a couple of exercises, then go back to your own work, incorporating what you've just learned. When you begin to get frustrated, take a break. Later—hours, days or weeks later—try another lesson. And don't forget to breathe.

Rule #1: Always keep one finger on the ⌘ key (CTRL for Windows). Whether you are using a mouse or a pressure-sensitive tablet, the hand you are not drawing with should be resting on the keyboard, with one finger (or thumb) on the ⌘ key. This position will make that all-important Undo (⌘-Z) instantly accessible.

Rule #2: Undo if you make a mistake. This is so crucial an aspect of working in the computer environment that I am willing to be redundant. If there is only one key combination that you memorize, make it ⌘-Z, Undo.

Rule #3: The ⌘ (Ctrl) key turns your cursor into a selection tool. In Illustrator, the ⌘ key does a lot more than merely provide you with easy access to Undo (⌘-Z). The ⌘ key will convert any tool into the selection arrow that you last used. In the exercises that follow, you'll soon discover that the most flexible selection arrow is the Direct-selection tool.

Rule #4: Watch your cursor. If you learn to watch your cursor, you'll be able to prevent most errors before they happen. And if you don't (for instance, if you drag a copy of an object by mistake), then use Undo and try again.

Rule #5: Pay careful attention to *when* you hold down each key. Most of the modifier keys operate differently depending on *when* you hold each key down. If you obey Rule #4 and watch your cursor, then you'll notice what the key you are holding does.

Rule #6: Hold down the key(s) until after you let go of your mouse button. In order for your modifier key to actually modify your action, you *must* keep your key down until *after* you let go of your mouse button.

Rule #7: Work in Artwork mode. When you are constructing or manipulating objects, get into the habit of working in Artwork mode. Of course, if you are designing the colors in your image, you'll need to work in Preview, but while you're learning how to use the power-keys, you'll generally find it much quicker and easier if you are in Artwork mode.

Remove "Easy Access"! (Mac)

When you're using Illustrator, you must take the Apple program called *Easy Access* out of the Extensions folder (in the System folder). Although *Easy Access* was developed as an aid to mouse movements for people with limited manual mobility, it interferes with Illustrator's normal functioning. If you have limited manual dexterity, try using QuicKeys to simplify menu selection, keystrokes and object creation.

1 Finger Dance (⌘) Grabbing a selected object and moving it

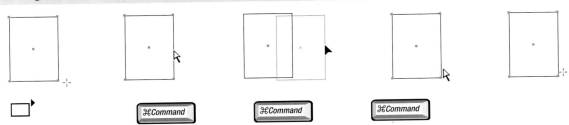

2 Finger Dance (⌘) Deselecting an object, selecting a path and moving it

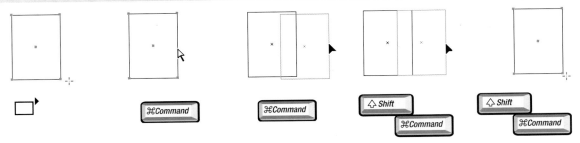

3 Finger Dance (⌘-Shift) Moving a selected object horizontally

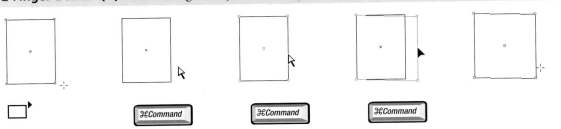

4 Finger Dance (⌘-Shift) Deselecting an object, selecting a path and moving it horizontally

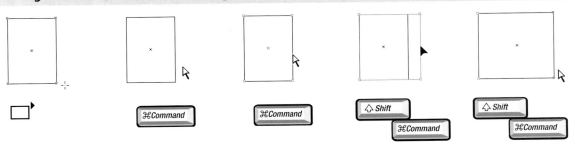

5 Finger Dance (⌘, then ⌘-Option) Moving a copy of a selected object

6 Finger Dance (⌘, then ⌘-Option) Deselecting an object, moving a copy of a path

7 Finger Dance (⌘, then ⌘-Shift-Option) Moving a copy of a selected object horizontally

8 Finger Dance (⌘, then ⌘-Shift-Option) Deselecting, moving a path copy horizontally

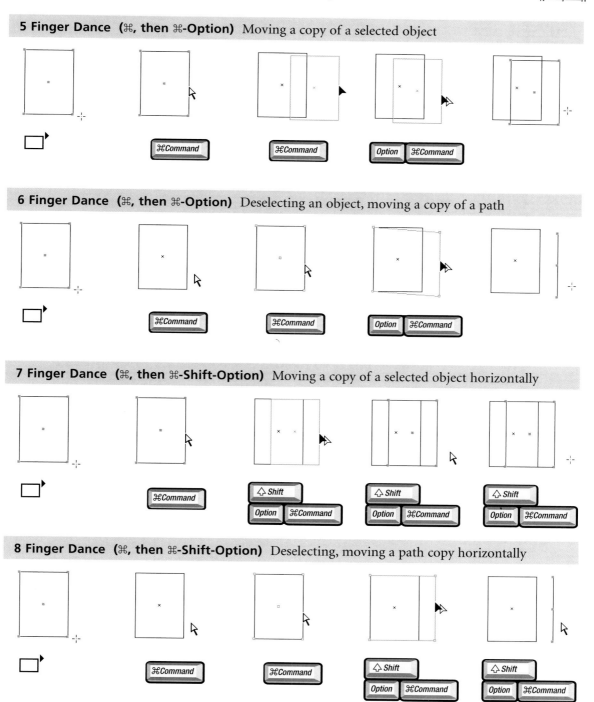

Note: *Before you begin this sequence of exercises, choose the Direct-selection tool,* *then select the Rectangle tool and drag to create a rectangle.*

9 Finger Dance (⌘-Option, then ⌘-Option) Deselecting, Group-selecting, moving a copy

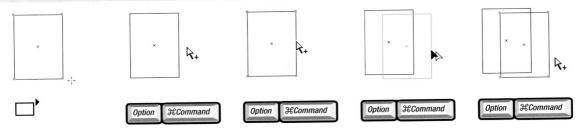

10 Finger Dance (⌘-Option, ⌘-Shift) Group-selecting, moving an object horizontally

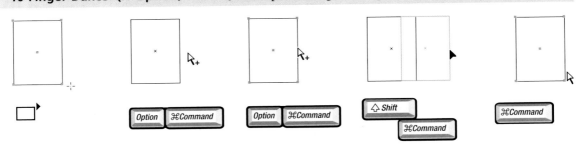

11 Finger Dance (⌘-Option, ⌘-Option-Shift) Moving copies horizontally, adding selections

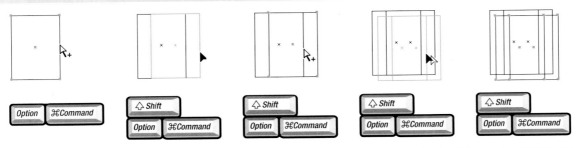

12 Finger Dance (⌘-Option, ⌘-Option-Shift, ⌘) Moving a copy, adding a selection, moving

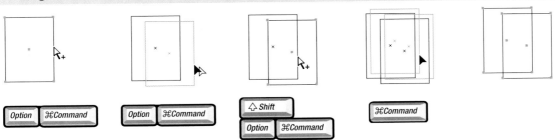

Lines, Fills & Colors

3

Lines, fills and colors are at the core of creating with Adobe Illustrator. There are now even more new tools to add power to your ability to draw, express and explore your artwork. If you look carefully, you'll discover that virtually all the techniques in this chapter are used (as basics) in combination with some of the flashier techniques found in the chapters that follow. Illustrator, mixed with a healthy dose of careful observation and attention to detail, can help you create quick, simple and elegant images without any of the fuss or muss of complex tricks or special effects.

The many palettes for working with color

Illustrator now uses separate palettes for Color, Swatches, Stroke and Gradient. To set a Fill or Stroke for an object, select the appropriate Fill/Stroke icon found at the bottom of the Toolbox and then use one of the palettes. (See Tip at right and "Working with Palettes" in *Chapter 1*.)

You'll find some new additions to the Color palette, a fill of None and a Last Color icon (displays when you change to either a pattern or a gradient fill). New pop-up menu options let you Invert or find the complement of a selected color (though the complements don't seem to correlate to art school color wheels).

You can drag and drop colors between palettes and to and from the swatches in the Toolbox. To store any colors or styles you wish to save with the document, drag from either the Color or Gradient palette or from the Toolbox into the Swatches palette (don't drag *objects* to the Swatch

---

Illustrator's color palettes

- **The Color palette** lets you mix colors and change color modes from the palette pop-up or by Shift-clicking the Color ramp. (See the *Chapter 10* warnings and tips for working in RGB.)

- **The Swatches palette** contains a default set of color swatches, gradients and patterns and can store any colors you want saved in your file. Using or pasting a style from a Custom Library adds that color to your Swatches palette.

- **The Stroke palette** lets you set the line, cap, miter and dash styles of a stroke (see page 49).

- **The Gradient palette** is used to create gradient fills (see *Chapter 5* for more).

- **Swatch Library palettes** let you open swatch palettes for specific color systems via Window: Swatch Libraries, or then choose Other Library to access styles from any *unopened* document.

Note: *You can't access styles from documents that are already open.*

Caution when deleting colors!

When you click the Trash icon to delete swatches in the Swatches palette, Illustrator does *not* warn you—even if you're deleting colors used in that document! Illustrator converts the colors in objects filled with deleted global colors to non-global colors, and converts deleted spot colors to non-global process colors.

To be safe, *always* choose Select All Unused swatches *immediately* before clicking the Trash.

Pencil tool paths disappearing?

If paths disappear when you draw them close together, check the options for the Pencil and Smooth tools. Disabling the Keep Selected option deselects each path as you create it so you won't accidentally reshape or lose it while you draw.

   "K" Paint bucket tool
"I" Eyedropper tool

Filling open objects

Illustrator allows you to fill both closed *and* open objects (see page 114 for a practical example).

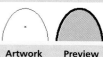

Artwork   Preview

Preference: Add Stroke Weight

When this is selected, the calculated size (width and height) of stroked objects displayed in the Info and Transform palettes (but not Align) includes stroke weight.

palette or you'll create a pattern!). Whenever you copy and paste objects that contain custom styles stored in the Swatches palette from one document to another, you'll be pasting those *styles* into the new document as well.

A new addition to Swatch Options is Global or Non-Global Process colors. Deselecting (not checking) the Non-Global checkbox means that when you change the mix (sliders) or definition of the color, all objects filled with it will update to the new color (see page 54).

Color modification filters

The Adjust Colors filter lets you adjust the tint of Global colors and convert them among CMYK, RGB and Grayscale color modes. The Saturate filter (which integrates Saturate, Saturate More, Desaturate and Desaturate More filters) lets you adjust the saturation of objects and image objects via sliders or numerically. (See index for examples using these filters.)

More tools and palettes

Two easily overlooked Illustrator tools are the Eyedropper (which *picks up* line, fill, color styles and text formatting) and the Paint-bucket (which *deposits* line, fill, color styles and text formatting). These two tools offer some useful shortcuts for copying and applying styles from one object to another. To set the default styling for your next object, click an object with the Eyedropper or click an object with the Paint-bucket to fill it with the current styling. With one tool selected, access the other by holding down the Option key. Use the Eyedropper tool to sample colors from any object (including a bitmapped one).

You can also use the Eyedropper to copy a style from one object to another. Select the object you would like to change, and with the Eyedropper tool, click an object that has the style you like. *Voilà!* Your selected object is now styled to match the one you clicked on, including dashes, line weights and custom fills. By default, both the Eyedropper and Paint-bucket tools copy the styling of an object, but double-clicking either of these tools in the

Toolbox allows you to customize the settings for both.

To copy Type attributes using the Eyedropper, select the type block or portions of type you want to affect. Then using the Eyedropper, click on the type whose attributes you wish to copy (see *Chapter 7* for more).

The end of the (path) line

One of the aspects of Illustrator that seems mysterious to newcomers is the way path lines end. There are many times when it's easier and more efficient to work in Artwork mode, but you may discover someday that, although a set of lines seems to contact perfectly when viewed in Artwork mode, they visibly overlap in Preview. You'll find the solution in the Stroke palette. Access it by choosing Window: Show Stroke.

By selecting one of the three Caps styles for your line endings, you can determine how the endpoints of your selected paths will look. The first (and default) choice is called a Butt-cap; it causes your path to stop at the end anchor point. Butt-caps are essential for creating exact placement of one path against another. The middle choice is the Round-cap, which rounds the endpoint in a more "natural" manner. Round-caps are especially good for softening the effect of single lines or curves, making them appear slightly less harsh. The final type is the Projecting-cap, which can extend lines and dashes at half the stroke weight beyond the end anchor point. You should also know that in addition to determining the appearance of path endpoints, Caps styles also affect the shapes of dashed lines.

You can also adjust the corners in an angled path if they appear too flat or stick out too far behind the anchor points. The default Miter-join with a limit of 4 usually looks just fine, but if you want to round or bevel your corners, simply choose the Round-join or Bevel-join. Each line weight has a particular Miter-limit at which the joins switch from blunt to pointy; the thicker the line, the higher the limit will be. Miter-limits can range from 1 (which is always blunt) to 500.

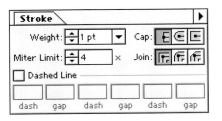

The Stroke palette

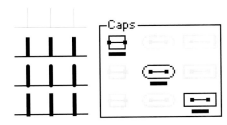

The same lines shown first in Artwork, then in Preview with Butt-caps, Round-caps and Projecting-caps

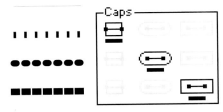

A 5-pt dashed line with a 2-pt dash and 6-pt gap shown first in Artwork, then Preview with a Butt-cap, Round-cap and Projecting-cap

A path shown first in Artwork, then in Preview with a Miter-join, Round-join and Bevel-join

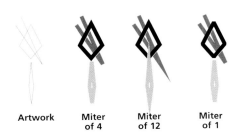

| Artwork | Miter of 4 | Miter of 12 | Miter of 1 |

Objects with 6-pt strokes and various Miter-limits, demonstrating that the angles of lines, as well as weight, affect Miter-limits

Simply Realistic

Realism from Geometry and Observation

Overview: *Re-create a mechanical object using and altering the Rectangle or Oval tools; place all inner enclosed objects while finding the right values; add selected highlights and offset shadows and reflections.*

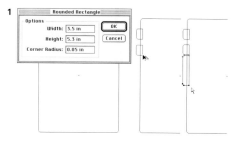

Creating and adjusting rounded rectangles to construct the basic forms

After choosing Grayscale from the Color pop-up menu, filling objects with tints of black, stroked with a .5-pt, 100% black line

Many people believe the only way to achieve realism in Illustrator is with elaborate gradients and blends, but this illustration by Patrick Lynch proves that artistic observation is the real secret. For his *Manual of Ornithology* (with Noble S. Proctor, for Yale University Press), Lynch needed equipment illustrations to aid in birdwatching.

1 Re-creating a mechanical object with repeating geometric shapes, by altering copies of objects. Most artists find that close observation, not complex perspective, is the most crucial aspect to rendering illustrations. To focus your attention on the power of basic shapes, select a simple mechanical device to render in grayscale, and choose Grayscale from the Color pop-up menu. Experiment with the Oval, Rectangle and Rounded Rectangle tools to place the basic elements. Especially with mechanical devices, components often tend to be similar; thus, look for opportunities to adjust a copy of an object, rather than create another that might not align perfectly. For his personal stereo/radio knobs, Lynch dragged a copy of one knob (holding Option-Shift), stretched it by selecting one end with the Direct-selection tool and dragging it down (with the Shift key), creating a sequence of knobs with the same height, but different widths.

2 Using tints to fill the objects. Select all your objects and choose a .5-pt black stroke from the Stroke and Color palettes. Then select an object (or set of objects), set the Fill to Black and Option-click on the New Swatch icon to name it "Black" and set the Color Mode to Spot Color. Click OK and create a tint using the Tint slider in the Colors palette. Continue to fill and adjust the tints for individual objects until you are happy with the basic value structure. Lynch used percentages from 10–80%, with the majority of the objects being 80% black.

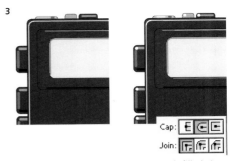

Carefully placing a few lighter-tinted, filled circles and lines with Round-caps for highlights

3 Creating a few carefully placed highlights. Look closely at your object and decide where to place selected highlights. Start with a couple of thin, lighter-tinted lines, making sure to choose Round-caps for the lines (in the expanded Stroke palette). In a couple of instances, place shorter and slightly heavier lines of an even lighter tint on top of the first lines. For lines that follow the contour of your object, select part of your object's path with the Direct-selection tool and copy and Paste In Front that part of the path. Use your cursor-keys to offset the contour and use the Eyedropper to double-click on one of your highlight lines to set the contour with the highlight line style. If you need to trim contours, use the Scissors tool and delete the unwanted portion of the path. Lastly, using a light tint as a fill, with no stroke, create a small circle at the confluence of two lines (try leaving a small gap between the lines and the circle). Option-drag the circle if you wish to place it in other locations. For his highlights, Lynch used lines varying in weight from .5 to 2 points, in tints from 0 (white) to 50%, and five carefully placed white circles.

Creating text and LED numbers, then offsetting objects and giving offsets a darker gray tint

Making subtle changes in value to create the illusion of transparency

4 Creating shadows and transparencies. Follow the same procedure as above, but this time use darker tints to create shadows and transparencies. Make sure to offset shadows behind the object, especially if the shadows have solid fills. ☽

The Artwork view of the final illustration

Combining Circles

Cutting and Joining Overlapping Objects

FOX/BLACKDOG

LINO BOY'S MOTTO: "I AM HIGHLY RESOLVED!"

Overview: *Design an illustration using overlapping objects; cut and remove overlaps and join objects.*

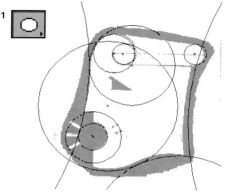

1

Using the Oval tool to trace circles over the PICT template

Illustrator is a flexible enough program to accommodate many different illustration styles. Mark Fox has always designed using a compass to draw perfect circles, an unusual drawing style that translates easily to computer illustration. Use this technique to join any two objects, but don't forget also to look at filters (*Chapter 6*).

1 Placing your objects. Fox scanned a sketch he made with his compass, saved it as a PICT, and opened it as a template. Chose File: Open, locate the image you wish to use as a template and enable the "Template" option (see pages 80–83 for more template help). Create your objects without worrying about how they overlap. Holding down the Shift key, Fox traced circles with the Oval tool.

2

Selecting an object and locking everything else, then using the Scissors tool to cut overlaps

2 Cropping the objects, removing the excess and joining the objects. To lock all *unselected* objects, select one object, hold Option and choose Arrange: Lock (⌘-Shift-Option-2). With the Scissors tool, click on the path where this object will overlap and join with others. Then choose Arrange: Unlock All (⌘-Option-2) and repeat the above procedure for other objects to be joined. After selecting and deleting excess paths, Direct-select each pair of points you want to join (one pair at a time), and Average-Join them by holding Option and choosing Arrange: Join (or ⌘-Shift-Option-J).

The first cut section, selecting pairs of anchors after moving the excess paths out of the way, then Average-Joining the pair

Gallery: Mark Fox / BlackDog

Mark Fox's whimsical design style hasn't visibly changed since his transition from ink and compass to Adobe Illustrator. The sketch to the right above for "Horse of a Different Color" shows Fox's notations for compass centers, as well as the circles. Although most people rely primarily on the Pen tool when drawing in Illustrator, Fox creates all his logos by cutting and joining rectangles and circles—occasionally using the Pen tool (for straight lines) and the Rotate tool.

Line Construction

Lines and Brushes Form Roads and Rails

Overview: *Use sequences of Copy and Paste In Front to create variations in line styles to form highways; make a Pattern Brush for railroad ties.*

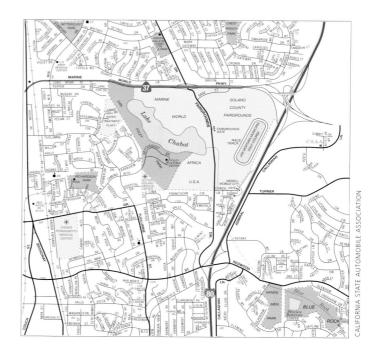

Not Non-global not confusing?

Illustrator uses a term called "Non-global" to describe process colors. When this box is checked in Swatch Options, the color is "Non-global"—that is, objects filled with this color do not change if the color definition changes. Deselecting this box makes a color *not* "Non-global." This double negative means the color *is* global and objects filled with it will be updated.

The black path that will "outline" the highway

More line styles and brushes

Find premade brushes, as well as Actions that create line-styles, in your installed "Adobe Illustrator" folder and on the *Wow!* disk.

The California State Automobile Association (CSAA) uses overlapping line styles in its road maps to represent streets and highways, and uses Pattern Brushes to make railroad tracks (for more on brushes see pages 68–71, *Chapter 6*, and pages 178–179). CSAA uses "global" process CMYK colors (see Tip at left) to ensure that color changes will auto-update objects filled with those colors, and color names are visible in the Colors palette (for help making colors see pages 60–61).

1 Creating the black "outline." Using the Pen tool, draw some paths, making sure you're in Preview mode so you can work in color (⌘-Y toggles Artwork and Preview modes). Select the paths you want to make into road map highways. Set the Fill to None, the stroke to Black (press "X" to toggle Fill and Stroke) and in the Stroke palette, set the weight to 2.4-pt. Keep these paths selected and copy (⌘-C). (To trap the highway lines, see Tip opposite.)

2 Pasting a copy in front and styling it in a color. Next, choose Edit: Paste In Front (⌘-F) to paste a copy exactly on top of the original objects, then style this copy in a color at a 2-pt line weight.

3 Pasting a final black line down the center of the highway. To create the dividing lines on the highway, use ⌘-F to paste another copy in front and style the line with a .4-pt black stroke.

4 Creating a Pattern Brush for railroad ties. Create a short horizontal line with the Pen tool (click then Shift-click) with .3-pt black stroke. To make a crosstie, draw a short .3-pt black line perpendicular to the first line and flush to its right end. Select both lines, choose Window: Align and click "Vertical Align Center." Next click the New Brush icon in the Brushes palette, choose New Pattern Brush, click OK, then name your brush, choose the "Stretch to fit" option and click OK. Now select the path that you want to make into a railroad line and click on your new brush. To change the spacing between the ties or the length of the ties, resize the objects that created the first brush, repeat the new brush creation and apply the new brush to your paths. 🪨

Manually trapping with knockout and Overprint

To manually create a .2-pt trap of the highway in this illustration, you can insert a white "knockout" path (white always knocks out!) between your black path and your color path, and then set the overlapping color path to "overprint." To do this, with your black path copied (i.e., between Steps 1 and 2), choose Edit: Paste In Front (⌘-F) and set this copy to a white 1.6-pt stroke. Next copy this path and follow the instructions for creating the color path (Step 2), though this time, with the color path selected, check "Overprint Stroke" in the Attributes palette.

Note: *If you need help inserting the white knockout path into an already completed set of paths, see the introduction to* **Chapter 4,** *especially "Controlling the Stacking Order."*

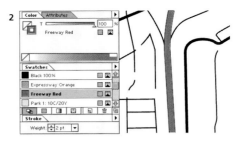

The highway color applied; only if white knock-out strokes were used

The black line down the center of the highway

Brush objects with Vertical Align Center applied

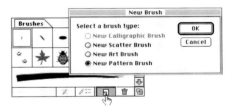

Making a New Brush with the selected objects and choosing New Pattern Brush; naming the brush and choosing Stretch to fit; specifying the new brush listed by icon and then by name

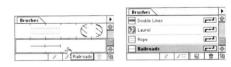

Before and after applying the railroad brush

Isometric Systems

Cursor-keys, Constrain-angles & Formulas

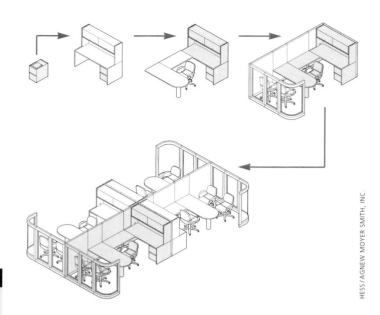

Overview: *Create detailed views of an object from front, top and side; use an isometric formula to transform the objects; set "Constrain-angle" and "Cursor key" distance; use cursor-keys with snap-to-point to adjust and assemble objects.*

Stubborn snapping-to-point

Sometimes if you try to move an object over slightly, it will annoyingly "snap" to the wrong place. If this happens, move it away from the area and release. Then regrab the object at the point from which you'd like to align it and move it so that it snaps into the correct position. If you still have trouble, zoom in. As a last resort, you can disable "Snap to point" in General Preferences.

1

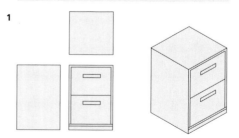

Separate views, then after transformations

2

Scaling, skewing and rotating

Technical illustrations and diagrams are often depicted in isometric perspective, and Adobe Illustrator can be the ideal program both for creating your initial illustrations and for transforming them into this perspective. The artists at Agnew Moyer Smith (AMS) created and transformed the diagrams on these pages using their three-step perspective. For both the initial creation and manipulation of the isometric objects in space, AMS custom-set "Cursor key distance" and "Constrain angle," and made sure that "Snap to point" was enabled—all from Preferences: General and Keyboard Increments.

1 Creating detailed renderings of the front, side and top views of your object to scale. Before you begin a technical illustration, you should choose a drawing scale, then coordinate the settings in General Preferences to match. For instance, to create a file drawer in the scale of 1 mm = 2", set the ruler units to millimeters and "Cursor key" distance to .5 mm, and make sure that the "Snap to point" option is enabled. With these features enabled and matching your drawing scale, it's easy to create detailed views of your object. With your ruler units set to the correct scale, choose Window: Show Info to keep easy track of your object sizing as you work. If a portion of the real object is inset 1" to the left, you can use the ← cursor-key to move the path one increment (.5 mm) further left. Finally, snap to point will help you properly fit together and assemble your various components. Select and group all the components of the front view. Separately group the top and side so you'll be able to easily isolate each of the views for transformation and assembly. AMS renders every internal detail, which allows them to view "cut-always" or adjust individual elements, or groups of elements, such as opening a drawer.

2 **Using an isometric formula to transform your view-points.** The artists at AMS created and transformed the diagrams on these pages using their three-step process, which is fully demonstrated on the *Wow!* disk. To transform your objects, double-click on the various tools to specify the correct percentages numerically. First, select all three views and scale them 100% horizontally and 86.6% vertically. Next, select the top and side, shearing them at a −30° angle, and then shear the front 30°. Lastly, rotate the top and front 30° and the side −30°.

3 **Assembling the top, front and side.** With the Selection tool, grab a specific anchor-point from the side view that will contact the front view, and drag it until it snaps into the correct position (the arrow turns hollow). Next, select and drag to snap the top into position. Finally, select and group the entire object for easy reselection.

4 **Using the constrain-angle and cursor-keys to adjust objects and assemble multiple components.** Look at the Movement chart to determine the direction in which to move. Try using the Direct-selection tool to select a portion of the object, setting the constrain-angle to 30° (or −30°), then using the ← and → cursor-keys to slide your selection along that isometric axis. Or, use the Selection tool to select entire objects and snap them into position against other objects. ✎

4

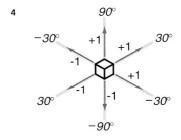

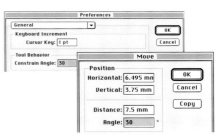

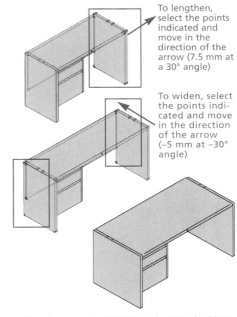

To lengthen, select the points indicated and move in the direction of the arrow (7.5 mm at a 30° angle)

To widen, select the points indicated and move in the direction of the arrow (−5 mm at −30° angle)

Transforming one object into the next, by Direct-selecting the appropriate anchor points and using the Move command, or by setting and using custom constrain-angle and cursor-keys

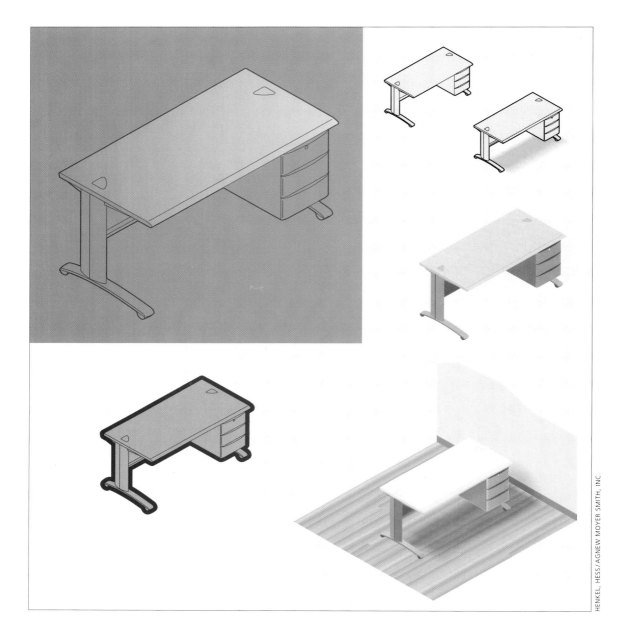

Gallery: Rick Henkel, Kurt Hess / Agnew Moyer Smith, Inc.

Creating a technical illustration in Illustrator may save you time over traditional graphic methods, but the real time savings lies in producing variations on a theme. Agnew Moyer Smith's artists use Illustrator because it provides so much flexibility in altering an illustration after construction of objects is complete. These different presentations of desks for Steelcase office furniture demonstrate how dramatically different the visual effect can be just by altering the stroke and fill styles of an object and its immediate surroundings. The shadow on the wood floor was set to the Overprint option.

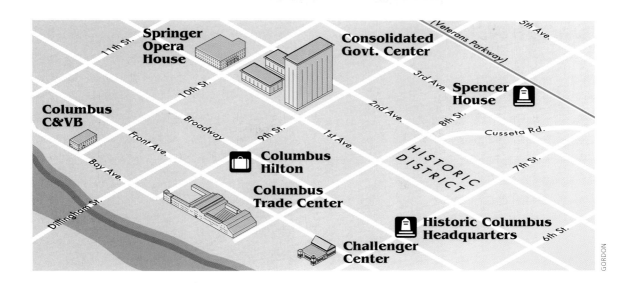

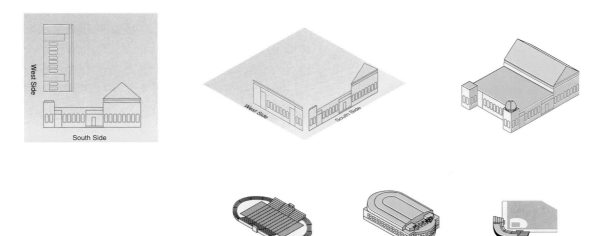

Gallery: Steven Gordon

For this map of Columbus, Georgia, cartographer Steven Gordon compiled building information from aerial photographs, postcards, sketches and architectural drawings. Gordon began by drawing the building sides and roofs, the street grid, and positioning the street names. All elements were rotated 45°. Building roofs and the streets and their names were scaled 100% horizontally and 57.74% vertically. All building sides were scaled 57.74% horizontally and 100% vertically. The west-side shapes were rotated 30°; the south-side shapes were rotated −30°. The two sets of shapes were then fitted together to compose the building. Gordon found that while isometric formulas work correctly for perpendicular sides and flat, horizontal roofs, the formulas could not produce the curved walls, domes and pitched roofs of buildings like those to the right; those shapes were drawn by hand. Gordon applied the Round-join to all building lines to avoid spikes at corners (see page 49).

Objective Colors

Custom Labels for Making Quick Changes

Overview: *Define custom spot colors, naming colors by the type of object; repeat the procedure for each type of object; use Select filters to select types of objects by spot color name to edit colors or objects.*

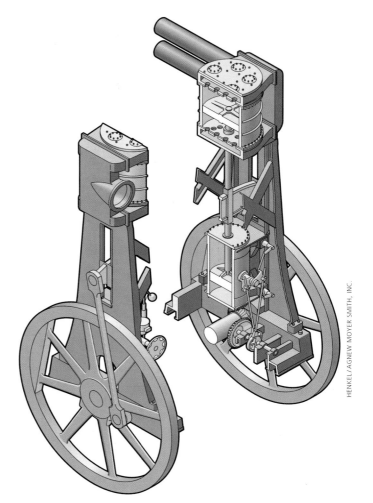

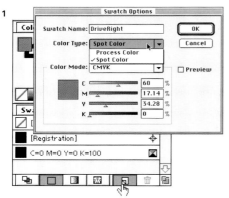

Option-clicking on the New Swatch icon to directly access Swatch Options; naming the color, then setting the color to be a Spot Color, which allows global changes and tinting

A spot color swatch with its custom label

When you need to create technical illustrations that require frequent adjustments of color, it's essential to develop a method of organizing your colors. This illustration by Rick Henkel demonstrates how his firm, Agnew Moyer Smith (AMS), uses colors to label different categories of objects, making it simple to isolate and update colors. This method also makes it easy to find all objects in a category in order to apply any *other* global changes, such as changing the stroke weight or scaling.

1 Creating custom spot colors. AMS uses spot colors even for process color jobs to allow easy access to tints. In the Swatches palette, Option-click on the New Swatch icon. If you have premixed a color in the Colors palette, this color will be loaded in the color mixer. If you are not pleased with the color, then edit it accordingly. Now give your color a name that signifies the type of object you plan to fill with the color and choose "Spot" from the Color Mode pop-up. Rick Henkel used labels such as "CamRight" and "DriveLeft" to label the colors he would use in his illustration for the Pittsburgh History & Landmarks Foundation. To help in the selection of reliably reproducible colors, Henkel used the Agfa *PostScript Process Color Guide* to look up the color he actually wanted and then entered the percentages of CMYK indicated. (For more about color in Illustrator, see *Chapter 1*.)

2 Repeating the procedure for all colors and labels, changing color definitions as necessary. Create colors for each type of object to be styled differently, naming each color for the objects it will fill (to speed creation, see Tip at right). Henkel created spot colors, properly labeled, for each type of object included in this engine.

The spot color system makes it easy to change definitions of colors. From the Swatches palette, double-click on the color you want to change to open Swatch Options, where you can change the color recipes. Click OK to apply the changes to all objects containing that color.

3 Using the labels to find all like objects. To select all like objects, for example, those colored with "CamRight," click on that color name in your list and choose Edit: Select: Same Fill Color. Once selected, you can reposition or recolor them all at once. Instead of repeating this procedure for your next selected color, just press ⌘-6! ☁

Creating custom spot color swatches for each category of object to be styled differently

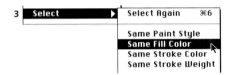

With a color swatch label selected, choosing Edit: Select: Same Fill Color to find the objects filled with that color

Finding the objects filled with a next selected swatch with Select Again (⌘-6)

From one swatch to another

When defining with custom parameters in Swatch Options, such as Spot colors or *not* Non-global process colors (see Tip on page 54), instead of having to continually set similar parameters, simply select a swatch that approximates the kind of color you want, then Option-click the New Swatch icon to redefine and name the Swatch.

Spot colors for four-color-process jobs

Illustrator's process colors don't update globally by default (see Tip on page 54), so some artists may still choose to define all swatches as spot colors. If you do, just make certain that you've enabled "Convert to Process" options when generating separations.

Organizing Color

Arranging an Artist's Palette of Colors

Overview: *Work with color swatches to choose initial colors; make adjustments to, and rename, custom colors; save a palette of your custom colors.*

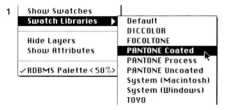

Opening one of the Pantone spot color palettes

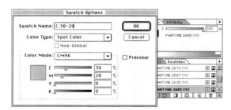

Respecifying and renaming custom spot colors to form an orderly, accessible palette

Moving multiple sliders

With the Shift key down, grabbing one color slider moves all colors together. Grabbing the right-most slider gives the greatest control. Drag to the right to 100% to saturate the color fully. Drag left to desaturate.

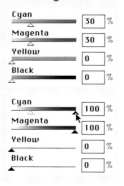

As any colorist knows, a well-organized palette can go beyond providing you with mere colors; it can facilitate the creative process. Progress Software Company's product signature color is the deep Pantone Violet #2685, so when art director Deborah Hurst commissioned artist Jean Tuttle to create a series of illustrations for a "family" of Progress sales literature, they worked closely to develop a limited palette that would feel related to the signature color. Tuttle developed a method to organize the colors so she could work with them in an intuitive manner.

1 Using swatches of printed colors to choose ranges of colors to work with. As is mentioned in *Chapter 1*, color on the screen is not a reliable predictor of the color you will get in print. Therefore, start with one of the computer-to-print color matching systems to choose your initial colors. Since Hurst was in Boston and Tuttle was in upstate New York, the two used the Pantone spot color system as a reference in choosing swatches of color to consider for the palette. Once they had agreed upon the general color scheme, Tuttle could open the Pantone

Coated color palette (Window: Swatch Libraries) and gain access to the computer version of the colors from within Illustrator. For each color she was considering, Tuttle put a square filled with that color into the document. After using the basic colors she wanted, she could close the Pantone palette—leaving her with just the color swatches she had chosen for her palette in the document.

Tuttle renamed each color in her palette based on five color groupings: Blues, Purples, Blue Violets, Red Violets and Accents. Because Illustrator by default lists custom colors alphabetically, Tuttle preceded each color grouping by a letter that would automate how Illustrator grouped the colors. Using a process color matching book as a guide, Tuttle then rounded off the CMYK percentages for each individual color, incorporating the color formulas in the name (B.50-50, for example, would be Purples: 50% Cyan / 50% Magenta), and created variants on each of the colors as well, saving each color swatch into her palette. To visually separate the color groupings as they list in the Swatches palette, she created a series of white swatches to use purely as name placeholders—for example, one white was named "B. Purples" (the space before the "P" makes it list ahead of the numbered purples in the list)—while making sure that each of these white custom colors used as a label was placed into a square in the palette as well. To develop your custom set of swatches, select each palette object, Option-click on the New Swatches icon to specify the name, and choose "Spot" from Color Mode (see the previous lesson for more on making spot colors).

2 Accessing and tinting colors with your palette.

Another benefit to using spot colors in your palette is that you can easily specify tint percentages for any color. Just select the color and adjust the Tint slider in the Colors palette or type in a percentage in the text box. For each illustration Tuttle produced for this series, she had access to her entire set of colors and their tints. With this palette, Tuttle was able to create a "smoky blue" color environment to use for the entire family of illustrations. ✑

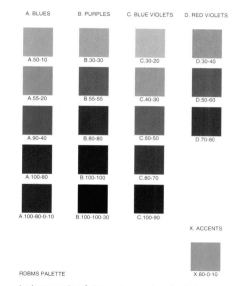

A chart made of the custom colors for future access to the full palette, including a rectangle for each white made as a name placeholder

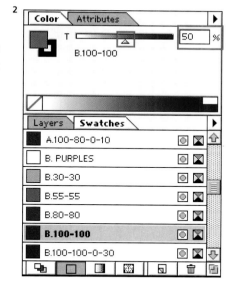

Specifying a tint of a custom color

Tints will "stick" until changed

The tint percentages of your last selected object will set the tint of your next fill and stroke color, unless you manually change them.

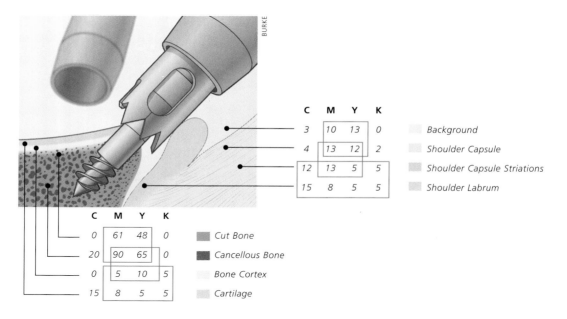

C	M	Y	K	
3	10	13	0	Background
4	13	12	2	Shoulder Capsule
12	13	5	5	Shoulder Capsule Striations
15	8	5	5	Shoulder Labrum

C	M	Y	K	
0	61	48	0	Cut Bone
20	90	65	0	Cancellous Bone
0	5	10	5	Bone Cortex
15	8	5	5	Cartilage

Gallery: Christopher Burke

When printed using the CMYK four-color process, Adobe Illustrator's smooth, crisp edges can be a registration nightmare. Even the slightest misregistration of inks can create visually disturbing white gaps between colors. So, although you shouldn't have to worry about what happens to your illustration once it's completed, the reality is that in this phase of computer graphics evolution, you still have to help your printer along. "Trapping" is a technique of printing one color over the edge of another—usually achieved by creating overprinting strokes that overlap adjacent objects. However, work-around solutions exist; Christopher Burke, for example, constructs the colors in his images in such a way as to ensure "continuous coverage" for at least one (preferably two) of the color plates in every region of his image. As long as adjacent objects share at least 5% of at least one color, no white gaps can form, and trapping will naturally occur! (Also see the Tip below and on page 23.) This method of keeping just enough in common between adjacent colors allows Burke to maintain a full-spectrum palette. (The background of the image is an Illustrator drawing rasterized in Photoshop and placed back into Illustrator as an EPS—see Chapter 4 for placing EPS images, and Chapter 9 for more on rasterizing Illustrator images.)

Manual trapping of gradients and pattern fills

Since you can't style strokes with gradients or patterns, you can't trap using the Pathfinder Trap filter either. To trap gradients and patterns manually, first duplicate your object and stroke it in the weight you'd like for a trap. Then use Object: Path: Outline Path to convert the stroke to a filled object, which you should fill in the same style as the object you'd like to trap. Lastly, enable the Overprint Fill box in the Attributes palette. If necessary, use the Gradient tool to unify gradients across objects (page 108), and manually replicate pattern transformations.

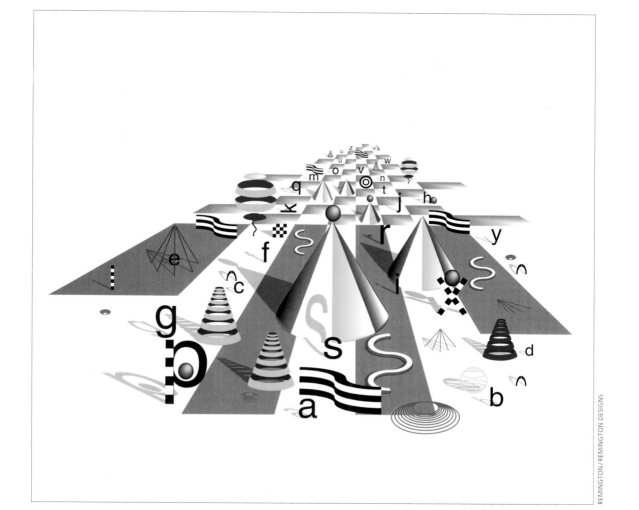

Gallery: Dorothy Remington / Remington Designs

Color printers are notoriously unpredictable in terms of color consistency, so Dorothy Remington developed a method to increase consistency from proof to final output. When Remington constructs an image, she freely chooses colors from any of the CMYK process color models (Pantone Process, TruMatch, Focoltone and Toyo) that come with Illustrator, provided that she has the matching color swatchbooks. When she sends the computer file to the service bureau for proofing, as well as for final output, she also sends along the color swatches representing colors used in the image. Remington asks the service bureau to calibrate the printer to match the enclosed swatches as closely as possible. Although requesting such special attention might result in a small surcharge, it can save you an immense amount of time (in back-and-forths to the service bureau) and expense in reprinting the image because colors did not turn out as expected.

Gallery: Hugh Whyte / Lehner & Whyte

To celebrate Letraset's distribution of a new Pantone line of blacks, Hugh Whyte was commissioned to produce a thematic illustration for Letraset to silk-screen on T-shirts. The beauty of using the Pantone custom colors was that when he had them printed to positive separations, the films were perfectly registered for the different screens in silk-screening. The printer could then mix the inks to Whyte's exact specifications using the Pantone swatchbook to match.

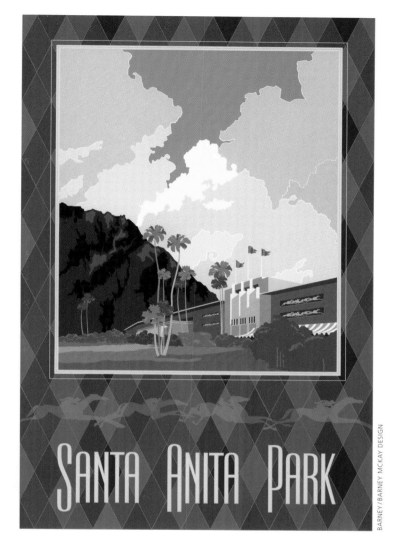

Gallery: Jeffrey Barney / Barney McKay Design

When Santa Anita Park decided to produce a commemorative poster, Jeffrey Barney chose this 1930s-style illustration to reflect the park's period elegance. The color proofs needed to match the actual colors used at the park, to be of large enough format to view at near poster size, and to be consistent with the colors that would result from the printing process. Given these parameters, Barney decided to calibrate all of his work against Iris prints (see the Resources *appendix). He therefore had his computer monitors professionally calibrated to match the prints. He also regularly brought the prints to the park and made color notes directing himself how to alter each color. In Illustrator, Barney created a set of custom spot colors labeled by name, so as he adjusted the CMYK formula for each color, all occurrences of that color, and corresponding tints, would automatically update (for more about tints, see page 60). Finally, after he proofed the final Iris prints, the service bureau matched the color separations to them.*

Brush Strokes
Making Naturalistic Pen and Ink Drawings

STEUER

Overview: *Adjust the Paintbrush Tool settings; customize a Calligraphic Brush; trace or draw your composition; make final adjustments.*

The digital photo saved as TIFF and placed as an Illustrator template

Maintaining your pressure

Only brush strokes *initially* drawn with pressure-sensitive settings can take advantage of pressure-sensitivity. Also be aware that re-applying a brush after trying another may alter the stroke shape.

It's easy to create spontaneous painterly and calligraphic marks in Illustrator—perhaps easier than in any other graphics program. Creating highly variable, responsive strokes (using a graphics tablet and a pressure-sensitive, pen-like stylus), you can now edit those strokes as *paths*, or experiment with applying different brushes to the strokes *after* the path has been made. This illustration, one of 150 figures I drew for Christina Sillari's teaching manual on Chakra Yoga, was created using one custom Calligraphy Brush and a Wacom ArtZ tablet.

1 If you'll be working from a source, prepare your template. Although you can draw directly into the computer, if you want to trace a sketch or a scan you'll need to prepare your template. For this series of illustrations, since the charcoal drawings were between 11" x 17" and 18" x 24", I took digital snapshots of the drawings instead of scanning. The grayscale TIFF version of this posture "Easy Pose" was then placed as a template into Illustrator (see pages 80–83 for template help). To toggle between hiding and showing the template, press ⌘-Shift-W.

2 Setting your Paintbrush tool preferences and customizing a calligraphy brush. Choose the Paintbrush tool and select one of the Calligraphy brushes in the Brushes Palette. In order to sketch freely and with accurate detail, the default Paintbrush Tool settings must be adjusted. Double-click on the Paintbrush tool to open Paintbrush Tool Preferences. Drag the Fidelity slider all the way to the left (.5 pixels), the Smoothness all the way to the right (100%), and disable both "Keep Selected" and "Fill new brush strokes" Options.

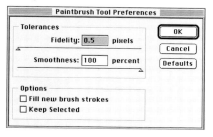

Customizing the Paintbrush Tool Preferences

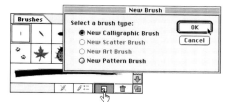

Creating a new Calligraphic Brush

To create a custom brush, select a Calligraphic Brush, click the New Brush icon and click OK to New Calligraphy Brush. Experiment with various settings, name your brush and click OK. For this series of yoga illustrations, I named the Calligraphic brush "6 pt oval" with settings of: Angle 60°, Random 180°, Roundness 60%, Pressure 40%, Diameter 6pt, Pressure 6pt. The Paintbrush is now set to use your current stroke color—if there is no stroke color, it will use the fill color! Now draw. If you don't like a mark, either choose Undo or use the Direct-selection tool to edit the path. (If you don't have a pressure-sensitive tablet, you may want to try Random as a variable in Brush Options, since Pressure won't have any effect.)

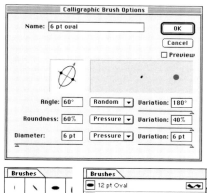

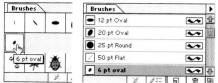

Customizing a Calligraphic Brush; the brush in the palette viewed with Tooltips and By Name

3 Experimenting with your image. First, save any versions that you are pleased with, then try applying different brushes to specific strokes and to the entire image (to hide/show the selection edges, ⌘-H). To access more Adobe-made calligraphy brushes choose Windows: Brush Libraries: Calligraphic—though you'll likely find that custom brushes provide more nuance (at right, see two of Adobe's brushes applied to the same strokes). For more on Calligraphic and "natural" brushes see pages 70–71 (for other brushes, see pages 54–55 and *Chapter 6*). ◗

Strokes made with customized brush (left); applying default 3pt Oval then 1pt Oval

Gallery:
Lisa Jackmore

Lisa Jackmore created a different custom calligraphy brush for each type of object in this colorful still-life (such as the vase, the flowers and the stripes). For the tablecloth, she drew one leaf and one dash, applied Object: Expand, defined each of them as an Art brush (see Chapter 6*) and then painted with the leaf and dash brushes. Haloing the illustration is a soft-edged background made of blended fills (see page 103 directions for creating a shadow).*

JACKMORE

ALSPACH

Gallery: Jen Alspach

For this portrait of her horse Murphy, Jen Alspach used a variety of default and custom calligraphy brushes—from 1-pt scribbly and scratchy to 20-pt broad and flat.

STEUER

Gallery: Sharon Steuer (with Sandee Cohen's variations)

Sharon Steuer first drew the original veggie illustration (top) using the Calligraphic brush for the black strokes, with the flat colors created in layers below (see pages 84–85). Sandee Cohen then created five variations of the squash by creating and applying several custom Art brushes (shown next to each version and on the Wow! disk). In the first two, Cohen applied a brush which was created by expanding a stroked oval and applying the Roughen filter; the first version colored the strokes and maintained the background colors, while the second deleted the background colors and used only black strokes. The third was created by deleting the strokes and applying a brush directly to the background colors. In the fourth, the stroked paths were duplicated and different brushes were applied to each set of paths. For the fifth, Cohen applied a brush with wispy ends to simulate the look of an actual paintbrush.

Intricate Patterns

Designing Complex Repeating Patterns

Advanced Technique

Overview: *Design a rough composition; define a pattern boundary and place behind everything; use the box to define guides; place small lines to use as registration while dragging; define and use the pattern.*

1

Arranging objects into a basic design

Placing a confining rectangle (defining the pattern tile), guides and registration lines

Pattern tiles into objects

To retrieve a pattern tile, just drag the pattern swatch onto your work area. To convert an applied pattern fill into editable objects, choose Object: Expand Fill.
Note: *Expand Fill won't work on very complex patterns, like this one.*

Included with Illustrator are many wonderful patterns for you to use and customize, and the *User Guide* does a good job of explaining pattern-making basics. But what if you want to create a more complex pattern?

A few simple guidelines and registration marks can help you minimize what could be a painstaking process of trial and error. With some essential help from author and consultant Sandee Cohen, I was finally able to come up with a method that allowed me to experimentally design an intricate tile that would print properly as a repeating pattern. This fabric and wallpaper pattern was created for an upcoming children's book by Matt Lake.

1 Designing your basic pattern, then drawing a confining rectangle and guides. Create a design that will allow for some rearrangement of the elements. Be aware that you cannot make a pattern tile from objects filled with gradients, rasterized or placed images, or other patterns. Use the Rectangle tool to draw a box around the part of the image you would like to repeat. This rectangle defines the boundary of the pattern tile. Send the rectangle to the back of the page or to the bottom drawing layer (if you would like help with layers, see *Chapter 4*). This boundary rectangle, which controls how your pattern repeats, *must* remain an unstroked, unfilled, nonrotated, nonskewed *rectangle.* Next, make sure that the "Snap to point" option is enabled (in General Preferences), then choose Show Rulers and pull out the guides to snap to each side of the rectangle (your cursor turns hollow as it snaps). Make sure you've selected the Lock Guides option (see pages 21 and 96 for more on guides).

Next, you need to create small lines that will help you to move objects while maintaining registration. On each of the guides, use the Pen tool to draw the lines outside of the pattern in a color not used in the pattern. These registration marks will help you to align elements as you move them from corner to corner.

2 Developing the repeating elements. In order for the pattern to repeat properly, you must place copies of any elements extending beyond the bounding rectangle in the area butting up against the overlapping object. For instance, if an object extends below the rectangle, you must place a copy of the continuing part of the object into the upper portion of the pattern. So, for the grass in the jungle pattern to repeat properly, I selected grass in front of the tiger and used Group (⌘-G) for easy reselection. In order to align the grass properly, I selected the bottom right horizontal registration mark with the grass that was to be moved. I grabbed the registration mark, and then, while holding down the Option and Shift keys (the Option key leaves the original, while the Shift constrains the dragging to vertical and horizontal movements), dragged a copy until it snapped into position along the upper horizontal guide. If you make a mistake, try again. (See "A Finger Dance" in *Chapter 2* for practice with Shift, Option and other modifier keys.)

3 Weaving your repeating objects in front of or behind others. One way to make a pattern interesting is to weave elements on top of some objects and behind others. After placing your copy of the repeating element

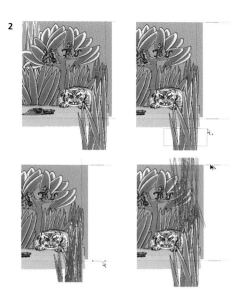

2

Moving grasses up into position

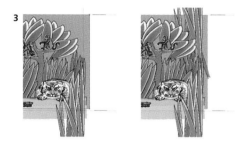

3

Cutting the copied grass and using Paste In Front to place it in front of the sky

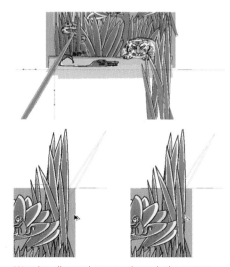

Weaving diagonal grasses through the pattern

4

Controlling patterns

Enable "Transform pattern tiles" in General Preferences to reset the default to transform patterns along with their objects. You can also transform patterns in any of the dialog boxes (with or without the object itself). To *manually* move, rotate, scale or skew the pattern tiles *alone*, start your transformation and hold down the "~" key as you drag (or use the cursor-keys). Relocate the ruler origin to set where the next pattern will begin. (For info about Pattern Brushes see *Chapter 6*.)

Speeding redraw with patterns

When your pattern-filled object is in position, put it on a separate layer set to Artwork mode (for help with layers see *Chapter 4*), or even rasterize it.

into its properly registered position, and while it's still selected, cut that copy to the Clipboard (⌘-X). Then choose an object or objects in your composition that you can easily Paste In Front of (⌘-F) or Paste In Back of (⌘-B). For the jungle, I cut the grass copy, then selected the blue sky and chose Paste In Front, which placed the copy in front of the blue sky but behind all other elements. Other grasses, such as the diagonal blades, needed to be on top of some grass while behind others. I used a combination of Paste In Front and Paste In Back with such elements to increase the complexity of the weaving.

4 Testing your pattern. When you're ready to test your pattern (to see if you like what you've done so far), make sure all the objects and layers you'll need are visible and unlocked (Object: Show All/Unlock All, or ⌘-Option-3/ ⌘-Option-2). Next, select your pattern elements (including the bounding rectangle), and either choose Edit: Define Pattern to name your pattern, or drag your selection to the Swatches palette (double-click the swatch later to customize its name). Then create a new rectangle and select the pattern as your fill from the Swatches palette to see how your pattern repeats within a filled object. If you redesign the pattern tile and then wish to update the pattern swatch with those changes, select your pattern elements again, but this time Option-drag the elements onto the pattern swatch you made before.

5 Simplifying and scaling your final pattern. The larger and more complex your pattern is, the more difficult and time-consuming it will be to print. When you finally get a pattern you like, do your best to minimize its complexity by deleting excess anchor points and trimming objects that extend beyond the defining border of the tile (see *Chapter 6* for Pathfinder filters that help you trim). Finally, from the Pattern dialog box, select unused patterns and delete them. Make sure you save this smallest possible version of the file with a new name. ✑

Gallery: Sharon Steuer

A reduced version of the final pattern (tile prescaled to 52%). In the original pattern tile, I used the Brush tool (see pages 68 through 71), multiple layers to separate the colored elements (see Chapter 4), and the Blend tool (see Chapter 5) to create the color transitions in the sky and leaves.

Templates & Layers

4

Layer palette navigation

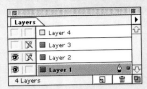

- To hide a layer, click its Eye icon. Click again to show it.
- To lock a layer, click in the box to its left (a Crossed-out Pencil displays). Click again to unlock.
- To select contiguous layers, Shift-click on one layer, then the other. To select or deselect *any* layers ⌘-click in any order.
- To open Layer Options, Double-click on a layer (see next page).
- To select all objects on a layer, Option-click on the layer name.
- To toggle lock/view options between only the current layer and all other layers Option-click on the appropriate icon.
- To move objects from one layer to another, see Tip on page 88.
- To duplicate a layer, grab and drag it to the New Layer icon.

See the *Quick Reference Card* for more layers shortcuts.

Used wisely, layers can dramatically improve organization of complicated artwork, thereby easing your workflow. There are a few helpful shortcuts when you're adding layers to the Layers palette. Click the New Layer icon to add a layer in numeric sequence above the current layer. Option-click New Layer to open Layer Options as you add the layer. To add a layer to the top of the Layers palette, ⌘-click New Layer. Finally, to make a new layer below the current layer ⌘-Option-click the New Layer icon. To delete selected layers click the Trash icon. **Note:** *To bypass the warning that you're about to delete a layer containing artwork, drag the layer to the Trash or Option-click the Trash. If you're not sure whether a layer has artwork or guides you may need, select the layer and click the Trash so you'll get the warning if applicable.*

The layers mindset

Try to think of layers as sheets of clear acetate, stacked one on top of the other, allowing you to separate dozens of groups of objects easily. You can rearrange the stacking order of the layers; lock, hide or copy layers; and move objects from one layer to another.

By default, the Layers palette (in Window: Show Layers) opens with one layer, though you can add as many layers as you wish. Unlike Photoshop, Illustrator layers affect your file size minimally.

Maximizing Layer Options

Double-click a layer name to set Layer Options to:

- **Name the layer.** In complicated artwork, naming layers keeps your job, and your brain, organized.

- **Change the layer's color.** A layer's color determines the selection color for paths, anchor points, bounding boxes and Smart Guides. Adjust the layer color so selections stand out against artwork (see "Color…" Tip at right).

- **Template Layer.** The ability to create a template has returned with gusto. Template layers will *not* print or export. There are three ways to create a template: You can double-click a layer to open the Layer Options and then check Template, select Template from the Layers pop-up menu or check Template when placing an image in Illustrator. Templates by default are locked layers (see pages 80–83). To unlock a Template (to adjust or edit objects) click the toggle lock to the left of the layer name.
  Hint: *Make a layer into a Template to ensure it won't print.*

- **Show / Hide layer.** This option functions the same way as the Show/Hide toggle, which you access by clicking the Eye icon (see Tip opposite). By default, hiding a layer sets it to *not* print (also see Tip on page 90).

- **Preview / Artwork mode.** Controlling which layers are set to Preview or Artwork is essential to working with layers. If you have objects that are easier to edit in Artwork mode, or objects that are slowing redraw (such as complicated patterns, live blends or gradients), you may want to set only those *layers* to Artwork mode. Set selected layers to Artwork or Preview in Layer Options, or toggle this option on and off directly by ⌘-clicking the Eye icon (see page 83).

- **Lock / Unlock layer.** This option functions the same way as the Lock/Unlock toggle, which you access by clicking to the left of the layer name (see Tip opposite).

- **Print / Suppress printing.** When printing from within

Layer Options (double-click a layer name)

Color-coding groups of layers

Select a set of layers using the Shift or Command keys. Double-click any of the selected layers to open the Layer Options dialog box. Then set the layer color for all selected layers (see David Nelson's map on page 178). You can also use this technique to adjust other options globally on a set of selected layers.

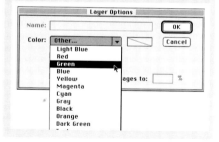

Objects on different layers

Here are three ways to move a group of objects from one layer on top of objects in another:
- Reorder the layers (see page 83).
- Move the bottom objects to the top layer (see Tip, page 88).
- Cut the bottom objects, select the topmost object and Paste In Front (⌘-F) with Paste Remembers Layers *off* (see "Paste In Front, Paste In Back," page 78).

Unlock and show all layers, then unlock and show all objects (from Object menu, ⌘-Option-3, and ⌘-Option-2), *then* press ⌘-A to Select All.

When a layer name is in *italic*, that means it's set to *not print from within Illustrator* (see "Print/Suppress..." on page 77 for limitations of nonprinting layers). If the name is italic *and* you see the Template icon, then it is reliably a nonprinting layer (see "Template..." page 77).

You can use layers to separate print production marks and notes. For instance, use separate layers for die tracing, blueline (or keyline), type, printer remarks, and one layer each for any linked or embedded art. Because you can toggle Hide/Show layers by deselecting or selecting the Eye icon on the Layers palette, you can hide certain layers when you want to proof your file from within Illustrator. —*Robin AF Olson* (Also see the Tip "WYSIWYG layers?" on page 90 for details on when layers print or don't print.)

Illustrator you can use this to override the default, which sets visible layers to print. If you need to ensure that a layer will *never* print in *any* circumstances (for instance, when placed into a page layout program) make the layer into a Template layer, or see Tip on page 90.

- **Dim Images.** You can dim *only* raster images (not vector Illustrator objects) from 1% to 99% opacity.

The Layers pop-up menu

You can perform the first four functions in the Layers pop-up via the layer icons, or Layer Options (see above). Template, Hide Others, Artwork Others and Lock Others all perform actions on unselected layers. Merge Layers is available when two or more layers are selected, and will place *visible* objects in the topmost layer. An alternative to Flatten Artwork is Select All, Copy and Paste with Paste Remembers Layers disabled (General Preferences).

Paste Remembers Layers is a great feature: when it's off, pasted objects go into the selected layer; when it's on, objects retain their layer order in exciting ways (see pages 92–93 for a technique using this feature).

Lastly, Small Palette Rows minimizes the layer display. This is a great help to artists who have complicated files with many layers (see page 178).

CONTROLLING THE STACKING ORDER OF OBJECTS

Layers are crucial for organizing your images, but controlling the stacking order of objects *within* a layer is just as essential. Following is a summary of the functions that will help you to control the stacking order of objects within a layer.

Paste In Front, Paste In Back (⌘-F, ⌘-B or Edit menu)

Illustrator doesn't merely bring or send an object in front of or behind all other objects when you choose Paste In Front/Back (⌘-F/⌘-B); it positions the object *exactly* in front of or behind the object you copied. A second, and equally important, aspect is that the two functions paste objects that are cut (⌘-X) or copied (⌘-C) into the exact same location—in relation to the *ruler origin*. This ability applies from one document to another, ensuring perfect registration and alignment when you copy and use Edit: Paste In Front / Back. See pages 92–93 for a practical application of this option, and the *Wow!* disk for exercises in reordering objects using pasting and layers.

Lock / Unlock All (⌘-2 / ⌘-Option-2 or Object menu)

When you're trying to select an object and you accidentally select an object on top of it, try locking the selected object (⌘-2) and clicking again. Repeat as necessary until you reach the correct object. When you've finished the task, choose Unlock All (⌘-Option-2) to release all the locked objects.

Note: *Use the Direct-selection tool to select and lock objects that are part of a group (see "Selecting within groups" in Chapter 1)—but if you select an unlocked object in the group with the Group-selection or other selection tools, the locked objects can become selected. Hidden objects stay hidden even if you select other objects in the same group.*

Hide / Show All (⌘-3 / ⌘-Option-3 or Object menu)

Another approach for handling objects that get in the way is to select them and choose Hide Selection (⌘-3). To view all hidden objects, choose Show All (⌘-Option-3).

Note: *Hidden objects may print if they're on visible layers and will reappear when you reopen the file.*

Bring Forward / Bring To Front and more...

Within a layer, Bring Forward (⌘-]) or Object: Arrange) stacks an object on top of the object directly above it. Bring To Front (⌘-Shift-]) moves an object in front of all other objects on its layer. Logically, Send To Back (⌘-Shift-[) sends an object as far back as it can go in its stacking order. Send Backward (⌘-[) sends an object behind its closest neighbor.

Note: *Bring Forward and Send Backward may not work on large files.*

If you can't select an object...

If you have trouble selecting an object, check the following:
- Is the object's layer locked?
- Is the object locked?
- Are the edges hidden?
- Is the Area Select box disabled (in General Preferences)?

If you keep selecting the wrong object, try again after you:
- Switch to Artwork mode.
- Zoom in.
- Hide the selected object; repeat if necessary.
- Lock the selected object; repeat if necessary.
- Choose View: Preview Selection to preview *only* your selected object, so you know what you're about to lock, hide or edit.
- Put the object on top in another layer and hide that layer, or select Artwork for that layer.
- Use the Move command: Option-click the Selection arrow in the Toolbox to move selected objects a set distance (you can move them back later).

Hide or lock all *except*...

To hide all *but* selected objects, choose Object: Hide Selection with the Option key down (or ⌘-Shift-Option-3). To lock all *but* selected objects, choose Object: Lock with the Option key down (or ⌘-Shift-Option-2).

Digitizing a Logo

Controlling Your Illustrator Template

Overview: *Scan a clean, enlarged version of your artwork; place the art as a template in Illustrator; analyze the curves of the template; trace the template; hide the template for adjustments; copy the finished illustration and paste it into a new document.*

Line art can be tinted easily!

If your image was scanned as a bitmap and saved as a TIFF, you can tint the placed image from within Illustrator: select the placed 1-bit TIFF and set a fill color to replace the black pixels with the color you selected. The white pixels will be transparent.
— *Sandee Cohen*
Note: *Since competing illustration programs allow the tinting of* gray-scale *images, with luck, Illustrator will also let us do* that *soon!*

You can easily use Illustrator to re-create traditional line art with the computer—easily, that is, if you know the tricks. Years after Rick Barry rendered the Breeders' Cup logo in black and white using traditional methods, he re-created it digitally in order to produce colorized versions. One version, using gradients, is shown above (for more about gradients, see *Chapter 5*).

1 **Preparing a large, clean scan.** Select a high-contrast image to re-create in Illustrator. Scan the image as black-and-white "line art" at 75 pixels per inch (ppi), but enlarged to 200–400%, and save it in TIFF format. An image scanned at 1" x 1" at 300 ppi contains the same number of pixels as a 4" x 4" scan at 75 ppi. Since that 75 ppi image would appear four times larger when viewed in Illustrator, this gives you more flexibility to zoom in and work on the tiny details of your artwork. Although the original logo was not very big, Barry had a "stat" produced at 12" wide and scanned it into the computer. Since his scanning software didn't permit adjusting the pixel-per-inch ratio, Barry scanned at 300 ppi and used Photoshop to set the image to 75 ppi without changing the actual number of pixels (*not* "Resampling") before using it as a template in Illustrator.
Note: *Don't be concerned if you encounter 72 ppi (the resolution of your screen)—72 or 75 ppi is fine for templates.*

1

Scanning a large, clean version of your artwork

2 Placing the TIFF as a template. Choose File: Place, click the Template option, then choose your scan, thus placing it into a new template layer. Template layers are automatically placed below the current layer and are set to be non-printing, dimmed layers. You'll be tracing in Layer 1.

3 Adjusting the page size for large images. Large templates may bleed over the edges of your paper size. An easy way to temporarily adjust an image to fit within a smaller paper size is to set a % reduction in Page Setup (⌘-Shift-P; Windows users will need to choose Printer's Properties, where most printer drivers allow a reduction).

4 Tracing the template. Look at the entire template and compare it to the original you have scanned. Are any of the curves or lines misrepresented in the template? Remember that the template is just a guide; if a discrepancy exists, follow the original. Working first in Artwork mode (from the View menu or ⌘-Y), use the Pen tool to trace your template (see the "Zen Lessons" on the *Wow!* disk for help). Place the minimal number of points necessary to complete the object, and don't be too concerned with how closely you're matching the contour. Then, zoom in close (with the Zoom tool, drag to marquee the area you wish to inspect) and use the Direct-selection tool to make adjustments to the length and angle of the direction lines until the Bézier curves properly fit the template.

5 Adjusting your views. As you work, use both Artwork and Preview modes, zoom in and out as necessary, and use Hide/Show Template (View menu or ⌘-Shift-W) to control whether your template layer is hidden or visible.

6 Scaling the final. To place the finished illustration into another program, save the original, then choose Select All (⌘-A), copy the image and paste into a new document. With the logo still selected, double-click the Scale tool to scale the final to meet your specific needs, making sure that you enable "Scale Stroke Weight."

2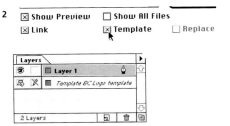

3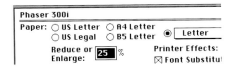

The large template bleeding over the page

Adjusting Page Setup so the image fits within the page margins

4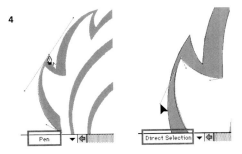

Using the Pen tool to draw curves and using the Direct-selection tool to adjust the curves (for info on Illustrator's cursors which change to reflect your action, see Chapter 1)

5

Hiding the template to make final adjustments

Tracing Details

Tracing Intricate Details with the Pencil

Overview: *Scan a photo and place it into a Template layer in Illustrator; adjust Pencil Options; trace the photo with the Pencil; create new layers; adjust layer positions and modes.*

Saving images for tracing

While EPS is often the preferred format for placed images (see the *Chapter 9* introduction), saving images in TIFF format will display more detail for tracing.

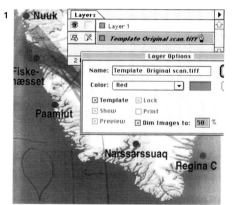

Double-clicking the Template layer to access Layer Options where "Dim Images" percentages can be customized

Double-clicking on the Pencil tool to set Options

Laurie Grace loves the way that the new Pencil tool permits her to trace details with more precision than ever before. Using the Pencil with custom settings and additional layers, she was able to create this map of Greenland for a *Scientific American* article on a comet path.

1 Scanning and placing the image into a Template layer. Scan the image you wish to use as a tracing template as grayscale and save it in TIFF format. In a new document in Illustrator, place your TIFF as a template (see pages 80–81). Your template will automatically be dimmed to 50%; to customize the percentage at which the template is dimmed, double-click the Template layer.

2 Setting up your Pencil Options for tracing. In order to draw with precision, you'll need to adjust the default settings for the Pencil tool. Double-click the Pencil tool and drag the Fidelity slider all the way to the left, to 0.5 pixels, keeping Smoothness at 0% (higher numbers in Fidelity and Smoothness result in less accurate, smoother lines). For this lesson, keep "Keep Selected" enabled, so you can redraw lines and easily connect a new line to the last.

3 Drawing with the Pencil tool into Layer 1. It's very simple to attach one line to the next, so don't worry about tracing your entire template in one stroke. Zoom in as much as you need to (see *Chapter 1* for Zoom help) and trace one section. When you finish drawing that section (and it's still selected), move the Pencil tool aside until you see "×" indicating that the Pencil would be drawing a new path. Next, move the Pencil close to the selected path and notice the "×" disappears, indicating that the new path will be connected to the currently selected one, then continue to draw your path. If you wish to attach a path to an unselected path, simply select the path you wish to attach to first. To draw a closed path with the Pencil (like the islands in Grace's map), hold the Option key as you approach the first point in the path. **Note:** *With the Option key down, if you stop before you reach the first point, the path will close with a straight line.*

4 **Creating and reordering new layers.** To add the background water and the coastline terrain details, Grace had to create additional layers. To create additional layers, click on the New Layer icon in the Layers palette (or Option-click the icon to name the layer). Clicking on a layer name activates that layer so the next object you create will be on that layer. To reorder layers, grab a layer by its name and drag it above or below another layer. Click in the Pencil column to Lock or Unlock specific layers.

5 **Hiding and Previewing layers.** To toggle Hide/Show for Template layers, press ⌘-Shift-W (View menu). To toggle any layer between Hide and Show, click on the left icon for that layer to show or remove the Eye. To toggle a non-template layer between Preview and Artwork mode, ⌘-click the Eye. (To move objects from one layer to another, see bottom Tip on page 88.) ☺

Zooming more means smoothing less...

You can control the amount of smoothing applied with the Smooth tool by adjusting screen magnification. When you're zoomed-out, the Smooth tool deletes more points; zoomed-in, the tool produces more subtle results.—*David Nelson*

3

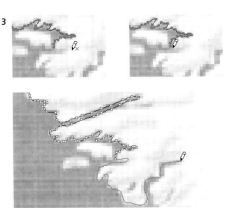

After drawing part of the coastline it remains selected, moving the Pencil close to the selected path then allows the next path to be connected; continuing the path with the Pencil tool

Drawing with the Pencil tool and holding the Option key to close the path

4

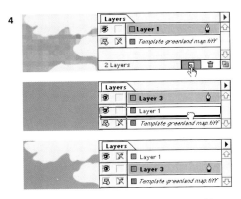

Making a New Layer; a blue object created in the new Layer 3 which is moved below Layer 1; Layer 1 locked with Layer 3 activated

5

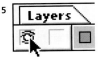

Toggling between Artwork and Preview mode for a specific layer by ⌘-clicking the Eye

Layering Colors

Coloring Black-and-White Images with Layers

Overview: *Create your black outlines; set up layers in Illustrator for the colors inside the lines and other layers for background elements; place black-and-white art into the upper layer; color the image; group outlines with their colors.*

The background for the illustration, created in the bottom two layers

An outline sketch

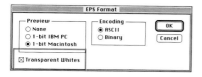

Choosing the "Transparent Whites" option when saving in EPS format

While the most obvious way to trace placed images in Illustrator is to put the image to be traced in a locked lower layer and use an upper layer to trace the new Illustrator objects, in some cases you'll want your tracing layer to be *below* a placed image. When illustrating a three-ringed circus for a Ringling Brothers Barnum & Bailey International Program, Michael Kline placed his sketches with the whites transparent into a locked upper layer so he could add color using Illustrator while maintaining a hand-sketched look.

1 Setting up your Illustrator layers. In Illustrator, create enough layers for the various background elements in your image. (For help making layers, see pages 80–83.) Assign each layer a different color to help keep track of which objects will be in each layer (selected paths and anchor points will be color-coded to match their layer). Then create the background of your illustration in these layers. When the background is ready, create at least two additional top layers for the figures you will be coloring. For his circus illustration, Kline established four layers— using the bottom layer ("Layer 4") to create the background itself and "Layer 3" to create the objects that would be directly on top of the background.

2 Sketching or scanning a black-and-white drawing.
Scan a hand-drawn sketch or draw directly into a bit-mapped program. Save it as an EPS file, with a black-and-white preview (1-bit) and the "Transparent Whites" option. Kline drew figure sketches with a soft pencil on rough paper, scanned them, then saved them individually as transparent, 1-bit, black-and-white EPS files.

The scanned drawing placed into Layer 1

3 Placing your drawings into the top layer. From the Layers palette, make the top layer active (click on the layer name) and use the Place command (from the File menu) to place one of your drawings into the top layer. Then, lock the layer (click in the box to the right of the Eye icon).

4 Coloring your drawings. You must tell Illustrator in which layer you will be drawing by activating and unlocking the second layer (to the left of the layer you should see the Eye and no Crossed-out Pencil). Now, using filled colored objects without strokes, trace *under* your placed sketch. To view the color alone, hide the top layer.

The colorized drawing with the line drawing visible and the line drawing hidden

5 Grouping your drawing with its colors. When you're finished coloring the first figure, select the placed EPS with the objects that colorize that figure and group them together. The colored, grouped figure will now be on the top layer, where you can easily reposition it within your composition.

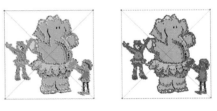

The drawing and the underlying color before and after being grouped together

Switching layers by selecting an object

If you are creating or editing objects with a number of layers unlocked, you don't have to use the Layers palette to switch your active layer. When you select an object from an unlocked layer, the layer that the selected object is on automatically becomes your new active layer. The next object you create will use the same paint style as the object you had selected and will be placed on that new active layer.

Moving the grouped, colorized figure around the composition

Multiple Layers

Creating a Poster from Multiple Sources

Overview: *Sketch and scan a composition; set up basic layers in Illustrator for the objects you will create; place art into temporary layers; trace the placed art; delete the temporary layers.*

1

Scanned photos of figures

Assembled collage and hand-traced sketch scanned

Scanned background photos

Multiple layers can be a lifesaver when you're constructing complex illustrations. Using these layers to isolate or combine specific elements will simplify your tasks substantially and save you an immense amount of production time. When The City Volunteer Corps (CVC) commissioned Nancy Stahl to design a New York City subway poster, she saved time and frustration by creating pairs of template-and-artwork layers for tracing and arranging various components of the poster.

1 Collecting and assembling source materials. Prepare your own source materials to use as tracing templates in Illustrator. For the CVC subway poster, Stahl took Polaroids of herself posed as each of the figures in the composition and scanned them into Adobe Photoshop, where she scaled them, and moved them into position. She then printed out the assembled "collage," roughly sketched in the other elements by hand and, with tracing paper, created a line version of the full composition to use as an overall template. She then scanned it into the computer.

Finally, Stahl scanned a number of photos showing different buildings in New York City's skyline for individual placement and tracing in Illustrator.

2 Setting up illustration layers. Before you begin to import any photos or drawings, take a few moments to set up layers to help you isolate the key elements in your illustration. (For help making layers, see pages 80–83.) For the subway poster, before she actually started her Illustrator image, Stahl set up separate layers for the background, the type, and the buildings that would make up the skyline, as well as one layer for each of the figures and a final layer for the foreground buildings.

3 Placing art to use as templates. You'll now need to create a few temporary layers for placing the artwork or scans you've collected to use as tracing templates. For each image you want to use as a template, make a new layer and use Place to select the scan or artwork to be placed into this layer. Then move the Template layer directly below the object layer upon which you will be tracing and lock it. Stahl created a layer, which she named "EPS Images," and then placed the buildings that she would be tracing for the skyline. Using the Layers palette, she then moved this new skyscraper template below her "buildings" layer, onto which she created the Illustrator buildings, and then locked the EPS Images layer.

4 Drawing into your layers. Now you can begin drawing and tracing elements into your compositional layers. Activate the layer in which you want to draw (click on the layer's name), unlock and view the layer (there should be an Eye in the Show box and an empty Edit box) and start to work. Use the Layers palette to lock, unlock or hide layers, as well as to toggle between Preview and Artwork modes (⌘-click the Eye icon), switch your active layer or add a new layer. By so maneuvering, Stahl could easily trace a group of skyscrapers, create type against a locked background or develop one figure at a time.

2

Setting up layers to isolate key elements

3

The temporary layer and choosing Place

Moving the layer and setting up the Edit and Show options for tracing

4

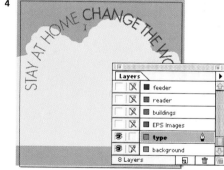

Isolating elements by viewing and unlocking only the essential layers

5

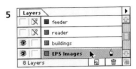

Clicking on a visible and unlocked layer to make it active for placing new art

6

Moving placed art within a layer to trace different objects

7

Clicking on the Trash icon, or choosing Delete from the Layers palette pop-up menu

---

Changing placed art

Select the image you wish to replace. Next open the Links palette (Window menu) and click on the Replace Link icon (the bottom left icon) or choose Replace from the Links palette pop-up menu. In the dialog box, locate the replacement image and click Place.

---

5 Adding new placed art to a lower layer. If you need to import art into an existing layer, you must first make the layer visible and unlocked (in the Layers palette, the Eye icon should show and the Edit box should be empty) and then make it the active layer. For the subway poster, when Stahl needed additional building references, she viewed and unlocked EPS Images, clicked on it to make it the active layer and then used the Place command.

6 Moving placed art within a layer. Stahl's reference photos showed New York's buildings clustered differently from the way she wanted them for her illustration, so she devised a way to space the buildings as she worked. After tracing over one building, she unlocked EPS Images, moved the cluster of buildings slightly and relocked the layer. She then traced a different skyscraper in the new location and repeated the procedure for each building.

7 Deleting layers when you finish using them. Extra layers with placed art can take up quite a bit of disk space, so when you finish using a template, first save the file. Then, in the Layers palette, click on the layer you are ready to remove and click on the trash icon, or choose the Delete option from the Layers palette pop-up menu. Finally, use Save As to save this new version of the illustration with a meaningful new name and version number (such as "CVC without EPS-3.0"). Stahl eventually deleted all the layers she created as templates so she could save her final poster with all the illustration layers but none of the templates or placed pictures. 🍪

Moving an object from one layer to another

To move a selected object to another layer: open the Layers palette, grab the colored dot to the right of the object's layer and drag it to the desired layer. To move a copy of an object: hold down the Option key while you drag.

Gallery: Nancy Stahl

Working with the computer, artists can now miraculously breathe new life into finished works. Nancy Stahl had created this image from one of her handpainted illustrations using Illustrator 3.2 (before there were layers). In order to simplify reworking this image, Stahl began by using Illustrator 5.5 to separate elements into distinct layers: the background, a layer for each of the figures, and a few layers to isolate the various foreground elements. She moved objects to the correct layers by dragging the colored dots representing them in the Layers palette. (See Tip at left, and reworked image on page 194.)

Viewing Details

Using Layers and Views for Organization

Overview: *Establish your working layers; use layers to organize distinct categories of elements; save zoom levels and viewpoints using the New View command.*

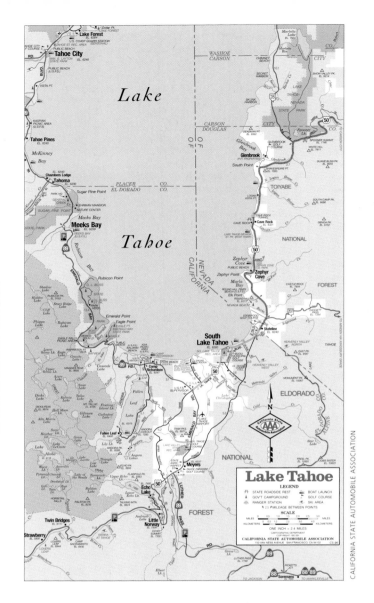

CALIFORNIA STATE AUTOMOBILE ASSOCIATION

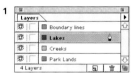

General organizational layers

Additional layers created to isolate categories of elements

In addition to providing an ideal method for overlapping compositional elements, layers can help organize complex illustrations, even when many of the elements appear to exist on the same visual plane. When the California State Automobile Association (CSAA) creates road maps using Illustrator, the cartography department uses layers to delineate the different categories of labeling information. Even on the fastest computers, however, you can waste a lot of time zooming in and out, hiding and showing layers and toggling various layers between Preview and Artwork modes. That's why the CSAA saves frequently used views to navigate quickly and easily around its large format maps.

1 Creating organizational layers. In addition to layers you create for compositional elements (such as background or figures), try creating separate layers for each category of labeling information you're including. If you construct your image with layers organized by the category of element, it becomes very simple to view and change all similar text or objects at once. For its Lake Tahoe map, the CSAA created individual layers for park lands, creeks, lakes and boundary lines, as well as layers for roads, type, symbols and the legend.

2 Saving frequently used views. Instead of wasting precious time zooming in and out of your image and scrolling around to find a specific detail, you can preserve your current viewpoint for immediate return at another time. Along with "remembering" the specific section you zoomed to, saved views remember which of your layers were in Preview or Artwork modes. To save your current view, simply choose View: New View, name your current view and click OK. Your view will then be added to the bottom of the View menu. Each successive view you save will appear at the bottom of the menu. The CSAA saved separate views for each area of the map requiring repeated attention, which included each of the four corners, the legend box and three additional locations.

3 Using views. To recall a saved view, choose the desired view from the list at the bottom of the View menu. Using Edit Views, you can rename or delete views, although you cannot, unfortunately, change the viewpoints themselves. Another glitch is that Edit Views lists the most recently created or renamed view last, not alphabetically, so getting your layers to list in a specific order takes a bit of organization.

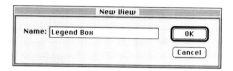

Saving and naming a viewpoint using New View

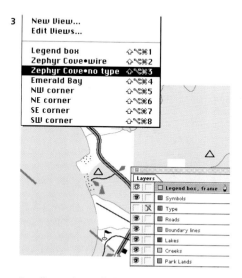

Recalling a view, which resets the zoom level, what portion of the image is visible, and which layers are visible or hidden, locked or unlocked

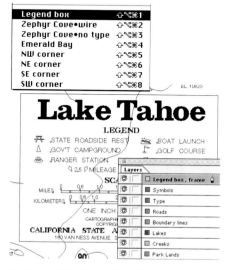

The Legend Box View, with all layers in Artwork

Layer Registration

Paste Remembers Layers' Magic Alignment

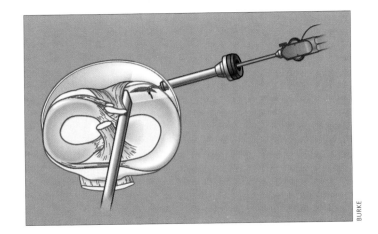

BURKE

Overview: *Create enough layers for all stages of your sequence; use New View to save settings for which layers are visible for each stage; control which layers print for proofing; set "Paste Remembers Layers" for separating stages for final printing.*

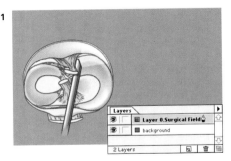

The background layer (the filled rectangle only) and main surgical layer, "Layer 0"

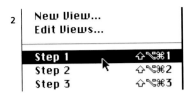

Choosing the View and Layers reset for "Step 1"

Organizing a series of interrelated illustrations in perfect registration with each other is simple using layers. This medical illustration shows three of the nine stages in a series that Christopher Burke created for Linvatec Corporation demonstrating the surgical procedure for repairing a knee injury once the fiber-optic light / camera is in place to illuminate the injury site.

1 Creating layers to illustrate the unifying aspects of the series. Create the necessary layers into which you'll construct basic elements common to the whole series of illustrations (for layers help, see pages 80–83). Burke's basic layers for this surgical technique illustration were the surgical layer illustrating the knee, and the background.

2 Simplifying the creation, viewing and proofing of the various stages of your illustration. Once the unifying aspects of your illustration are in place, use additional layers for creating variants. Use the Layers palette to hide and show various layers and thus isolate each of the different versions. Burke created all stages for the suturing technique in the same document. As he created a layer for a specific stage of the procedure, he would include that stage number in the layer name. For the numbering system, Burke named the main surgical layer "Layer 0"; this layer would appear in every stage. He numbered each progressive layer above it "1, 2, 3…" and then used "-1, -2, -3…" for each subsequent layer below.

When using layers to create a series of related illustrations, the New View command (View menu) can help track which layers need to be visible, hidden, locked or unlocked for each individual stage. Be aware, Views also remember Zoom level and location, and whether each layer is in Artwork or Preview mode. After setting the Layers palette for a stage of your illustration, choose New View, then name and save these settings. Repeat this procedure for each stage. To recall the Layers palette settings for any stage, select its view from the View menu.

When you're ready to print proofs, Illustrator will, by default, print only visible, non-template layers. To avoid having to make unnecessary changes to multiple documents, keep the file together as long as you can, using Views to help you keep track of which layers should be hidden or visible for each stage.

3 Preparing final versions for printing. In the Layers pop-up menu, enable "Paste Remembers Layers." This option ensures that your objects will stay in the correct layers, and that layers will be automatically replicated (or unlocked) as you move them into other files.

To print the final illustrations, you'll have to copy each completed stage into its own file. Select your saved views for the first stage, making sure all layers necessary to the illustration are visible and unlocked (all Eye icons should be visible and the Edit column should be empty). If you've hidden or locked any elements individually, choose from the Object menu: Unlock All and Show All (or ⌘-Option-2 and ⌘-Option-3). Then select and copy this version and, in a new document, use Paste In Front (⌘-F). When you use Paste In Front, all needed layers will miraculously appear in the Layers palette and the image will be in perfect registration so you can still move objects back and forth between files. Repeat this step for each stage of the illustration. If you're printing from another application, save these in EPS format (see *Chapter 1* for more information on saving in EPS). 🌀

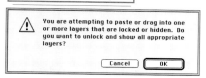

Setting "Paste Remembers Layers" in Layer Options and the warning you'll get if you try to paste copied objects to locked or hidden layers (see page 88 for moving objects to other layers)

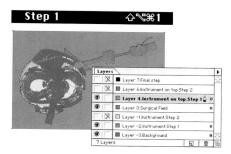

Choosing Step1 view, then selecting all needed layers for copying and pasting into a new file

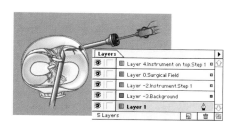

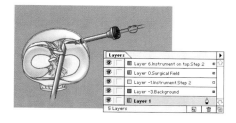

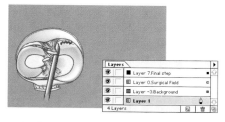

Each of the three stages pasted into its own document, with layers appearing automatically

BARNEY (illustrator), FRANSON (designer)/ BARNEY MCKAY DESIGN

Gallery: Jeffrey Barney / Barney McKay Design

For this image, serving as part of a five-tier pop-up promotion for The
Secret Garden, *Jeffrey Barney used dozens of layers to isolate various elements. Barney began by creating seven separate documents which, from
front to back, were Ivy, Poppies, Roses, Irises, Mary (the girl), Sunflowers
and Tree/Sky—each of the files containing between four and twelve
named layers. To arrange elements into the final five files for the pop-up
properly, Barney kept the "Paste Remembers Layers" option enabled (see
page 92). In this way, he could move objects between files while keeping
them on the correct layers and in perfect registration. He needed other
arrangements of different layers for other materials, including the close-
ups of Irises and Sunflowers for a CD cover (shown with an "onionskin"
overlay) and other print materials designed with Scott Franson.*

Gallery: Dorothea Taylor-Palmer

For this image, artist Dorothea Taylor-Palmer used the technique of placing one of her drawings on a top layer and painting the colored swatches in layers below (see page 84). She began with a traditional sketch and experimented with running it through a copier while moving it slightly until she captured the illusion of movement she had in mind. After scanning the sketch into Photoshop, Taylor-Palmer saved it as a transparent, 1-bit EPS file, which she then placed into Illustrator. After locking the layer with the EPS, she created another layer and moved it below the first. Into the lower layer, Taylor-Palmer painted swaths of color to show through the white portions of the placed sketch.

TAYLOR-PALMER

PALMER

Gallery: Charly Palmer

Although a professional illustrator for many years, Charly Palmer has only recently begun using Illustrator, under the tutelage of his wife, Dorothea Taylor-Palmer. Even though his method of working is fairly similar to that which Taylor-Palmer used for the image above, his own vision and hand are strongly evident in this profile. After placing a scanned drawing that was saved as a transparent EPS onto an upper layer and locking it, Palmer used colors and blends to complete the composition.

Varied Perspective

Analyzing Different Views of Perspective

Advanced Technique

Overview: *Draw and scan a sketch; establish working layers using your sketch as a template; in a "Guides" layer, draw a series of lines to establish perspective; make the perspective lines into guides; using layers to control what is visible, construct your image according to the applicable perspective guides.*

1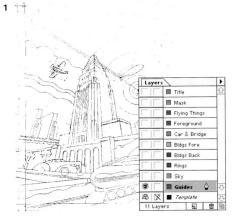

The template with a custom layer ready for placement of guides

2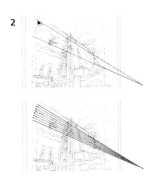

Dragging a perspective line to form a "V," then blending to create in-between perspective lines

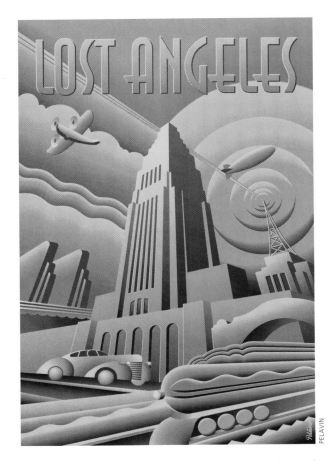

Since the Italian Renaissance, the conventions of vanishing-point perspective have helped artists to organize their two-dimensional artwork. You can use Adobe Illustrator to establish vanishing points with the help of object guides. The following few pages include perspective approaches by two different artists. This section will not so much teach you how to construct an image using vanishing points as it will help you to translate your knowledge of perspective into techniques to use within Illustrator. The slightly distorted perspective in Danny Pelavin's "Lost Angeles" demonstrates how that knowledge can translate into results that are quite fantastic.

1 With a scanned sketch as a template, setting up the necessary layers. Draw a sketch of your composition establishing some basic perspective guidelines. Scan the sketch, save it in TIFF format and open it as a template in Illustrator (see pages 80–83). Once in Illustrator, create the essential number of layers to isolate the various compositional elements, plus one extra layer for your guides.

2 Establishing the location of vanishing points. Activate your "Guides" layer (by clicking on the layer name) and lock all other layers. Using your template as a reference, decide where to place the first vanishing point and use the Pen tool to draw a line along the horizon line through the vanishing point. (It's fine if your vanishing point extends beyond the picture border.) With the Direct-selection tool, select the anchor point from the end of the line that is opposite the vanishing point. Grab the point, then hold down your Option key and swing this copy of the line up so it encompasses the uppermost object that will be constructed along the vanishing point. You should now have a "V" that goes from your horizon line through your vanishing point, then to an upper portion of your composition. To create in-between lines through the same vanishing point, select both of the original lines, use the Blend tool to click first on the outer anchor point of one of the lines, then on the outer anchor point of the other line, and next specify the number of in-between steps. For each different vanishing point, repeat the above procedure. While creating his perspective guides in Illustrator, Pelavin discovered that his previous technique of using a thumbtack and a piece of string was nowhere near as accurate.

3 Making your perspective lines into guides. Once you have completed your perspective lines, choose Edit: Select All (⌘-A), then choose View: Make Guides (⌘-5). You have now transformed the lines into nonprinting guides (set guides to "dash" line style in Preferences: Grids and Guides). In addition to being able to lock or hide your guides from within the Layers palette, you can take advantage of some unique properties. If you wish to select, align, or manipulate your guides, then disable

3

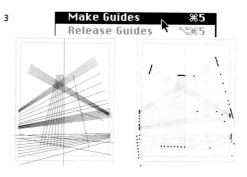

Perspective lines before and after being made into guides

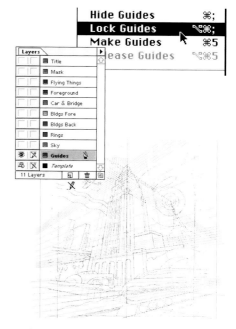

Locking guides by using the Lock/Unlock toggle from the View menu and locking the layer

More guide guidance

- When guides are unlocked, you can select any guide as an object and move it.
- You can move, hide, scale and rotate guides grouped with related objects along with their associated objects.
- You can only "snap to" guides that are on unlocked layers.

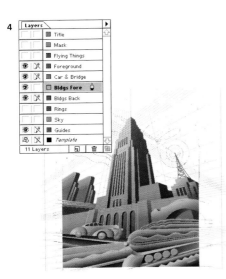

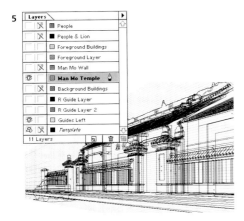

4

Hiding, showing and locking specific layers

5

"Guides Left" layer shown with buildings drawn in Artwork mode on Man Mo Temple layer

Tate's final image

TATE

the View: Lock Guides option (by selecting it). Note, however, that the Lock/Unlock Guides option will affect all open documents. If you wish to transform your guides back into objects, unlock them, select the guides you wish to convert, and choose Release Guides from the View menu.

4 Creating your illustration using guides and templates as necessary. As you actually create your illustration, control what you're viewing on the screen at any one time with the View and Object menus. Also, from the Layers palette, toggle to control which layers are visible, hidden, locked, unlocked, or in Preview or Artwork mode.

5 Variations on a theme. Other artists use similar techniques adapted to their personal working styles. For his "Man Mo Temple," instead of reserving one layer for perspective guides, Clarke Tate used three separate layers. Because of the nature of the architectural detailing he was creating, Tate wanted more than just general perspective lines; he wanted to be able to actually create every building line from his perspective grid. Since having so many lines is visually distracting, Tate created two layers for his right-facing perspectives, each containing every other line, with a third layer reserved for the left-facing perspective. With this system, Tate could use the Layers palette to show only the specific perspective lines he required for the construction of each object.

Scanning true horizontals and verticals for tracing

When preparing templates for detailed renderings that rely on true horizontal and vertical lines (such as the architectural images in this technique or the Andrea Kelley computer renderings on pages 114 and 158), you must scan your template image into the computer perfectly straight. Take an image (or copy of an image) and cut the edge of the paper perfectly square to the image so you can line up the paper edge to the edge of the scanner bed itself. — *Andrea Kelley*

Basic Blends & Gradients

5

LIVE BLENDS

Think of blends as a way to "morph" one object or color, or shape and color, to another. You can now blend between multiple objects, which can even be gradients (see later in this intro for more on gradients) and compound paths (such as letters; see *Chapter 8* for more on compound paths). Blends are now "live," meaning once you've blended, you can edit the key objects by altering their shape, color, size, location or rotation, and the in-between blend will automatically update. Lastly, you can even distribute a blend along a custom path. Be aware that complex blends require a lot of RAM when drawing to the screen, especially gradient-to-gradient blends.

The simplest way to create a blend is to select the objects you wish to blend and choose Object: Blends: Make (⌘-Option-B). The number of steps you'll have in between each object is based on either the default options for the tool or the last settings of the Blend Options (details following). Adjust settings for a selected blend by double-clicking the Blend tool (or Objects: Blends: Blend Options).

A more reliable method of creating smooth blends in many circumstances is to *point map* between two objects using the Blend tool. First, select the two objects that you want to blend (with the Group-selection tool), then use the Blend tool to point map by clicking first on a selected point on the first object, then on the correlating selected point on the second object.

When a blend first appears, it is selected and grouped.

"W" Blend tool
"G" Gradient tool

Nancy Stahl's illustration with blends in place

Before blending; after blending (with the path that will replace the "spine"); after replacing the spine; Stahl's blends with replaced spines

To insert objects into a blend...
Direct-select a key object and Option-drag to insert a new key object (the blend will reflow) that you can Direct-select and edit.

John Kanzler created the fairy (top) with multi-object blends and a replaced spine; Rick Henkel used gradient-to-gradient blends for the pedestal of his table (see his explanation, "Henkel-AMS flared effect," on the Wow! *disk for full details)*

Minimizing banding

Long blends and gradients may *band* when printed, appearing as hard-edged strips, not smooth color transitions. To avoid this:

• Keep blends shorter than 7.5"
• Try to avoid long blends made of dark colors or that change less than 50% between two or more process colors.

Recolor after expanding blends

If you've expanded a blend, you can use *filters* to recolor blended objects. Direct-select and recolor the fill for the start and/or end objects, then select the entire blend and choose Filter: Colors: Blend Front to Back. Your objects' fill colors will reblend using the new start and end colors (this won't affect strokes or compound paths). Also try Blend Horizontally or Vertically, Adjust and Saturate.

If you Undo immediately, the blend will be deleted, but your source objects remain selected so you can blend again. To modify a key object, Direct-select the key object first, then use any editing tool (including the Pencil, Smooth and Erase tools) to make your changes.

Blend Options

To specify Blend Options as you blend, use the Blend tool (see above) and Option-click the second point. To adjust options on a completed blend, select it and double-click the Blend tool (or Object: Blends: Blend Options). Opening Blend Options without any blend selected resets the default for blends created *in this work session*; these Options reset each time you restart.

• **Specified Steps** specifies the number of steps between each pair of key objects. Using fewer steps results in clearly distinguishable objects, while a larger number of steps results in an almost airbrushed effect.
• **Specified Distance** places a specified distance between the objects of the blend.
• **Smooth Color** allows Illustrator to calculate automatically the ideal number of steps between key objects in a blend to achieve the smoothest color transition. If objects are the same color, or are gradients or patterns, then instead, the calculation equally distributes the objects within the area of the blend, based on their size.
• **Orientation** determines if blend objects rotate as the path curves. **Align to Path** (the default, first icon) allows the blend objects to rotate as they follow the path. **Align to Page** (the second icon) prevents objects from rotating as they are distributed along the curve of the path.

Blends along a Path

There are two ways to make blends follow a curved path. The first way is to Direct-select the "spine" of a blend (the path automatically created by the blend) and then use the Add/Delete-anchor-point tools, Direct-selection, Convert-direction, Pencil, Smooth—or even the Erase tool—to curve or edit the path; the blend will redraw to fit the new spine. The second way is to replace the spine with a customized path: select both the customized path and the blend and choose Object: Blends: Replace Spine. This command moves the blend to its new spine.

Reversing, Releasing and Expanding Blends

Once you've created and selected a blend, you can:

- **Reverse** the order of objects on the spine by choosing Object: Blends: Reverse Spine.
- **Release** a Blend (Object: Blends: Release) if you wish to remove the blended objects between key objects and maintain the spine of the blend (be forewarned—you may lose grouping information!).
- **Expand** a Blend to turn it into a group of separate, editable objects. Choose Object: Expand.

GRADIENTS

Gradients are color transitions. To open the Gradient palette: double-click the Gradient tool icon on the toolbox, click the gradient icon at the bottom of the Swatches palette, or choose Window: Show Gradient. Gradients can be either radial (circular from the center) or linear. Make your own gradients by placing and spacing pointers (stops) representing colors along the lower edge of the color scale in the Gradient palette, and by adjusting the midpoint of the color transition by sliding the shapes along the top of the scale.

You can adjust the length, direction and centerpoint location of selected gradients, as well as unify blends across multiple objects, by clicking and dragging with the Gradient tool (pages 108–111).

To fill type with gradients, convert the type to an outline (see page 138). To create the illusion of a gradient within a stroke, convert the stroke to a filled object (see Tip on page 64). To turn a gradient into a grouped, masked blend, use Object: Expand (see *Chapter 8* for more on masks and masked blends).

Note: *For details on Gradient Mesh see* Chapter 6.

Adding color to your gradient

- Drag a swatch from the Color or Swatches palette to the gradient slider until you see a vertical line, indicating where the new color stop will be added.
- If the fill is a solid color, you can drag color from the Fill icon at the bottom of the Toolbox.
- Hold down the Option key to drag a copy of a color stop.
- Option-drag one stop over another to *swap* their colors.
- Click the lower edge of a gradient to add a new stop.

Super-size gradient palette

If the Gradient palette isn't docked with other palettes: 1) you can make it both taller and wider; 2) it pops more clearly into view.

Don't lose that gradient!

Until gradients can be updated, you must take steps to ensure you don't inadvertently lose the gradient you are masterfully creating:

- To design a gradient for only one object, keep your object selected and see your gradient develop within the object itself.
- To design a gradient for later use or for multiple objects, drag the initial gradient square from its palette to the Swatches palette to store it. Keep Option-dragging from your gradient square to that initial swatch to update the stored gradient.

Examining Blends

Learning When to Use Gradients or Blends

Overview: *Examine your objects; for linear or circular fills, create basic gradients; for contouring fills into complex objects, create blends.*

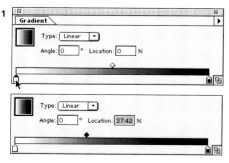

Adjusting the placement of colors, and then rate of color transition in the Gradient palette

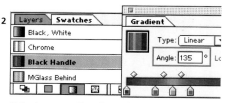

Selecting a gradient from the Swatches palette and setting the gradient Angle

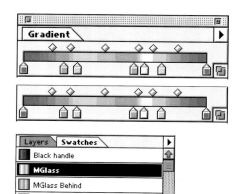

One gradient duplicated and altered for application to different related objects

You need to take a number of factors into consideration when you're deciding whether to create color transitions with blends or gradients. Steve Hart's magnifying glass, created for *Time* magazine, is a clear-cut example demonstrating when to use gradients or blends.

1 Designing gradients. Select an object you'd like to fill with a linear gradient. Open the Gradient palette. Click on the gradient icon at the bottom of the Swatches palette. Choose Name from the Swatches pop-up menu and click on the "Black, White" gradient. This initially minimal gradient has two colors: white (at the left) and black (at the right). Click on the left pointer to display its position on the scale from 0–100% (in this case 0%). Slide the pointer to the right to increase the percentage displayed in the scale, and increase the black area of the gradient. Click on the bottom edge of the scale to add additional pointers. Click on a pointer to access its numeric position, or to change its color or tint. Between every two pointers is a diamond shape indicating the midpoint of the color transition (from 0–100% between each color pair). Grab and drag a diamond to adjust the color transition rate, or type a new position into the percent field.

2 Storing and applying gradients and making adjustments. To store a new gradient you've made within a selected object, Option-click the New Swatch icon and name your gradient. For help adding color to gradients, see Tip below and the intro to this chapter. Hart filled his magnifying glass handle with a gradient set at a 135° angle (in the Gradient palette). He created slightly different variants for gradients representing the metal rings around the outside, along the inside, and inside behind the glass. To create variants of a current gradient, make color adjustments first, then Option-click the New Swatch icon to name your new gradient. Although you can experiment with changing the angle of a gradient, be forewarned that continued adjustments to a gradient in the Gradient palette will not update the gradient stored in the Swatches palette! (See the intro to this chapter.)

3 Using blends for irregular or contoured transitions.
A blend is often best for domed, kidney-shaped or contoured objects, such as shadows (for Gradient Mesh, see *Chapter 6*). Scale one object to create another and set each to the desired color. With the Blend tool, click an anchor point on one, then Option-click a related point on the other. The default blend setting, "Smooth Color," often means many steps; however, the more similar the colors, the fewer steps you actually need. You can manually choose "Specified Steps" from the pop-up and experiment with fewer steps. Hart specified 20 steps for the glow in the glass, 22 for the handle knob and 12 for the shadow. To respecify steps of a selected blend, double-click the Blend tool (if you're using Preview, press Tab to update). To blend selected objects using previous settings, click with the Blend tool without the Option key. ●

Automatically updating colors
Changing a spot-color definition (see *Chapter 3*) automatically updates all gradients and live blends containing that color. Blends between tints of the *same* spot color (**Hint:** *Tints of 0% = White*) will be updated when changes are made to that spot color, even if the blend isn't "live." —*Agnew Moyer Smith, Inc.*

3

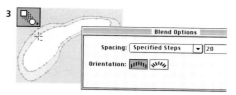

With the Blend tool, clicking first on a selected point of one path, then Option-clicking on a selected point of the other to open Blend Options; choosing Specified Steps from the pop-up and entering 20; the blended objects

Selected paths before and after a 22-step blend

Before and after a 12-step blend to create a shadow

The final image as it appeared in **Time**

Shades of Blends
Creating Architectural Linear Shading

Overview: *Create an architectural form using rectangles; copy and paste one rectangle in front; delete the top and bottom paths and blend between the two sides.*

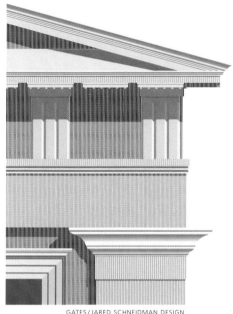

GATES / JARED SCHNEIDMAN DESIGN

1

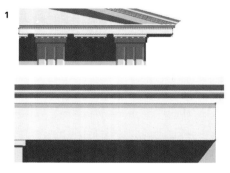

A selected rectangle copied and pasted in front in full view, and in close-up

2

The top and bottom deleted with the sides selected

The full blend and a close-up detail (⌘-H hides—or shows—selection edges; see page 19)

Without much difficulty, Illustrator can help simulate the traditional artistic conventions for rendering architectural details. Jared Schneidman Design developed a simple but exacting method to apply vertical line shading.

1 Creating an architectural structure. After establishing the overall form, color and tonality of your illustration, select and copy one rectangle. Choose ⌘-F (Edit: Paste In Front) to place the copy on top, then set the fill to None and the stroke to .1-pt Black. Choose Window: Show Info to note the line's width in points (to change your ruler units, see Tip, "Changing measurement units," page 21). Calculate the width of the rectangle divided by the spacing you'd like between lines. Subtract 2 (for the sides you have) to find the proper number of steps for this blend.

2 Deleting the top and bottom and blending the sides. Deselect the copy, Shift-Direct-select the top and bottom paths and delete, leaving the sides selected. With the Blend tool, click on the top point of each side and specify the number of steps you determined above. 🖱

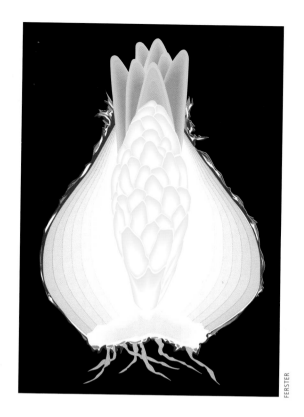

Gallery: Gary Ferster

For his client Langeveld Bulb, Gary Ferster used blends to create the in-between layers in this flower bulb. He began by styling the outer peel with a .5-pt stroke in a dark brown custom color and filled the object with a lighter brown custom color. He then created the inner layer, filled it white and gave it a .5-pt white stroke. Selecting both objects, Ferster specified a six-step blend that simultaneously "morphed" each progressive layer into the next while lightening the layers towards white. Blends were also used to create the leafy greens, yellow innards and all the other soft transitions between colors.

Popular San Francisco Buildings

S.F. Opera House

Davies Symphony Hall

Orpheum Theatre

S.F. Museum of Modern Art

Palace of Legion of Honor

Fish in the San Francisco Bay

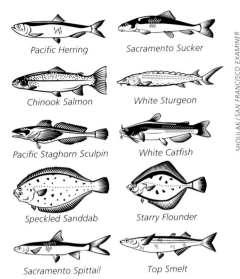

Pacific Herring

Sacramento Sucker

Chinook Salmon

White Sturgeon

Pacific Staghorn Sculpin

White Catfish

Speckled Sanddab

Starry Flounder

Sacramento Spittail

Top Smelt

San Francisco Museum of Modern Art

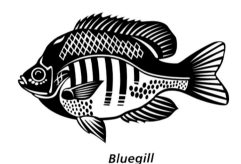

Bluegill

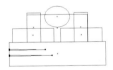 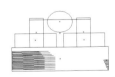

Gallery: Joe Shoulak / *San Francisco Examiner*

Joe Shoulak frequently uses blends to create in-between repetitive shapes. Given the deadlines at a busy newspaper, the Blend tool has proved an essential production tool for generating the horizontal and vertical lines in buildings (for an article on "Retrofitting the Arts") as well as the sequence of organic shapes (as in the fins of fish for the series "Bay in Peril"). Shoulak also relies heavily on filters—using the Offset Path filter to create white inset shapes that follow the contours of outlines, and the Outline Path filter to convert all stroked lines in final images to filled objects (so he doesn't accidentally resize without properly scaling the line weight). See Chapter 6 *for more on filters.*

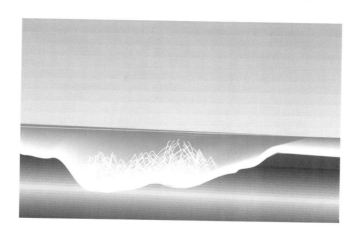

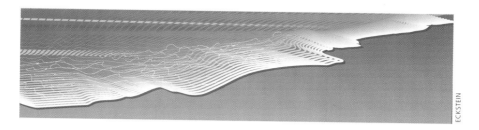

ECKSTEIN

Gallery: Linda Eckstein

Linda Eckstein created these beautiful seascapes in Illustrator using blends. Instead of merely controlling the regularity of blends to depict the ocean, Eckstein needed to control the irregularity of the blends as well. On the back layer of her image are blends that establish both the general composition and the broad color schemes. On top of these tonal-filled, object blends are irregularly shaped linear blends that form the waves and surf. Using the Direct-selection tool, she isolated individual points and groups of points to stretch and distort the waves.

Unified Gradients

Redirecting Fills with the Gradient Tool

Overview: *Fill objects with gradients; use the Gradient tool to adjust fill length, direction, center location, and to unify fills across multiple objects.*

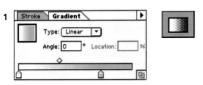

The Gradient palette, and the Gradient tool
(This tool has the same name and icon as the one in Photoshop, but is completely different.)

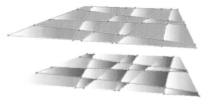

Filling the first group with the cyan gradient fill, then the other group with the purple gradient

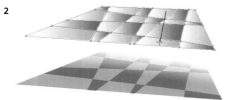

Clicking and dragging with the Gradient tool to unify the gradient fill across multiple objects, and to establish the gradient's rate and direction

How long can a gradient be?

Click and drag with the Gradient tool anywhere in your image window; you don't need to stay within the objects themselves. Also, see the *Wow!* disk for Eve Elberg's "Comet" Gradient tool exercise.

The Gradient tool allows you to customize the length and direction of gradient fills, and to stretch gradients across multiple objects. For this *Medical Economics* magazine illustration, Dave Joly used the Gradient tool to customize each gradient and unify the checkerboard floor.

1 Filling objects with the same gradient. Select multiple objects and fill them with the same gradient by clicking on a gradient fill in the Swatches palette. Keep your objects selected.

2 Unifying gradients with the Gradient tool. Using the Gradient tool from the Toolbox, click and drag from the point you want the gradient to begin to where you want it to end. Hold down the Shift key if you want to constrain the angle of the gradient. To relocate a radial gradient's center, just click with the Gradient tool. Experiment until you get the desired effect. To create his checkerboard, Joly used the Knife tool to segment the floor, grouped every other tile together and filled these with a cyan-to-white gradient fill. He then duplicated the gradient, changed the start color to purple and applied this purple gradient to the remaining tiles. With all tiles selected, he again applied the Gradient tool. 🖱

GORSKA

Gallery: Caryl Gorska

Caryl Gorska created "Bountiful Harvest" as a package design for Nunes Farms' dried fruits, nuts and chocolates. She used the Gradient tool to customize her radial blends (made of process colors). Parchment paper, scanned in Photoshop and saved in EPS, is the background layer (see Chapter 4).

Resetting gradients to the default settings

After you make angle adjustments with the Gradient tool, other objects that you fill with the same or other gradients will still have the altered angle. To "re-zero" gradient angles, Deselect All (⌘-Shift-A) and fill with None by pressing the "/" key. When you next choose a gradient, angles will have the default setting. Or, for linear gradients, you can type a zero in the Angle field.

Gallery: Kerry Gavin

Kerry Gavin is the first to admit that without the Gradient tool, he couldn't have created the image "Golden Parachutes." The miniature version of "Parachutes" at the right shows the figure in the room without the benefit of the Gradient tool. The sense of place and light that is so present in Gavin's final version is noticeably absent in the miniature, where the fills aren't customized.

Gallery: Hugh Whyte / Lehner & Whyte

In this image designed for a spring calendar, Hugh Whyte used gradients and the Gradient tool to create a colorful, cut-out look that is both flat and volumetric. The Artwork view at the right reveals that Whyte constructed the image entirely of gradients, with no blends.

Unlocking Realism

Creating Metallic Reflections with Blends

Overview: *Form the basic shapes of objects; create tonal boundaries for future blends that follow the contours of the objects; copy, scale, recolor and adjust the anchor points of tonal boundaries; blend highlights and shadows.*

1

Designing the basic objects and choosing a base tone (Note: Gray strokes added to distinguish objects)

Creating tonal boundaries for future blends by following the contours of the objects

Achieving photorealism with Illustrator may appear prohibitively complex and intimidating, but with a few simple rules-of-thumb, some careful planning and the eye of an artist, it can be done. Brad Neal, of Thomas•Bradley Illustration & Design, demonstrates with this image that you don't need an airbrush to achieve metallic reflectivity, specular highlights or warm shadows.

1 Preparing a detailed sketch that incorporates a strong light source, and setting up your palette.
Before you actually start your illustration, create a sketch that establishes the direction of your light source. Then, in Illustrator, set up your color palette (see *Chapter 3*). Choose one color as a "base tone," the initial tint from which all blends will be built, and fill the entire object with that value. After you create the basic outlines of your illustration, work in Artwork mode to create separate paths—following the contours of your objects—for each of your major color transitions. After completing the initial line drawing of the lock set, Neal visually and then physically "mapped" out the areas that would contain the

shading. He added a few highlights and reflections in the later stages of the project, but the majority of blends were mapped out in advance.

2 Using your color transition paths to create blends.
Next, use the contouring paths you've created to map out your tonal boundaries. Choose one of the objects and fill it with the same color and tonal value as its underlying shape. In the Neal locks, this initial color is always the same color and value selected for the base color. Then, copy the object and use ⌘-F to Paste In Front. Next, fill this copy with a highlight or shadow value, scale it down and manipulate it into the correct position to form the highlight or shadow area. You can accomplish this step by one of two methods: by scaling the object using the Scale tool or by selecting and pulling in individual anchor points with the Direct-selection tool. In order to ensure smooth blends without ripples or irregular transitions, the anchor points of the inner and outer objects must be as closely aligned as possible and should contain the same number of points. To then complete this highlight or shadow, use the Blend tool to *point map* (see the intro to this chapter for details). The blend in Figure 2 required eight in-between steps. If your blend isn't smooth enough, then use the Direct-selection tool to select anchor points on the key objects and adjust their position or Bézier handles until the blend smoothes.

3 Blending in smaller increments. Some blend situations may require more than two objects to achieve the desired look. For instance, to control the rate at which the tone changes or the way an object transforms throughout the blended area, you may wish to add an intermediate object and blend in two stages, instead of one.

4 Using blends to soften hard transitions. Always use blends when making tonal transitions, even when you need a stark contrast shadow or highlight. A close look at Neal's shadow reveals a very short but distinct blend. ◔

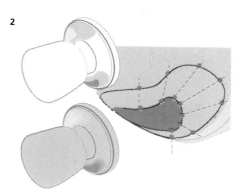

2

Pasting In Front a scaled down and adjusted copy with the same number of aligned points

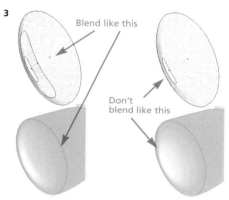

3

Blend like this

Don't blend like this

Adding an in-between contour to help control the rate and shape of blends; blending with too few contours flattens the image

4

Long, close-up and Artwork close-up views of highlight and shadow transitions

Blending Realism

Keeping Blends Clean and Accessible

Overview: *Delete the side of a rectangle; offset the top and bottom open ends horizontally; blend this open object with another smaller, darker object; place caps on top and bottom; create contouring blends on the sides.*

The final illustration in Artwork mode

1

Two copies of a rectangle pasted on top with right side removed and points shifted left

Before and after blending offset objects

A quick look at an illustration in Artwork mode usually reveals a lot about how an image is constructed. However, when you look at Andrea Kelley's Apple Computer product illustrations in Artwork mode, you would probably mistakenly guess that she uses gradients to create her tonal changes. But since her renderings are used on-screen as well as printed, Kelley often uses blends for more exacting control over her tones (gradients can look banded on the screen even if they print well). Her techniques can help you create a monitor screen with a soft, ambient lighting effect.

1 Creating an "offset" blend. Make a rectangle and fill it with a 35% tint of black. Copy and Hide (Object menu, or ⌘-3) the rectangle, then use Paste In Front (⌘-F) to place the copy on top. Direct-select and delete the right side of the path. Since open objects remain filled in Illustrator, the object looks identical in Preview mode. With the Direct-selection tool, grab the top right point and slide it to the left slightly (about .25"), using the Shift key to constrain movement horizontally. Then grab the lower right point and slide it over to the halfway point on the rectangle (again, use your Shift key). Now select and copy the adjusted object, use Paste In Front to move the copy and change the tint of this new object to 65%. Use the same technique you did before, but this time slide the bottom right point all the way to the left and the top right point over towards the left corner. (This polygon should look almost like a triangle.) Next, select the top right points of the two objects you just made, click on each point with the Blend tool and use the recommended number of steps. In Artwork mode, instead of the expected sea of diagonally blended lines running across the screen, your monitor should appear "clean" and uncomplicated.

Rounded "caps" put on top and bottom of the blended screen

2 Creating the rounded top and bottom. Object: Show your hidden back rectangle (⌘-Option-3). With the Pen tool, draw a bow-shaped "cap" filled with a 35% tint of black that overlaps the top of your blend with a long, almost horizontal curve. Have the points meet beyond the blend on either side, arcing into a bow shape above. To add shadow detail, copy the bottom path of the bow (the long, almost horizontal line) and Paste In Front to place a copy of the path. Change the Fill style of this path to None, with a .25-pt stroke weight at a 40% tint of black. Lastly, copy and reflect the full filled cap along the horizontal axis, place it along the bottom of the blended monitor screen and set it to a 10% tint of black.

Placing three rectangles of different shades on the left side of the screen (deleting the sides to reduce clutter), then blending the middle object first to the dark, then to the light

3 Contouring the sides. To create the illusion that the monitor is inset, create three long, overlapping rectangles on the left edge of your blended monitor screen, running from cap to cap. (Adjust the points as necessary so the objects run flush against the cap.) From left to right, make the rectangles 10%, 50% and 45% tints of black. Select the right two rectangles and blend between them, then lock the blend so you can easily blend the left two rectangles. Repeat from the right side of the monitor with rectangles of 5%, 10% and 25% (from left to right). You can make the monitor case the same way as the screen, but shade the case with 10% on the left, blending to 25% on the right. (See *Chapter 8*'s Advanced Techniques for blending and masking curved objects.) 🖱

Placing three rectangles of different shades on the right side of the screen (again, deleting the sides to reduce clutter), then blending the middle object first to the light, then to the dark

The final monitor screen in Preview

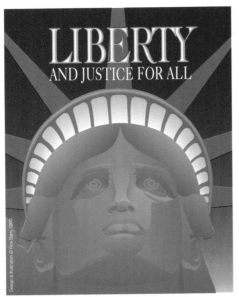
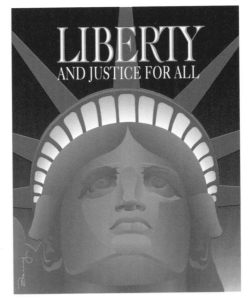

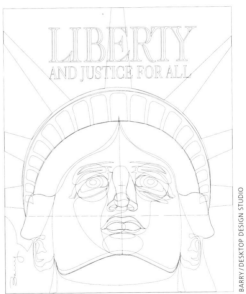

Gallery: Rick Barry / DeskTop Design Studio

To demonstrate the difference between blends and gradients, Rick Barry took an image he created with blends in Illustrator 3.2 (upper left Preview, lower left Artwork), selected the blends (by clicking twice with the Group-selection tool on one of the blend objects) and deleted them. The objects used to create the blends remained, and Barry filled these objects with custom gradients and then adjusted the rate and range of the gradients with the Gradient tool (upper right Preview, lower right Artwork).

Path Creativity

6

Once you're comfortable with basic path operations, you'll be ready to explore some of the more creative features of Illustrator: namely, the Pathfinder filters, the exciting Brush tools, Hatches, and the Gradient Mesh tool. With these tools and filters you'll save time in constructing images and perhaps even expand your vision of what Illustrator can do. Be aware that most of these effects require a lot of RAM (64 MB). Have fun exploring the possibilities!

BRUSHES FOR CREATIVITY

Brushes are so flexible and powerful that they have been integrated throughout this book: from Pattern brushes that create mapping line styles (54–55 and 178–179), to Calligraphy and Art brushes that allow you to draw lines of various weights and textures (68–71). In this you'll find a lesson that focuses instead on creating and applying brushes that broaden the ways you can draw and *paint* in Illustrator (pages 126–127).

Double-click the Brush tool to set general preferences for all brushes maintained in your Illustrator program. With Fidelity and Smoothness, lower numbers are more accurate, higher numbers are smoother. "Fill new brush strokes" determines if the brush will take on the fill color if there isn't a stroke color set (instead of filling the interior of the brush path). When "Keep selected" is enabled, the last path drawn stays selected and drawing a path close to it will redraw that selected path. Disabling this option allows you to draw paths near each other, because

Expanding brush opportunities

- Paste paths containing brushes to paste the brush as well.
- Convert an applied brush into editable artwork, select the path and choose Object: Expand.
- Drag a brush out of the Brushes palette to get an editable version of the brush itself.
- To create a brush out of a brush, blend or gradient: expand it first.

Closing a brush path

To close a path using the Brush tool, hold down the Option key *after* you begin creating the path, then let go of the mouse button just before you're ready to close the path. Or, apply the brush to an already-drawn closed path.

Constraining a brush

You can't use the Shift key to constrain the Brush tool to draw a straight path, so draw the path first with the Pen tool, *then* select the desired brush in the Brushes palette. —*Robin AF Olson*

Scaling and brushes

There are different ways to handle scaling artwork that contains applied brushes:

- Expand (Object menu) the brushed path first, then scale the artwork.
- Scale the artwork after placing it into a page layout program.

Note: *When you apply the Scale tool to brushed paths in Illustrator, enabling Scale Stroke Weight scales the size of the brush art itself.*

Adam Z Lein's bison images before and after Photo Crosshatch filter (settings shown)

After applying Photo Crosshatch, Adam Z Lein combined the rasterized hatches with two copies of the original photo in Photoshop (see Chapter 9 for more on rasterizing)

once drawn, a path is automatically deselected.

There are several ways to edit a brush: double-click it in the Brushes palette to change Brush options, or drag it out of the Brushes palette to edit the brush itself and then drag the new art into the Brushes palette. To replace a brush, see Tip on page 179.

Each of the brushes provides a myriad of options to experiment with, and following the Brushes lessons in this chapter (126–127) will help you understand many of these options. Among the most powerful Brush options is the ability of Art, Scatter and Pattern brushes to take on stroke color and tint (also see Adobe's tips in the individual Brush option dialog) based on a key color (click with the Eyedropper tool in the preview *within* the dialog). Other great features are the ability of Calligraphy and Scatter brushes to vary according to pressure (when initially drawn using a pressure-sensitive tablet), the incorporation of randomization, and a scaling option.

HATCH EFFECTS

Hatch Effects allow you to apply textural effects to vector images. Select a solid or gradient-filled object and choose Filter: Pen and Ink: Hatch Effects to open a dialog box with endless possibilities. See pages 127 and 128 for examples of how to use this filter, as well as artist Victor von Salza's wonderful explanation "VictorVS Wow! Hatches.pdf" on the *Wow!* disk.

Photo Crosshatch (Filter: Pen and Ink: Photo Crosshatch) converts raster objects (such as photos) into vectors that simulate grayscale hatch effects with black lines. Use the histogram sliders to move the shadow and highlight points, and to adjust the density of hatches in specific tonal regions of your image. To get more detail from the filter, start with an image of larger dimensions—but remember, the more detail, the more RAM you'll need. Since there are so many adjustments to make (and no preview!), work on a *copy* of your image, adjust the options one at a time to see how they'll affect your image, and undo immediately if you don't like the results.

GRADIENT MESH

You can apply a gradient mesh to a solid or gradient-filled object in order to create smooth color transitions from multiple points (but you can't use compound paths to create mesh objects). Once transformed, the object will always be a mesh object, so be certain that you work with a copy of the original if it's difficult to re-create.

Transform solid-filled objects into gradient mesh either by choosing Object: Create Gradient Mesh (so you can specify details on the mesh construction) or by clicking on the object with the Gradient Mesh-tool. To transform a gradient-filled object select Object: Expand and enable the Gradient Mesh option. Use the Gradient-Mesh tool to add mesh lines and mesh points to the mesh. Select individual points or groups of points within the mesh using the Direct-selection tool or the Gradient-Mesh tool in order to move, color or delete them. For details on working with gradient meshes (including a warning tip about printing mesh objects) see pages 129–132. *Hint: Instead of applying a mesh to a complex path, try to create the mesh from a simpler path outline, then mask the mesh with the complex path.*

PATHFINDER FILTERS

Pathfinder filters allow you to combine and separate objects with a simple command (see techniques that follow). You'll now find Pathfinder filters in their own palette (Window: Show Pathfinder), or you can import *Wow! Actions* (on the *Wow!* disk) that allow you to apply Pathfinder filters by name. Use the palette pop-up menu to view all options. The charts on the next pages demonstrate Pathfinder filters as applied to simple geometric objects, and to *Wow!* artists' work as further explanation (also see the Plug-ins folder for printable charts detailing the settings for the more complex filters). Keep in mind that filters can irrevocably change your objects, limiting their editability, so either work on copies of your objects in files that are backed up or be prepared to undo immediately if the results aren't what you expected.

Other helpful filters

The Distort filters (Filter menu) **Scribble and Tweak, Punk and Bloat, Zig Zag** and **Roughen** all distort paths based on the paths' anchor points. They either move, randomly distort, or add anchor points to create distortions, and Preview lets you see and modify the results as you're experimenting with the filters.

Though the filter Free Distort may return, you now perform much of this function with the **Free Transform** tool by dragging a corner of the bounding box, *then* holding ⌘ while you continue dragging.

To uniformly **Add Anchor Points** to your path or object, use Object: Path: Add Anchor Points, or use the *Wow! Action* (on the *Wow!* disk) so you can easily reapply it. Having trouble selecting all but a few objects? Select the few you don't want, and choose Edit: **Select Inverse**. A wonderful filter is Edit: **Select Stray Points**, which selects lone points so that you can delete them before they cause trouble. Illustrator's Object: **Path Cleanup** can also delete stray points. But beware: it could also delete unstroked, unfilled objects that you need (such as masks). **Note:** *Selecting a lone point by accident can prevent you from joining properly, or could even cause your objects to disappear if you choose mask when a point is on top!*

Pathfinder Filters

The default settings for 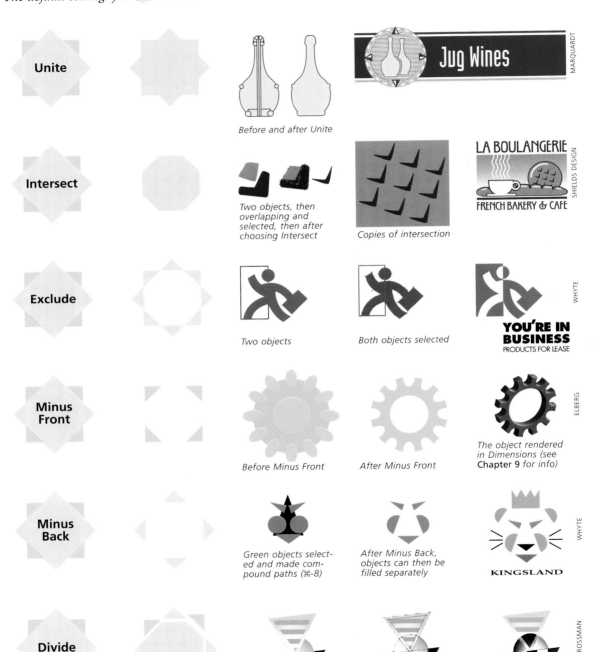 *were used unless otherwise noted. Artists' work may use custom settings.*

Unite

Before and after Unite

MARQUARDT

Jug Wines

Intersect

Two objects, then overlapping and selected, then after choosing Intersect

Copies of intersection

LA BOULANGERIE
FRENCH BAKERY & CAFE

SHIELDS DESIGN

Exclude

Two objects

Both objects selected

YOU'RE IN BUSINESS
PRODUCTS FOR LEASE

WHYTE

Minus Front

Before Minus Front

After Minus Front

The object rendered in Dimensions (see **Chapter 9** *for info)*

ELBERG

Minus Back

Green objects selected and made compound paths (⌘-8)

After Minus Back, objects can then be filled separately

KINGSLAND

WHYTE

Divide

(Objects moved to show results)

Four objects

Objects divided

Each newly divided object filled

GROSSMAN

Pathfinder Filters *(continued)*

The default settings for *were used unless otherwise noted. Artists' work may use custom settings.*

 Outline

(Objects moved and line weights **increased** to .5-pt to show results)

Before Outline

After Outline, and resetting line weight

STEUER

 Trim

(Objects moved to show results)

Before Trim; in Preview and Artwork

After Trim; overlaps are reduced, BUT strokes are lost

SHIELDS DESIGN

 Merge

(Objects moved to show results)

Before Merge in Artwork

After Merge; like fills are united, BUT strokes are lost

STAHL

Crop

A copy of the fish in front to use for Crop

After Crop; objects are now separated

DROBLAS GREENBERG

 Hard

Same color objects don't mix, so overlapping objects were colored differently

After Hard filter; Each overlap is now a separate object

After using the Eyedropper to switch the colors in the front objects

MARGOLIS PINEO (digitized by Steuer)

 Soft

Before Soft filter; the blue wave overlaps the detail along the bottom of the rocks

After Soft filter (see "SandeeC's Mix Soft Chart" in the Plug-ins folder on the **Wow!** disk)

FERSTER

Practical Path-cuts

Preparing for Blends with Pathfinder Filters

Overview: *Use a bisecting path with Intersect; combine drawn elements and copies using Unite; create see-through details using Exclude.*

1

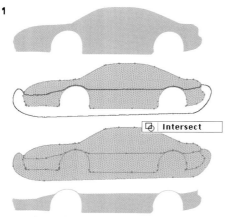

An object; drawing a bisecting path; selecting and intersecting

2

Drawing a fender-well; selecting it with copies of tires to unite; the final path united

3

The outer portion of the wiper and drawing the inner objects; selecting them both to exclude

Pathfinder filters can be astounding time-savers. To form the basic shapes then used for photorealistic blends, Thomas Neal (of Thomas•Bradley Illustration & Design) used to painstakingly cut and join paths using the Scissors tool with Average and Join (see page 52 for cutting and joining, and pages 112 and 162 to see the resulting blends). Pathfinder filters practically automate Neal's tasks for preparing objects to use for blending. (See *Chapter 4* for help hiding, locking and reordering objects.)

1 **Using Intersect to create a subsection of your car.**
Copy your car-body object, Lock it (Object menu or ⌘-2) and use Paste In Front (Edit menu or ⌘-F) to paste a copy exactly on top. Using the Pen tool, draw a path bisecting the car, then loop the path around to create a closed path surrounding the car so that the car can only be divided along your bisecting path. Select both objects and choose Pathfinder: Intersect which deletes the paths that lie outside of the car subsection.

2 **Using Unite to create the undercarriage.** Using the Pen tool, draw a path that defines the shadow in the fender-wells. Copy and Paste In Front (⌘-F) the four wheels, and use ⌘-G to group them. With the Shift key, select the fender-wells with the grouped wheels and choose Pathfinder: Unite.

3 **Creating see-through details.** Create an object that forms the outline of your wiper. Using filled black objects, draw the areas you want to cut out of the outline. Select the outer and inner objects and choose Pathfinder: Exclude. 🌀

Gallery: Michael Kline/Acme Design

When Michael Kline uses Pathfinder filters, he always uses a copy of the object in case he needs that object again for something else. With this illustration for Kids Discover *magazine, Kline kept an earlier version of the house handy so that, if he needed to, he could quickly copy the original and use Paste In Front to place that into the working version.*

For the lines in the roof, Kline used the Brush tool, set at 2.5 points, 130° calligraphic angle, and 60% black. Once all the lines were drawn, he used Pathfinder: Crop to "cookie-cut" the basic shape of the roof. He used the same treatment for most of the siding. (The bushes were given a random look with the calligraphic Brush tool in varying shades of green, then "ruffled" using Distort: Roughen.) Kline also used Pathfinder filters in the "cookie-cutting" of objects into other objects. He did almost all the detail in the shadows using Pathfinder: Soft at varying percentages—again, using a copy of all his objects to retain the integrity of originals in case he needed to reuse them.

Fanciful Filtering

Creative Experimentation With Filters

Advanced Technique

Overview: *Create objects as the basis for filtering; use various filters on different groups of objects; make color and object adjustments as necessary.*

1

The template with grid before and after the first ovals and lines are drawn and text is placed

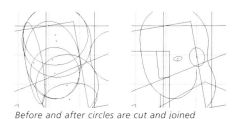

Before and after circles are cut and joined

2

Three objects selected in Artwork and Preview

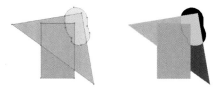

The Soft filter applied, then objects recolored

A wonderful way to learn new techniques is through creative experimentation. When Ron Chan was commissioned to create artwork for the University of Minnesota, he used the opportunity to experiment with filters. Don't forget that many different ways exist to achieve the same effect, and you might gravitate towards an entirely different set of filters.

1 Preparing your basic objects from which to work.
Create the objects that will form the basis for your filtering. Chan used methods discussed elsewhere in the book to prepare the initial objects, including scanning a sketch to use as a template (page 80), creating a custom drawing grid (see Tip on page 137) in its own layer (page 96) and making a masking layer (page 152). He also cut and joined circles to form the head (page 52). In final preparation for filtering, Chan drew bisecting lines with the Pen tool, which he later used as guides in applying filters.

2 Selecting overlapping objects and applying the Pathfinder: Soft filter. After creating a few overlapping objects, you might choose to see how those objects "cut into" each other. First, select the objects with any selection tool (you can even select part of an object using the Direct-selection tool). Although you can use Pathfinder: Divide to create separate objects for each point where the objects intersect, Chan prefers to use the Pathfinder: Soft filter, because the Soft filter creates new colors where objects overlap, making the intersections easy to see. He can then recolor like-colored objects as a unit by Direct-selecting one color and using the Edit: Select: Select Same Fill Color filter, which selects all objects of that color. Chan also uses Direct-select on particular divided objects for recoloring individually.

3 Offsetting and outlining paths. To create an offset of a path, choose Object: Path: Offset Path and specify how much larger or smaller the offset path should be. Chan offset the jaw path smaller at −6 points, used Direct-select on the original and offset paths' endpoints to join (⌘-J) them and then filled the new joined object. Since strokes can't contain gradients or patterns (see *Chapter 5* for gradients; *Chapter 3* for patterns), use Object: Path: Outline Path to convert stroked paths into filled objects that can be styled with more flexibility.

4 Cropping copies for an overlay look. To create a transparent overlay look in a section of your image, first select and copy all the objects that will be affected. Then deselect everything (Shift-⌘-A), and use Paste In Front (⌘-F) and Group (⌘-G) on the copy. Using any tools you wish, create a closed object to define your cropping area and, with your Shift key down, use the Selection tool to select the grouped copy and its cropping object; then choose Pathfinder: Crop and group the cropped objects. Try experimenting with the Colors: Adjust Colors filter until you achieve a color cast you like (see pages 129-132). Or, just Direct-select objects to customize their styling.

3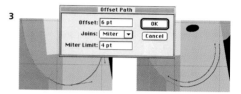

Before and after offsetting the path −6 points

Joining the two paths and then changing style

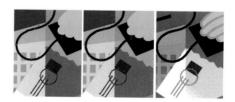

Lines selected, then outlined, then customized

4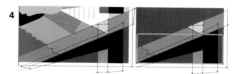

Objects copied, then after Paste In Front and being selected with a defining rectangle

After Pathfinder: Crop, then recolored

Organic Creation

Painting with Brushes, Hatches and Mesh

Advanced Technique

Overview: *Create Scatter brushes of stars; draw with a "hue-tinted" Art brush; create bark textures with Art brushes; automate drawing of grass with Pattern brushes; add Hatches and Gradient Mesh.*

STEUER

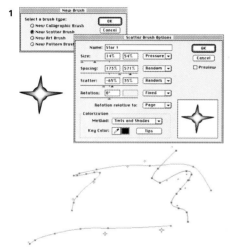

Dragging the star objects into the brushes palette to specify Scatter Brush; the settings for one of the four stars; three selected paths with different star Scatter brushes applied

The leaf Art brush (left) with the Hue Shift Colorization option; the final color strokes for the leaves shown without the Art brush applied

This organic landscape was painted using exclusively brushes, hatches, gradients and gradient meshes.

1 Defining a star Scatter brush. Create a star. The stars in this image were created following Guilbert Gates's instructions for creating a glowing star (page 164). Drag your star to the brushes palette, then choose Scatter Brush. In Options, name the star and play with various options—but keep the "Rotation relative to" Page. Set the colorization to Tints and Shades. With the Brush tool and new star brush selected, draw some paths—notice your stroke color will tint the star. For brush variations, drag the star brush to the New Brush icon, then double-click the brush to rename it and reset settings.

2 Drawing leaves. Make a straight leaf. Drag it into the Brushes palette, choose Art Brush, then name the brush and choose Hue Shift for Colorization. With the Brush tool and this brush loaded, choose a stroke color (hue) that this brush will be based on, and draw. I first mixed and stored about a dozen colors, then drew leaves with a Wacom tablet. Though I chose stroke colors as I brushed with the leaves, I also edited the paths (with Direct-selection) and changed stroke colors as the image developed.

3 Creating tree trunks. Create objects to use as a trunk. In order to make a brush of blends or gradients, choose Object: Expand (see *Chapter 5*). Drag the trunk into the Brushes palette and choose Art Brush. Apply this trunk brush to a path. If it's too thin or thick for the path, double-click the brush and change the Size %. I made a second trunk brush—slightly narrower and paler—and gave it a different scaling percentage. I applied the thinner trunk to a slightly offset copy of the first trunk path. For texture, draw some strokes and make an Art brush of the strokes with Hue Shift colorization. Selecting a path styled as you want sets the default for the next path.

4 Creating a Pattern brush to generate grass. Design a pattern tile with 20–30 blades of grass. Drag the grouping of grass into the Brushes palette and choose Pattern Brush. Set the direction to be perpendicular to the grass and Tints and Shades Colorization. Draw a curvy path and select the grass Pattern brush to apply it.

5 Creating water effects. Create a gradient-filled object on one layer (see *Chapter 5*) and drag this layer to the New Layer icon to duplicate it. Select the top gradient and choose Filter: Pen and Ink: Hatch Effects. Choose "Wood grain Light" then enable the "Match Object" hatch color option. Play with various other settings (see "Victor V's Hatches Explainer" on the *Wow!* disk). Offset a copy of the hatches (Option-drag) for more texture.

6 Final Gradient Mesh details. A Gradient Mesh was applied by Expanding the sand gradient. A mesh was also applied to a circle on top of the moon gradient (for details about Gradient Mesh, see pages 129–132). 🌙

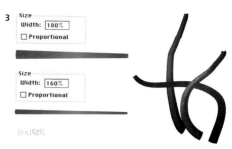

The three Art brushes used in the trunks (the top two with size scaled in Options); the trunks shown (from left to right) with one, two, and all three brushes applied

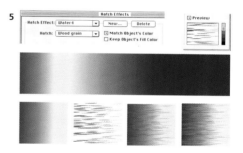

The Grass objects that make up the Pattern brush; then the brush applied to a path

The full two-piece gradient; then the left gradient, turned into Hatches, combined with the original gradient, then hatches Option-dragged

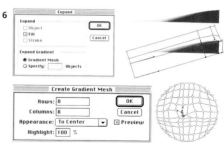

Expanding a gradient-filled object into a mesh (which was then adjusted to curve around the slope of the hill); for the moon, choosing Object: Create Gradient Mesh to convert a circle into a mesh (which was then manipulated using the Direct-selection tool and colored)

Gallery: Diane Hinze Kanzler & Sandee Cohen

*Starting with Diane Hinze Kanzler's "Goldfish" illustration (near right), Sandee Cohen used the Pen and Ink filter to add texture. The coral was given a plain pink fill. The Pen and Ink filter was then applied using the "Swash" hatch. The same hatch was also used on the top fin. The body of the fish was created using the "Dots" hatch. The two fins at the back were filled with the "Wood grain" hatch. The front fins were filled with the "Vertical lines" hatch, set for different angles. The middle fins were filled with the "Worm" hatch. Finally, a hatch was defined for the bubble. Then a large rectangle was created over the entire illustration and filled with bubbles. (**Hint:** The bubble could also be a Scatter Brush; see the previous lesson.)*

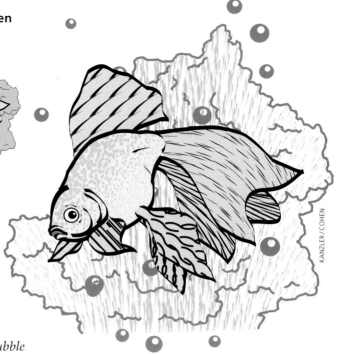

KANZLER / COHEN

Gallery: Kevin Barrack

Kevin Barrack began "Batik Dancer" by applying Streamline to one of his scanned drawings (see Chapter 9*). In Illustrator, he then filled the body shapes with gradients (see* Chapter 5*), and on a separate layer, he created "blobby" shapes for the background. In another layer, called "Ink Pen," he created a new "blobby" object with a green fill. To this object he applied Filter: Pen and Ink: Hatch Effects, and set Hatch = Worm; Match Object's Color; Density = 75%; Dispersion = Constant 180; Thickness = Constant 70; Scale = Linear 56–610, 270°; Rotation = Random 10–180; Fade = None; and the fourth "color" box in the indicator scale. Lastly, Barrack added thick strokes to the black solid-filled shapes outlining his figure.*

BARRACK

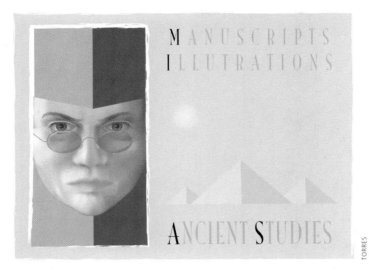

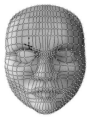   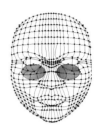

Gallery: Ivan Torres

Ivan Torres began this image by drawing an oval, then choosing Object: Create Gradient Mesh, entering approximately 30 rows, 15 columns and Flat appearance. Working in Artwork mode (⌘-Y), Torres Direct-selected horizontal rows and moved them closer or farther from other rows to cluster more rows around the eyes, nose and lips (he wanted at least three rows around the lips, for instance). To form more vertical structures (such as the nose), he used the Direct-
selection tool to select and move the columns. To create more diagonal lines, he Direct-selected a section of the mesh and used the Shear tool (with the Shift key down). In some cases he needed to use the Convert Direction Point tool to reset direction handles. He Direct-selected and then colored points using the Colors palette. Once he set base colors, he used the Eyedropper tool to pick up color from elsewhere to deposit into the selected anchor points. He used the Pen tool to draw the basic eyebrow shape, along with several overlapping angular objects to represent hair. He selected all eyebrow objects and cut the angles out of the brow with Pathfinder: Hard Mix (he selected one cut-out shape and used Edit: Select: Same Fill Color to find the rest of them so he could move them out of the way). For the glasses he made two ellipses, chose Object: Compound Path: Make and then made this into a mask with a copy of the mesh face, to which he then applied the Colors: Adjust Colors filter to increase the cyan and yellow (see the technique following for details). On layers above and below Torres created the other details, including the eyeglass frames and a "charcoal" Art Brush, which added texture to borders (see page 71).

Mastering Mesh

Painting with Areas of Color Using Mesh

TORRES

Advanced Technique

Overview: *Create simple objects to make into gradient mesh; edit and color mesh objects; create compound-path masks for copies of mesh; make a mesh with no grid to reshape.*

1

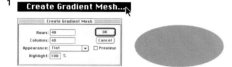

The original oval; choosing Object: Create Gradient Mesh; setting the Mesh options

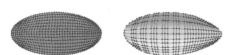

The mesh created; after Direct-selecting points and deleting to create a pattern in the mesh

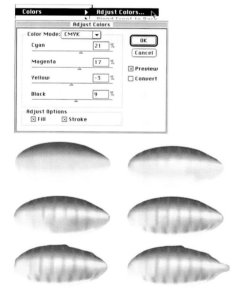

Recoloring selected rows and columns using the Colors palette and the Adjust Colors filter

With a background in painting, sculpture and 3D imaging, Ivan Torres knew immediately that the Gradient-mesh tool would allow him to paint in a powerfully unique way. In the creation of this fish illustration, he demonstrates how, unlike *any* other medium, the mesh allows him to *move a stroke of color* without changing the relationship between colors.

1 Creating the fish's body. Create a solid-filled oval; while it's selected, choose Object: Create Gradient Mesh. Set fairly high numbers for rows and columns; for his fish (shown above at about 30% actual size) Torres set 17 rows, 35 columns. Set Flat for Appearance, 100% Highlight and click OK. Next, to make the base for the fish's stripes, you'll need to create an irregular pattern within the mesh. With the Direct-selection tool, select anchor points and delete—the connected rows and columns will be deleted along with the points. Torres deleted 8 columns and 10 rows. Marquee horizontal anchor points with the Direct-selection tool. If you have trouble selecting the points you want, try working in Artwork mode, or turn off Use Area Select in General Preferences. With horizontal rows of points selected (make sure you are now in Preview), mix or choose new colors in the Colors palette (use the ⌘-H toggle to show/hide selection edges). Torres horizontally selected sections of the mesh, changing colors to create a sense of volume. For more subtle color transitions, select an area and choose Filter: Colors: Adjust Colors to adjust the color cast of your selection. Carefully Direct-select points and reposition them to form the fish body.

2 Making the fish's tail and fins. Create several colored rectangles and ovals and convert each object to a gradient mesh as before, but this time assign a low value for columns. Direct-select sections of each object and use the Adjust Color Filter to create gradual changes in tone (⌘-Option-E reopens the last-used filter). Direct-select points on the objects and adjust them to form tail and fin shapes. Move each object into position on a separate layer for easy editing (for help with layers see *Chapter 4*).

3 Creating the fish's eye and lips. Create three circles: one small, one medium and one large. Convert the medium-size circle to a gradient mesh this time by clicking on the circle with the Gradient-mesh tool. Add additional rows or columns by clicking again with the tool; delete by Direct-selecting points, rows or columns and deleting. Torres ended up with unevenly spaced rows and columns (five of each), which he colored to achieve a wet, reflective-looking surface. When you are pleased with the glossy part of the eye, combine all the circles and adjust the outlines of some to be less perfect.

To create the fish's mouth, begin with a rectangle on a layer above the fish. Convert the rectangle to a gradient mesh using Object: Create Gradient Mesh, and enter different low values for rows and columns, maintaining Flat for Appearance. Select areas of the object and use the Eyedropper to load colors from the fish to create smooth color transitions between the mouth and the body. Move this object into position and reshape it to form a mouth.

4 Creating the shadows for the fish. Duplicate the layer containing the fish's body by dragging that layer to the

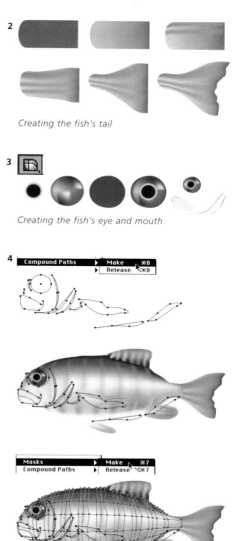

Creating the fish's tail

Creating the fish's eye and mouth

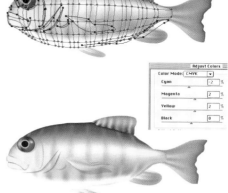

Drawing areas for shadow areas; making them into a compound path; masking a copy of the fish with the compound path; using Filter: Colors: Adjust Colors to darken a copy of the fish; the final fish shown with completed shadows

5

An oval

After applying a mesh with values of 1, deleting the original oval anchor points (in orange)

The remaining points moved and colored

After reshaping is complete, a copy is created, reflected and skewed, and colors are inverted

---

New Layer icon in the Layers palette. On a layer above this one, use the Pen tool to draw a contour defining each shadow as a closed object. Select all the shadow objects and make them into one compound object by choosing Object: Compound Path: Make. You then use these shadow objects as a mask for the copy of the fish body. Select both the compound objects and the copy of the fish body (in the Layers palette, ⌘-Shift-click the shadow and fish-copy layers to select all objects on those layers) and choose Object: Mask: Make. Selecting the masked copy of the fish, use the Adjust Colors filter to darken the area and reduce the contrast to simulate shadow colors. Torres wanted to create a shadow that contrasted the cyan color cast of the fish, so he decreased cyan and increased yellow and magenta—each in increments of 2 to 5%. After applying the filter, with selection edges hidden (⌘-H) he reapplied the filter (⌘-E) until he had achieved the desired effect.

5 Creating the border "bone" shape. Create an oval; while it's selected, choose Object: Create Gradient Mesh, assigning 1 for rows and columns and Flat. Using the Delete-point tool, delete the four original points of the oval, leaving only mesh points. Reposition the remaining points to create an arcing effect, and assign colors to each point. Next, use the Reflect tool to flip a copy of this object horizontally. With the copy selected Torres chose Filter: Colors: Invert Colors. Lastly, he used the Skew tool to adjust the copied image to touch the original border object (see *Chapter 2* for help reflecting and skewing). 🌙

Adding to the mesh

To add new rows and columns to your mesh, click on the mesh object with the Gradient Mesh tool. To add a new mesh row, click on a column mesh line. To add a new mesh column, click on a row.

Printing gradient mesh objects

Gradient mesh objects rely on PostScript Level 3 (PS3) printing technology. Gradient mesh objects printed to older printers will convert to a 150-pixel-per-inch JPEG! If you can't print to a PS3 printer, you may wish to use Illustrator's Rasterize or Export commands, or open the file in Photoshop 5.02 or higher to rasterize it there. **Note:** *See also Tip "Grouping masks" on page 154.*

Type & Layout

7

Illustrator is a powerful tool for graphically controlling type. Although you're likely to prefer a page layout program (such as QuarkXPress or PageMaker) for multipage documents like catalogues and long magazine articles, and PageMill or BBEdit for web page layout, this chapter will show you many reasons to stay within Illustrator for single-page documents. The Type chapter of Adobe's *User Guide* covers the creation and manipulation of type in great detail, so this introduction will focus on essentials, "what's new" and production tips.

For creating and manipulating type, there are two palettes you can open from the Type menu: Character (⌘-T, for Type) and Paragraph (⌘-M). When you first open these palettes, they may be in a collapsed view. To cycle through display options for either palette, double-click its name tab (or use the Palette pop-up menu).

There are three major type options in Illustrator accessible through the Type tool (press T): *Point Type, Area Type* and *Path Type*. The flexible Type tool lets you click to create a Point-Type object, click-drag to create an Area-Type object or click within any existing type object to enter or edit text. You can gain access to type created in other applications by using the File: Open or File: Place commands from the desktop menu.

Select letters, words or an entire block of text by dragging across the letters with the Type tool, or use a selection tool to select text as an *object* by clicking on or marqueeing the type's baseline (the baseline is the line that the type sits on, and is visible in Artwork mode).

The Type tool, Area-Type tool, Path-Type tool, Vertical-Type tool, Vertical Area-Type Tool, Vertical Path-Type tool — striking Option-T cycles through these type tools

One option you may not want
By default, Type Area Select is *on*. If you keep accidentally selecting type when you're trying to select an object, disable this in Preferences: Type & Auto Tracing: Type Area Select. You still be able to select type by clicking on, or Direct-select-marqueeing, its baseline.

Linking multiple blocks of text
Link multiple text objects so text flows from one to the next; select the desired objects (making sure the baselines are selected), and choose Type: Blocks: Link Type.

Typographic controls
Set keyboard-accessible typographic control defaults in Preferences: Type & Auto Tracing, but set units of measurement for type, in Preferences: Units & Undo.

- **Point Type.** Click with the Horizontal-Type or Vertical-Type tool anywhere on the page to create Point Type. Once you click, a blinking text-insertion cursor called an "I-beam" indicates that you can now type text using your keyboard. To add another line, press the Return key. When you're finished typing into one text object, click on the Type tool in the toolbox to simultaneously select the current text as an object (the I-beam will disappear) and be poised to begin another text object. To just select the text as an object, click on a selection tool.

- **Area Type.** If you click-*drag* with the Type tool, you'll create an Area-Type rectangle, into which you can type. Once you've defined your rectangle, the I-beam awaits your typing, and the text automatically wraps to the next line when you type in the confines of the rectangle. If you've typed more text than can fit in your text rectangle, in Artwork mode you'll notice a plus sign along the right side of the rectangle. To enlarge the rectangle to allow for more text, use the Direct-select tool to deselect the text block, then grab one side of the rectangle and drag it out, holding down the Shift key to constrain the direction of the drag. To add a new text object that you will link to an existing text object in Artwork mode, use the Group-select tool to grab the rectangle only (not the text), hold down the Option key and drag a copy of the rectangle. Text will automatically flow to the new rectangle.

  The other way to create Area Type or Vertical Area Type is to construct a path (with any tools you wish) forming a shape within which to place type. Then choose the Area-type or Vertical Area-type tool (click and hold down on the Type tool to access it, or press Shift-T to cycle to it) and click on the path itself to place text within the path. Distort the confining shape by grabbing an anchor point with the Direct-selection tool and dragging it to a new location, or reshape the path by adjusting direction lines. The text within will reflow.

  Note: *If you use the Vertical Area-type tool, you'll see that your text will flow automatically, starting from the right* *edge of the area flowing toward the left! For those of you who use non-CJK (Chinese, Japanese and Korean) fonts and typographic standards, you really won't have much use for this tool since non-CJK type flows from left to right. (For more on Multinational fonts, see Tip at right.)*

To set up tabs for Area Type, choose Type: Tab Ruler. To create paths for custom tab alignment, first create paths that align with the tab markers, then Direct-select your text object with your paths and choose Type: Wrap: Make. You can also use text-wrapping to flow text around objects. After paths are wrapped to text objects, reshaping the paths causes text to reflow. To add a new path, ungroup (⌘-Shift-G) the current text and path objects, then reselect the text with the old and new paths and choose Type: Wrap: Make. (For more information on tabs and wrapping text around objects, see the *User Guide*.) **Note:** *You'll have to use Type: Wrap: Release or Ungroup before you can apply some types of filters to wrapped text.*

- **Path Type.** The Path-type tool allows you to click on a path to flow text along the perimeter of the path (the path will then become unstroked or unfilled). To reposition the beginning of the text, use a Selection tool to grab the special Path-type I-beam *itself* and drag left or right. Drag the I-beam up or down (or double-click it) to *flip* the text so it wraps along the inside or outside of the path (also see Tip on page 136).

As with Area Type, use the Direct-selection tool to reshape the confining path itself; the Path Type path will automatically readjust to the new path shape.

ADDITIONAL TYPE FUNCTIONS (FORMER FILTERS)
- **Check Spelling**, **Find Font**, **Find** and **Smart Punctuation** all work whether or not anything is selected, although some of these filters give you the option to work within a selected text block if you have one selected.

More about Find Font: If you try to open a file and don't have the correct fonts loaded, Illustrator warns you, lists

---

Multinational font support

Illustrator supports Multinational fonts, including CJK (Chinese, Japanese, Korean). Access the Multinational portion of the Character palette by double-clicking the palette tab to expand it fully. To utilize the CJK font capabilities you must have the proper fonts and character sets loaded into your system, as well as special system software. Be aware that some options don't work on non-CJK fonts, such as U.S. and U.K. English language fonts.

The quick-changing Type tool

When using the regular Type tool, look at your cursor very carefully in these situations:

- If you move the regular Type tool over a closed path, the cursor should change to the Area-Type icon.
- If you move the Type tool over an open path, it will probably change to the Path-Type icon.

Type-tool juggling

To toggle a Type tool between its vertical and horizontal mode, first make sure nothing is selected. Hold the Shift key down to toggle the tool to the opposite mode.

If you don't have the fonts...

Missing fonts? Don't be afraid to open the file, make changes, save, copy, paste the missing type or resave the file, because Illustrator remembers which fonts you're *supposed* to be using. However, you won't have accurate text flow and the file won't print correctly until you load or replace the missing fonts (see "More about Find Font" on previous page).

Making a new text object

Reselect the Type tool to end one text object; the next click will start a new text object. Or, deselect the current text by holding down the ⌘ key (temporarily turning your cursor into a selection tool) and clicking outside the text block.

Type along the top and bottom

To create the illusion that Path Type is falling along the top *and* bottom of a path, hold down the Option key as you drag the I-beam to flip a *copy* of the type.

the missing fonts and asks if you still want to open the file. You need the correct fonts to print properly; so if you can't load the missing fonts, choose Find Font to find and replace the missing fonts with ones you do have.

When you open the filter, the top list displays the fonts used in the file; an asterisk will indicate the missing fonts. In order to access all fonts that you can use as replacements, deselect the options you don't want to use (e.g., TrueType); any different choices will force you to make your selections all over again. When you're ready to select font replacements, click on the fonts you'd like to replace from the top list; note that Illustrator shows you the type of font and where it occurs. After you choose a replacement font from the bottom list, you can individually replace each occurrence of the font by clicking Change and then clicking Find Next. Otherwise, simply click Change All to change all occurrences of the top fonts with the font selected from the bottom list.

- **Change Type Orientation** lets you change orientation from horizontal to vertical or vice versa by choosing Type: Type Orientation: Horizontal or Vertical.

- **Change Case** lets you change the case if you've selected text with the Type tool *before* you use the filter.

- **Rows & Columns** can be used on any selected rectangle or Area Type. Use a Selection tool (not the Type tool) to select the entire text object, and double-click the palette tab. You can enter your text first, or simply begin setting up your columns by choosing Rows & Columns. In this filter, specify the number and sizes of the rows and columns and whether you wish to use Add Guides. This creates grouped lines that you can make into Illustrator guides with View: Make Guides (⌘-5) (see page 96 for more on guides). Keep Preview checked to see the results of your specifications while you work, and click one of the Text Flow options to choose whether text will flow horizontally or vertically from one block to another.

- **MM Design** stands for Multiple Master fonts. Adobe includes a Multiple Master font in the Fonts folder of the *Adobe Illustrator Application CD-ROM*. There's also a separate MM Design palette to aid in customizing your Multiple Master fonts on the fly (see the documentation that ships with your fonts for how to modify them). At this writing, Illustrator is the only vector drawing program with this capability.

- **Fit Headline** is a quick way to open up the letterspacing of a headline across a specific distance. First, create the headline within an area, not along a path. Next, set the type in the size you wish to use. Select the headline, then choose Type: Fit Headline, and the type will spread out to fill the area you've indicated. This works with both the Horizontal and Vertical-type tools.

- **Show Hidden Character** reveals soft and hard returns, word spaces and an odd-shaped infinity symbol indicating the end of text flow. Toggle it on and off by choosing Type: Show Hidden Character.

- **Glyph Options** is a new feature and you can only access if you have the appropriate Japanese Kanji font loaded. This option is available only for Macintosh users.

CONVERTING TYPE TO OUTLINES

As long as you've created your type with fonts you have and can print, and provided you've finished experimenting with text as type elements (e.g., adjusting your line spacing or kerning/tracking, or wrapping text around a path), you have the option to convert your text objects to Illustrator Bézier curves with compound paths. Compound paths form the "holes" in objects, such as the transparent center of an **O** or **P**. You can use the Direct-selection tool to select and manipulate parts of the compound paths separately. To convert a font to outlines, select the type with a Selection tool and choose Type: Create Outlines (⌘-Shift-O). While the type is still

Paint Bucket and Eyedropper

To set what the Paint Bucket applies and the Eyedropper picks up, double-click either tool to open the Paint Bucket or Eyedropper Options dialog box.

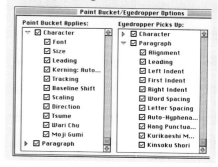

Eyedropper text

To restyle part of a text string or block, pick up a new sample with the Eyedropper tool, hold down the Option key to select the Paint-bucket tool and drag the cursor (as you would with the Text tool) over the text to be restyled.
—*David Nelson*

Text different sizes?

To resize a block of text or a text string that contains different sizes, select the text and use ⌘-Shift-> to increase all the font sizes proportionally or ⌘-Shift-< to decrease all the font sizes proportionally.

Bounding box warning

If you resize a text block by its Bounding Box handles (see *Chapter 1*), the text *won't* reflow (as it does in page layout programs), the text scales!—*Sandee Cohen*

Don't outline small type

If you're printing to a high-resolution image-setter, or using larger type sizes, you can successfully convert type objects to outlines. However, due to a font-enhancing printing technology (called "hinting"), a *small* type object converted to outlines won't look as good on the computer screen, or print as clearly to printers of 600 dots per inch or less, as it would have if it had remained a font.

Graphically transforming Bézier curves (artwork by Javier Romero Design Group)

Filling with patterns or gradients

Masking with type (see page 140) (artwork by Min Wang/Adobe Systems)

Transporting foreign or unusual fonts (artwork by Kathleen Tinkel)

Using pre-Illustrator 7 vertically scaled type (artwork by Pamela Drury Wattenmaker)

selected, choose Object: Group (⌘-G) to group the individual elements for easy reselection.

Why convert type to outlines?

- **So you can graphically transform or distort the individual curves and anchor points of letters or words.** Everything from the minor stretching of a word to extreme distortion is possible.

- **So you can fill type with patterns or gradients.**

- **So you can make type into a masking object.** See page 140 for an example of this technique.

- **So you don't have to supply the font to your client or service bureau.** Converting type can be especially useful when you're using foreign language fonts, or when your image will be printed when you're not around.

- **So you can work with vertically scaled type created in earlier versions of Illustrator.** Type is calculated differently in the various versions of Illustrator, so opening an earlier document with a later version of Illustrator may cause type to reflow. In lieu of editing, reopen the original version, if possible, and output directly, save as EPS or convert type to outlines.

- **If you *don't* want to convert to outlines, embed it and forget it.** Illustrator gives you the option to embed the fonts only if you're saving the file as EPS for placement into another document. This text can't be edited, and you don't *need* to transport the fonts with the artwork.

Choose your words, and letters, carefully!

Having access to dozens of fonts doesn't make you a type expert, any more than having a handful of pens makes you an artist. Experiment all you want, but if you need professional typographic results, consult a professional. I did. Barbara Sudick designed this book.

**Gallery: James Young /
Adobe Systems, Inc.**

*This alphabet (which would
have been a nightmare to create in QuarkXPress or Page-
Maker) was simple to con-
struct in Illustrator. James
Young arranged individual
Point-Type letters using the
Selection tool and resized each
visually using the Scale tool
with the Shift-key down (to
constrain scaling to propor-
tionate only; see page 38 for
scaling help). Because Young
created this graphic using the
Nueva Multiple Master
(MM) font, he was able to
select letters to change their
width and weight (see page
142 for more on MM fonts).*

Masking Type

Placing Type Within Type Using Masks

Overview: *Create a large letter and arrange other objects in relation to it; convert the letter to outlines; bring the outlined letter to the front and make it into a mask for the other objects; set the fill and/or stroke style of the mask.*

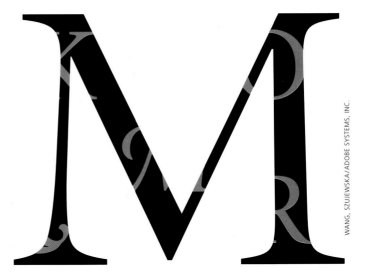

1 | Create Outlines ⇧⌘O

Arranged type objects and the "M" outlined

2

"M" brought to front and all objects selected

| Masks | ▶ | Make | ⌘7 |
| Compound Paths | ▶ | Release | ⌥⌘7 |

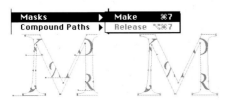

"M" after mask is applied, then only the mask selected so it can be styled with fill or stroke

Can't select within a mask?

Now that masks can actually be filled, it may be difficult to select objects within the mask. To solve this, Direct-select the mask and:

• choose Send to Back (this sends the mask behind its group), or

• Lock (⌘-2) the mask.

This **M** was created by Min Wang (Laurie Szujewska, art director) for the Adobe Minion type specimen book using masks. For more techniques using masks, including masking with *multiple* type objects, see *Chapter 8*.

1 Positioning type elements and converting the large letter to outlines. Using the Type tool, click to create a Point-Type object and type one letter. Choose a typeface of a heavy enough weight and in a large enough size for other elements to show through the letter form itself. Then arrange other type elements (or other objects) in relation to the large letter (you'll be able to move them later). Wang arranged separate Minion type characters in relation to a 297-pt **M**. Select the large letter with a Selection tool and choose Type: Create Outlines (⌘-O).

2 Creating the mask and filling it. Select the letter outline and Cut (⌘-X), then Paste In Front (⌘-F) so it's the top object. Select all objects and apply Object: Mask: Make (⌘-7). After the mask has been created, and while the objects are still selected, group the objects (⌘-G). To set a fill and/or stroke style, Direct-select the mask itself and set the desired styles. Finally, Direct-select individual objects to adjust their placement. ✐

SZUJEWSKA/ADOBE SYSTEMS, INC.

Gallery: Laurie Szujewska / Adobe Systems, Inc.

For Adobe's Poetica type specimen book, Laurie Szujewska was in-spired by a "love knot" poem from the book Pattern Poetry *by Dick Higgins, and created a similar spiral path with the Pen tool. She used the Path-Type tool to place the text on the path. She then meticulously kerned and placed spaces along the type path to prevent text overlaps, and to get things just right.*

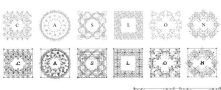

SZUJEWSKA/ADOBE SYSTEMS, INC.

Gallery: Laurie Szujewska / Adobe Systems, Inc.

For Adobe's Caslon type specimen book, Szujewska created these decorative ornaments by placing, rotating and reflecting groups of separate Point-Type objects filled with a gray color.

The Shape of Time

Trickling Type with Variations of Type Style

Overview: *Create the outside border and path baselines for your type; import text into the first line; cut and paste text into appropriate path lines, changing the typestyle each time; use Point Type for "trickling type" and baseline shifts for lines at the bottom.*

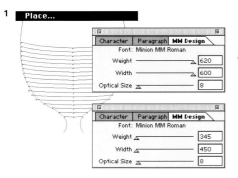

1

2

Weight

(Bold	-	Light)	÷(# of steps -1)	▼
(620	-	345)	÷ (17) =	16
Line 1				620
Line 2	620	-	16 =	604
Line 3	604	-	16 =	588
...				

Width

(Extended	-	Condensed)	÷(# of steps -1)	▼
(600	-	450)	÷ (17) =	8.8
Line 1				600
Line 2	600	-	8.8 =	591.2
Line 3	591.2	-	8.8 =	582.4
...				

Size

(12-point	-	6-point)	÷ (17) =	▼ .35
Line 1				12
Line 2	12	-	.35 =	11.65
Line 3	11.65	-	.35 =	11.30
...				

To illustrate the effects of varying the weight and width of a Multiple Master (MM) typeface, James Young (with Laurie Szujewska) created this interpretation of George Kubler's *The Shape of Time*. This lesson shows how to calculate exact instances for MM fonts using the MM Design palette (Type menu). To do this by eye (after entered your MM text), click on the Direct-selection tool, then use the sliders in the MM Design palette. You'll find some MM fonts in the "Fonts" folder on the Adobe Illustrator CD.

1 Creating your baselines. Draw an hourglass-shaped path with the Pen tool (see page 4 for help), and decide on a starting type size and style. Set your leading between lines one point larger than your type. Just move copies of your path *up* a distance equal to your leading; select the path, double-click the Selection tool, specify a Move equal to the desired leading, and click Copy. Then ⌘-D to make copies for each line of type. Young started with Minion MM Bold Extended at 7.88 points , with 8.88-pt leading, and 18 lines of type. To cut the paths to fit the hourglass, copy the hourglass, select the paths and Paste In Front (⌘-F) a copy. Shift-select the paths and this hourglass copy and choose Pathfinder: Outline, then select and delete the paths outside the hourglass.

2 Preparing your type. In a word processor, thoroughly proofread and spell-check your text, as making changes later will be difficult. Next, calculate and write down the variations in style to be placed on each path line, using the chart at left for help. Each MM typestyle has a numeric value that you'll be using for calculations. For the top line of type, Young used Bold Extended with a weight value of 620 and a width value of 600, and for the bottom, a Light Condensed with a weight of 345 and a width of 450. To

The number of ways for things to occupy time is probably no more unlimited than the large number of ways in which matter occupies space. The difficulty with delimiting the categories of time has always been to find a suitable description of duration, which would vary according to events while measuring them against a fixed scale. History has no periodic table of elements, and no classification of types or species; it has only solar time and a few old ways of grouping events, but no theory of temporal structure. If any principle of classing events be preferred to the impossible conception that every event will cluster during a given portion of time in an order varying between dense and sparse array. The classes we are considering contain events related as progressive solutions to problems of which the requirements are modified by each successive solution. A rapid succession of events is a dense array; a slow succession with many interruptions is sparse. In the history of art it occasionally happens that one generation, and even on e individual achieves many new positions not only in one sequence but in a whole set of sequences. At the other extreme a given need will subsist for generations or even centuries without fresh solutions. We have already examined these occurrences under the heading of fast and slow happening. They have been explained as contingent upon position in the series and upon the varying pace of invention in different centers of population. Let us now look at further varieties in the array of

YOUNG/SZUJEWSKA/ADOBE SYSTEMS, INC. with text from George Kubler's *The Shape of Time*

3

Changing the Cursor-key increments for typographic controls in General Preferences

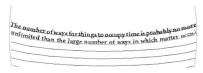

Cutting and pasting type into paths with the Path-Type tool

4

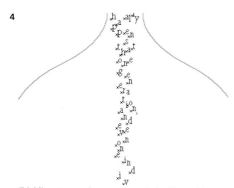

Trickling type using separate Point-Type objects

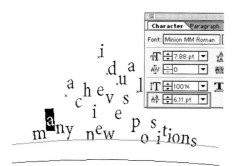

Graphically adjusting baseline shifts and viewing the shifts in an expanded Character palette

calculate the weight and width values for each of the in-between steps, he subtracted the lowest value from the highest and divided it by the number of steps (18) minus 1. The resulting value (16 for weight and 8.8 for width) represented the size of the steps from one line of text to the next. Starting with Bold Extended at 620/600, Young subtracted 16 from 620 to get the weight of the second step (604), and 8.8 from 600 to get the width of the second step (591.2). He subtracted the same values from the second step to calculate the third, and so on.

3 Placing type into baselines. With your Path-Type tool, click on the top path and choose File: Place to place your text onto the path. Direct-select the text-insertion I-beam and drag it until the text begins just inside the hourglass. Then click with your Type cursor at the end of the word closest to the right side of the hourglass (add a hyphen if you must), press ⌘-Shift-↓ to select all text beyond the line and cut the selected text. If necessary, place the Text cursor between words and kern slightly using Option-←/→ (set the units for Cursor-key distance in General Preferences). After adjusting the first line, click with the Path-Type tool on the second line and paste the cut text. Set the typestyle based on your "line 2" calculation, and repeat the above procedure until text is placed on all existing lines. Then click-drag to create an Area-Type object in which to paste the remaining text temporarily.

4 Creating the trickling type. Select and cut one letter at a time, then click within the hourglass to paste each letter as Point Type. Create the paths for the bottom of the hourglass, and calculate the values for increasing the weight/width (or size) of the styles. Click inside the temporary Area-Type object, press ⌘-A (Select All) and cut the text. With the Path-Type tool, place the text into the remaining paths at the bottom, placing fewer words just before the type hits the bottom. On these shorter lines, drag across individual letters with the Type tool and use Option-Shift-↑/↓ to create a baseline shift graphically. ☁

Gallery: Laurie Szujewska / Adobe Systems, Inc.

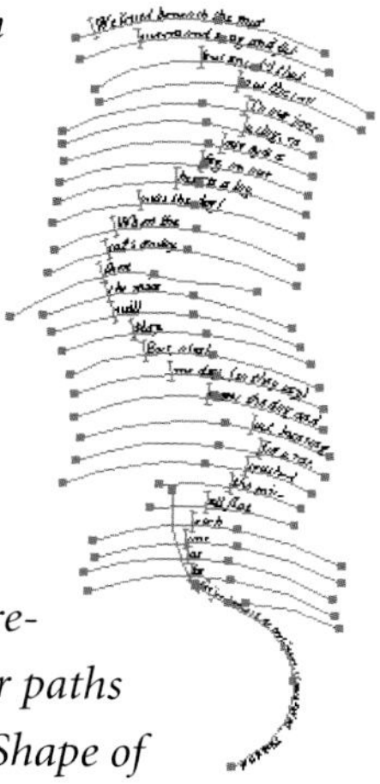

For the Adobe Caslon type specimen book, Laurie Szujewska created this reinterpretation of Lewis Carroll's handwritten, shaped poem from Alice's Adventures Underground. *Szujewska created the curved Bézier paths as described in "The Shape of Time" (page 142), but this time with a 14-pt distance for the leading and 28 duplications (⌘-D). After placing the appropriate text individually onto each line in 12-pt Adobe Caslon Italic (by clicking with the Path-Type cursor), Szujewska used the Direct-selection tool to adjust the angles of the curves. She then adjusted the starting point of each line of text by grabbing the I-beam and dragging it along the path. Finally, she individually selected each of the words in the last phrase (from "as he sat…") and progressively reduced them in size from "as he" at 11-pt to "Think of that!" at 6-pt.*

We lived beneath the mat
warm and snug and fat
but one, & that
was the cat!
To our joys
a clog, in
our eyes a
fog, on our
hearts a log,
was the dog!
When the
cat's away,
then
the mice
will
play.
But, alas!
one day, (so they say)
came the dog and
cat, hunting
for a rat,
crushed
the mice
all flat,
each
one
as
he
sat underneath the mat, warm, & snug and fat. Think of that!

Bookcover Design

Illustrator as a Stand-alone Layout Tool

DAY, EVANS

Overview: *Set your document size; place guides and cropmarks; place EPS files and make Area Type for columns and Point Type for graphic type; visually track type to fit.*

Page layout programs such as QuarkXPress and Page-Maker are essential for producing multipage, complex documents. However, Rob Day and Virginia Evans use Illustrator exclusively for their single-page design projects; for example, their book jacket designs.

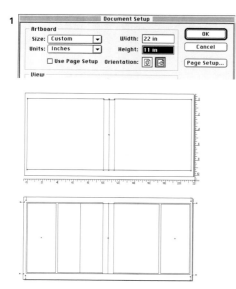

Setting up the Artboard and layout specs

1 Setting up your page. Choose File: Document Setup (⌘-Shift-P) to set up the Artboard for your design. Click on landscape or portrait page orientation and enter your Artboard size, making sure it's large enough for crop and/or registration marks (the "Size" parameter will automatically switch to "Custom"). Disable "Show Placed EPS Artwork" to keep your Artwork view uncluttered (placed images will always show in Preview). Choose View: Show Rulers and "re-zero" your ruler origin to the upper left corner of where your page will begin (see page 21). Although you can generate uniform grids with Preferences: Guides & Grid, for columns of varying sizes, Day and Evans numerically created two sets of rectangles, one for bleeds, and one for the trims. With the Rectangle tool (see page 8), click to make boxes sized for each trim area; Day and Evans made boxes for the front, side, flaps and spine. For bleeds, Option-click on the center of each trim area to numerically specify a box .125" larger in each dimension. To place an overall trim mark, select the boxes representing the entire trim area and choose Filter: Create: Trim Marks. If desired, make additional trim marks.

2 Customizing your guides. Select your trim and bleed boxes or columns (not the trim marks) and make them into guides (⌘-5), or View: Make Guides (see page 96 for more on guides). To shorten the trim marks, move the outside points inward until they touch the bleed guides (Direct-select an anchor point or Direct-select marquee multiple points and drag inward holding the Shift key).

3 Placing the elements. Choose File: Place to select EPS images to import into your layout. Use Area Type to place columns of text into your layout grid; use Point Type to place lines of type and individual type elements. To track type visually to fit a space, select a text object and use Option-←/→. (See the intro to this chapter for tips on how to change text and typestyles using filters.) 🖲

Creating "cropmarks," then "trim marks"

Create a rectangle that defines a cropping area, and choose Object: Cropmarks: Make. Cropmarks are visible in Illustrator but become invisible when placed into another program (such as QuarkXPress or PageMaker), except that they will reappear if you position objects beyond the cropmarks. To remove cropmarks, either choose Object: Cropmarks: Release, or make a new rectangle and choose again Object: Cropmarks: Make. More useful are the always-visible Trim Marks; select any objects (you don't need a rectangle) and choose Filter: Create: Trim Marks. Files can contain multiple trim marks, which you can customize (see Step 2 above), or make into dashed strokes for folds. To crop for export, create a "layer-mask" (see *Chapter 8*).

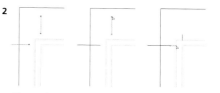

2

Shortening the trim marks; for folds, style with a dashed line (see page 54)

3

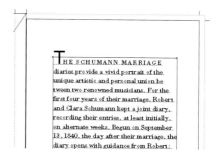

All of the elements placed into the layout

Close-ups of an Area-Type object

ROBERT & CLARA SCHUMANN

Close-ups of Point-Type objects

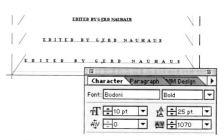

Tracking a line of Point Type with cursor-keys

Gallery: Pattie Belle Hastings, Bjørn Akselsen/Ice House Press & Design

When Ice House Press & Design (IHP&D) began to design labels for three different lines of oils and vinegars for an Italian client, they chose Illustrator as the production tool. Each line had to have a distinct identity, yet fit within the prescribed arched label shape. IHP&D found Illustrator ideal for designing such packaging labels, which combine graphics with highly modified type. IHP&D treated every block of type as a logo, manually kerning between each letter and word by clicking with the Type tool between letters and using the ← and → cursor-keys. (See the "Typographic Controls" tip on page 133.) IHP&D then manually selected and moved each graphic element and block of type until the spacing between the elements was just right. The ® mark, for instance, was individually created and placed as a separate element for each of the labels. Through this sort of meticulous manipulation, the type actually became graphical elements in a way not easily accomplished in a page layout program. For the Veritas line of organic olive oils, IHP&D chose to print in two PMS colors with gold foil for elegance (see Chapter 3 *for more on PMS colors). The Candoni line was designed for four PMS colors, while the third line (not pictured) was designed as a four-color process piece.*

Gallery: Javier Romero Design Group

Javier Romero Design Group converted the title in this illustration to outlines (Type: Create Outlines) and then manually distorted it. The resulting glowing effect, which the Design Group then applied to the type, can be used on any object—even regular, editable text objects. To replicate this effect, fill the top letter in a solid color, copy it and use Paste In Back (⌘-B) to place a copy of the letter behind the original. Set the Fill for this copy to None, with a 5.5-pt, medium-colored stroke (see page 54 for detailed instructions). Copy and Paste In Back this version and change the stroke weight to 7 points with a brighter color. Use Paste In Back again for an 11-pt, medium-colored stroke, and again for a dark, 16-pt stroke. (See Chapter 4 for help making layers to isolate the versions.)

JAVIER ROMERO DESIGN GROUP

GORSKA (design), BALDWIN (illustration)/MAX SEABAUGH ASSOCIATES

Gallery: Caryl Gorska / Max Seabaugh Associates

After commissioning Scott Baldwin to create a nutcracker illustration (he used Macromedia FreeHand to re-create his linoleum cut), Caryl Gorska scanned a traditional, copyright-free Dover Publications typeface into the computer. She saved the scanned typeface to use as a template (see page 80) and used the Pen tool to carefully trace the letters she needed. She then created the frame into which the type would be placed and, using the Selection tool, she "hand-set" the type by copying and pasting letter forms. Lastly, she fine-tuned the letter spacing, checking herself by printing myriad proofs—both actual size and greatly enlarged (increasing the percentage in Page Setup). Although her typeface, Newport Condensed, was available as a PostScript commercial font, instead of spending time and money tracking down and purchasing the font, Gorska preferred to spend the time typesetting the letters herself. "It keeps me in touch with the real letter forms and how they fit together, in a way that we often miss, just doing typesetting on the computer."

JAVIER ROMERO DESIGN GROUP

Gallery: Javier Romero Design Group

With a client as necessarily particular as Disney, Javier Romero needed the flexibility to create many design variations for children's clothing tags. And because the type needed to be fully integrated with the illustrations, Illustrator proved the most practical design tool. Of the dozens of designs that Romero presented, Disney selected as finals the designs shown in the photo above and to its right. Shown directly above are three of the comps, which include compositional elements contributing to the final design.

Masks & Special Effects

Advanced Techniques Chapter

8

This Advanced Techniques chapter builds upon techniques and exercises covered in earlier chapters and combines techniques found in different chapters. With the masking effects in particular, the techniques will be easier to follow if you feel comfortable with layers and stacking order (*Chapter 4*), as well as blends and gradients (*Chapter 5*), and are willing to try Pathfinder filters (*Chapter 6*). I'll continue to refer you to the proper chapter for more information on previously mentioned techniques.

Most techniques in this chapter make use of Illustrator's masks. Masks operate as stencils, or "clipping paths" that allow you to control which portions of objects will be visible. The simplest use of a mask is as a cropping tool. This defines the printable area of your page, cropping off from view or print any objects that extend beyond the boundary of the mask. Instead of using masks to define the printing boundary, many artists prefer simply to cover undesirable areas of an image with filled white rectangles. But the white rectangles end up being exported along with your image and creating false boundaries extending beyond the image. And if you export an image with a masked boundary, the masks will actually trim off parts of the image beyond the mask's border.

A better way to crop boundaries is to create a "layer-mask." Working with a file that already has an image, choose Show Layers from the Window menu, make a new layer titled "Mask" and create your masking object in that layer (again, see *Chapter 4* for more info on layers). Then select the mask, along with the backmost object in the

Artist Gary Newman converted text to outlines, then made a single compound path of the word **Careers**; he masked a copy of his background image with this compound word; he then selected the masked background objects and used Filter: Adjust Colors to create a darker version; the final image includes drop-shadows made from another compound mask and black type offset on top, and underneath the word **Careers** (for details on masking, masking with text and masking with compound paths, see 152–155, as well as pages 129–132 and 140)

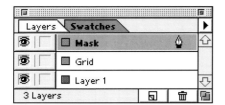

Ron Chan's Layers palette with a top Mask layer set to mask all lower layers

Grouping masks

Group an *object*-mask with its objects (⌘-G) for easy reselecting. However, if you group a *layer*-mask (see previous page) with its objects, it converts to an object-mask, with all objects moving to the mask's layer.

Note: *Use this technique with layer masks that don't rasterize properly.*

Inserting objects into a mask

To insert additional objects into a mask, make sure that Paste Remembers Layers is off (in the Layers pop-up menu), then cut (⌘-X) or copy (⌘-C) the objects you wish to insert into the mask. Next, select an object within the mask and use Paste In Front or Back (⌘-F or ⌘-B) to place the copied object into the mask (see page 78 for more on Paste In Front/Back).

Selecting within masks

Use the Direct-selection tool to edit individual masked objects. Use the Group-selection tool to select one object, and click again on the same object to select the rest of the objects in the mask set.

stacking order that you wish to mask, and choose Object: Masks: Make. Note that Illustrator masks any objects between the mask and the backmost object you selected. Move objects or layers above the mask or below that backmost object to prevent them from being masked.

But masks can do much more than simply create boundaries for printing and exporting. Masks can also directly affect objects or groups of objects. In an object-mask, the mask and the objects are all in the same layer with the masking object on top. To *create* an object-mask, select all the objects, including the top object, which will become the mask, and choose Object: Masks: Make (⌘-7). If you accidentally select objects on layers other than the one you want to mask, then you'll also mask all other objects in between the mask and the chosen object. To correct this problem, use Shift-Direct-select to deselect any objects that were inadvertently masked, then group (⌘-G) the mask with the desired objects. Grouping places all masked objects (including the mask) on the same layer and restricts the masking effect to those objects within the grouping.

Illustrator's masking feature provides extraordinary control over what portions of objects, blends or images are visible. Masks let you easily adjust both the contour of the masking object and the contents of objects being masked, through use of the Direct-selection tool to edit paths and the Group-selection tool to isolate objects.

MASK PROBLEM-SOLVING STRATEGIES

As you work with masks, there are bound to be times when a mask doesn't work right, or when Illustrator won't let you make an object into a mask. Here are some of the most common problems you may encounter when working with masks.

• **A type character isn't turning into a mask.** To use a type character as a mask, first apply Type: Create Outlines (⌘-Shift-O, as in "outline"). For step-by-step help with this technique, see page 140.

- **Text made into outlines and then a mask only has one letter of the word act as the mask.** This occurs once you've converted text into outlines (see above) and tried to mask using multiple letters. Because only the top-most object can be the mask, the last letter of the text is the only one that acts as the mask. Instead you must make a "compound path" of the entire text first (see page 151 for an example of masking with text).

- **You're trying to make a mask, but a dialog box says "selection cannot contain objects within different groups unless the entire group is selected."** This means that the objects you're selecting as a mask are only part of a group. Cut (⌘-X) and Paste In Front (with the Paste Remembers Layers toggle *on*), then make the mask.

- **Moving a mask from one layer to another stops the masking effect.** Moving a layer-mask (see earlier in this chapter) will release the masking effect. You'll need to reselect and reapply the masking command.

- **You're having trouble getting a masked object to print.** If you have tested to see if the mask is indeed the culprit (see Tip, "Memory-hogging masks," below), on a copy of your image, as long as your masked objects don't contain strokes, select the mask and its objects. Then apply the Pathfinder: Trim command (Trim deletes stroke styles!) to automatically trim hidden areas of the image. This can make it easier for the file to print (see pages 173 and 194 for examples).

Memory-hogging masks

Too many masks, or complex masking paths, may demand too much memory and prevent you from printing. To test whether a specific mask is a problem, select it with its masked objects, and temporarily hide them (Object: Hide, or ⌘-3), and see if printing is easier. **Note:** *Hiding only the mask will not alter the masking effect over the objects.*

Figuring out if it's a mask

If you're not sure whether a current selection contains a mask or is being masked, see if the Release option is enabled in Object: Mask, indicating that a mask is affecting your selection.

Finding masks

Deselecting all objects first and choosing Edit: Select: Masks should help you find most masks; layer masks (see earlier this intro), though, aren't always detectable.

When a mask isn't a mask

Masks were once the only way to achieve certain effects that you can now accomplish in other ways. For example, you can now use gradients to make transitions within complex objects both linearly and radially (see *Chapter 5* for more on blends and gradients). Also, Pathfinder filters can actually crop unwanted parts of objects that at one time required masking —a very useful example is the Trim filter. You'll find it by choosing Window: Show Pathfinder: Trim (see *Chapter 6* and page 173). Remember, applying these filters irrevocably alters the shapes of objects, sometimes creating distortions (such as deleting strokes), and will greatly limit your ability to make changes at a later time.

Colorful Masking

Fitting Blends into Custom Shapes

Advanced Technique

Overview: *Create a complex blend; mask it with a custom masking object; create a second mask-and-blend combination; make a two-object mask using compound paths.*

GRACE

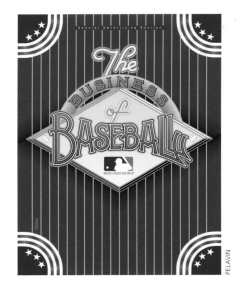

PELAVIN

The best way to learn how to mask is to make some masked blends. With Laurie Grace's pencils, you'll learn how to mask complex blends to fit into custom shapes. And with the patriotic corners of Danny Pelavin's baseball illustration, you'll learn how to mask one blend into two different objects by using compound paths.

The gradient for a pencil body

1 Creating the basic elements not requiring masking.
Create your basic objects. For her pencils, Grace created the long barrel of the pencil with a gradient fill.

Creating objects and blending them in pairs, then creating an object to use as a mask

Selecting the blends with an overlying object designed as a mask; the objects masked

2 Creating the first mask-and-blend combination. To prepare a mask for the pencils, create a closed object outlining the shaved wood and pencil tip, and Lock it (⌘-2 or Object menu). To ensure that your blend will completely fill the mask, make sure that each created object extends beyond the mask. Then select and blend each pair of adjacent objects (see *Chapter 5*). Grace created the slanted outside objects first and the center object last so the blends would build from back to front towards the center. Unlock (⌘-Option-2) your pencil-tip object, choose Arrange: Bring to Front (Shift-⌘-]), select the blends with the mask and press ⌘-7 (Object: Masks: Make). Then group (⌘-G) the mask and blend together.

3 Preparing the next masking objects and mask. Select and copy your mask, then select and lock the mask with the masked objects to keep from accidentally selecting any of them as you continue to work. Next, use Paste In Front (⌘-F) to paste a copy of your previous mask on top, and make any adjustments necessary to prepare this object as the next mask. Grace cut and reshaped a copy of the full pencil-tip mask until it correctly fit the colored lead at the top. Hide this new mask-to-be (⌘-3 or Object menu) until you've completed a new set of blends.

4 Creating a new mask that overlies the first. Create and blend new pairs of objects as you did for the previous mask. When your blends are complete, Object: Show (⌘-Option-3) your hidden masking object and Bring to Front to place the mask on top of these latest blends. Then select the colored-tip blends with this top object, ⌘-7 to make the mask and, as before, group them (⌘-G) together for easy reselection. Finally, unlock the first blends (⌘-Option-2), select the entire piece and group (⌘-G) it all together.

5 Making a mask from a compound path. Create a blend to be masked by two objects. As Pelavin did for his patriotic corners, start with a circle as a template. In Artwork mode, use the Pen tool with the Shift key to draw a straight line from the circle's center point to its bottom edge. With the Rotate tool, Option-click on the circle center to specify an 11.25° rotation and click Copy. Then press ⌘-D seven times to repeat the rotated copy a full quarter of a circle. Recolor every other line and blend from one to the next as above. Next, create two paths for a mask (Pelavin cut and joined quarters of concentric circles) and choose Object: Compound Paths: Make. Place the compound paths on top of the blends, select them all and choose Object: Masks: Make to see your blend show through both compound paths. Pelavin recolored a copy of the red blend with a range of whites, masked the white blend with a larger arc and placed it behind the reds. ↻

3

Completed objects selected and locked, then a copy of the last mask made into a new mask

4

New objects before and after blending, and after being masked

5

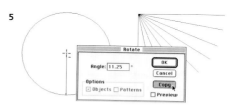

Rotating a copy of a line about a circle's center 11.25°, then using ⌘-D to transform 7 times

Coloring every other line and blending in pairs

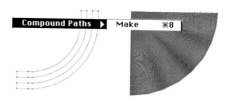

Compound Paths ▶ Make ⌘8

Compounding paths and getting ready to mask

Blends masked by compounds and a final corner (shown here also with a masked white blend)

Offsetting Colors

Using Masks to Create Relief & Shadows

LERTOLA/TIME

Advanced Technique

Overview: *Create a basic object stroked in white; offset a copy in a medium tone; copy and Paste In Front light and dark copies and mask them; Paste In Front the final color.*

1

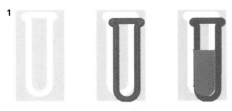

Creating the basic three positions and colors

2

Making highlight, shadow and masking-object

Masks ▶ Make
Release

Filling with no stroke or fill and creating the mask

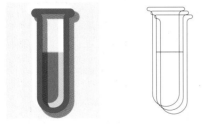

The final tube in Preview and Artwork modes

Creating the illusion of relief is a result of both finding the right colors and placing the objects in the correct relationship to each other. For a *Time* magazine article, "The Chemistry of Love," Joe Lertola relied solely on a limited palette, objects offset in three positions and Illustrator's masking feature to create this license plate.

1 Creating a simple object stroked in white, then off-setting copies. Set the ruler units to points (see *Chapter 1*). Select any object and set it to have a 2.5-pt white stroke and no fill (for help setting styles, see page 54). Hold down the Option key and drag a copy down and to the right 2.5 points, or Option-click on the Selection tool to open the Move dialog box, specify a 2.5 Horizontal and −2.5 Vertical move and click Copy. Style this copy in a medium blue-gray. Using the same technique, make another copy halfway between the objects (−1.25-pt horizontal and 1.25 vertical), remove the stroke and give it a fill of red. For the tubes, Lertola cut this red, topmost object so it appears half-filled (see page 52 and *Chapter 6* for different approaches to cutting an object).

2 Making the inner shadow and highlight. Copy the white object, deselect, choose Edit: Paste In Front (⌘-F) and change the stroke to a light tint of the red. Then copy the blue-gray object, deselect, Paste In Front and style it with a dark burgundy stroke. Copy the red-filled object, deselect, and Paste In Front, styling this copy with no stroke or fill. Select this last copy, the original red object, the light tint and the dark shadow, and choose Object: Masks: Make. Offset a final copy of the full object's outline on top, in the halfway position, and set a blue, 1.8-pt stroke. ◡

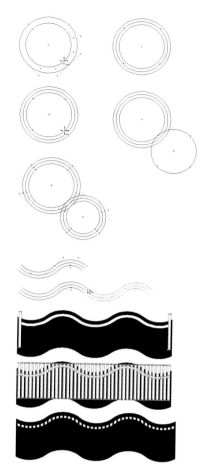

TUTTLE

Gallery: Jean Tuttle

In this Santa Barbara Film Festival image, Jean Tuttle created the wavy film sprockets by first setting the Constrain-angle to 45° (which rotates anchor points 45° off-center) and making a circle. From the center of this circle, she made a smaller, concentric circle by Option-Shift-dragging with the Oval tool. Selecting both circles, Tuttle used the Blend tool to create a third circle between them. Next, selecting the smallest circle, Tuttle Option-clicked with the Rotate tool on the lower right anchor point to rotate 180° and clicked Copy. From the center point of this copied circle, she made two smaller, concentric circles, dragging until they "snapped" to the next arc of the larger circle. She Direct-select marqueed the points on the circles above and below the wave shape and deleted, then selected and joined (⌘-J) each pair of overlapping anchor points. Tuttle next Option-Shift-dragged sideways a copy of the wave until it snapped into position so she could join it to the first. She dragged copies of the long wave downward and joined them to form both a wide black ribbon and a thinner, white path. After making two white rectangles and blending them to form regular strips across, Tuttle masked them with the thin wave path. She also recolored copies of the blended rectangles and used them elsewhere, such as the water (bottom of image) in which turquoise bars overlap a gradient rectangle made from tints of the same turquoise color.

Contouring Masks

Using Masks to Control Realistic Tonality

Advanced Technique

Overview: *Create the full outline for your image; copy an object representing a surface; create a blend and mask it with a copy of the surface outline pasted in front.*

1

Initial printer in Artwork mode (notice that objects don't overlap)

The top objects before blending

The top blended and selected with top object before masking

The top masked

There are a number of reasons why you should learn how to replicate the gradient effect (see *Chapter 5*) using blends and masks. First, blends which are made up of a limited number of steps print more quickly than gradients. Second, gradients that print smoothly won't necessarily look good for on-screen presentations. Finally, by learning this technique, you'll understand how to edit complex images saved in formats prior to Illustrator 5.

Since Andrea Kelley knows that her renderings for Apple Computer are often both printed in miniature (less than 1" tall) or viewed on computer monitors, she controls how the images will be displayed on the monitor, while reducing the printing time. Kelley uses blends and masked blends instead of gradients. For blends within straight-sided objects, she removes unnecessary paths to keep the blends clean in Artwork mode (see page 114). For rounded shapes, Kelley uses copies of an object's contour to mask her blends.

1 After creation of a full image outline, creating and masking blends. Create an outline version of your image, constructing each surface you'd like to mask out of one closed object (see page 122 for one way to create separate enclosed objects). Decide which surface you'd like to mask first, select the corresponding object and copy it, then choose Edit: Select All (⌘-A). Now Lock (Object menu, or ⌘-2) all the selected objects. Create a blend that extends beyond the surface parameters, then use Paste In Front to paste the copy of your surface (your new mask) on top. Select the blend along with the top object and choose Object: Masks: Make (⌘-7). Then group (⌘-G) the mask with its blend. To access the other objects in your illustration, choose Object: Unlock (⌘-Option-2). Then continue to follow the above steps for each surface requiring a different tonality or color. As you work, make sure to lock objects you don't want to select accidentally, and to group masks with their objects as soon as they're made. You may wish to group related objects further for easy reselection—for example, all of the objects forming the top of the printer.

Simplify your tasks by making and using custom layers to isolate objects as you work (see *Chapter 4* for details on layers). Try, for instance, pasting the next object you intend to use as a mask into a new, upper layer labeled "red." After you create the mask, grouping it with the masked objects will automatically move the masked objects into the upper red layer. By having this red layer, you'll be able to identify instantly and lock or hide all previously masked objects as you select the next surface to prepare it for masking. And there's no need to stop at one extra layer. Whenever you find it difficult to isolate particular elements, create a new layer (assigning it a new selection color) and move the appropriate objects to the layer by dragging the colored dots at the right of the current layer to the new layer (see layer Tip on page 88).

2 Creating details through careful observation. Kelley uses 100% blacks and whites with occasional small, thin lines as highlights or shadows. Use copied parts of paths as accents (see pages 50 and 114 for suggestions). ⌣

Magically transform gradients into masked blends
To transform gradients into masked blends, save a copy of the file in Illustrator 3 format; upon reopening, gradients will be replaced by masked blends! — *A. Kelley*

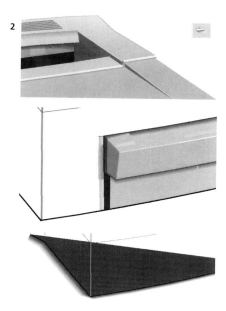

2

Details of the masked printer blends

The final printer in Artwork mode

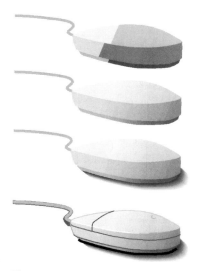

The mouse's mask-and-blend progression

Gallery: Kenneth Batelman

Kenneth Batelman used masks to fit blends into contoured shapes all through-out this "Banking Disaster" illustration. Shown directly above are the stages of creating the flames, from making pure blends, to masking with a flame shape, to layering flames upon flames. Batelman used a similar technique to fit blends within a poured shape for the glowing, radioactive slime, and to shape the tornado funnel. He also used masks to create splits in the earthquake image (each split contains an entire bank, masked to show only the desired portion), and in the clouds and waves.

MORRIS / SAN FRANCISCO EXAMINER

Gallery: Christopher Morris / *San Francisco Examiner*

Christopher Morris created "Mafia Chef" for a San Francisco Examiner *story about a Mafia member who, after entering the Federal Witness Protection Program, wrote a cookbook and then went out on tour promoting it, only giving interviews in clandestine hotel rooms. To create this darkly satirical illustration, Morris constructed blends that fit roughly into compositional outlines that he had drawn with the Pen tool. He then used his compositional outlines as masks to fit the rough blends snugly into these contours. Shown directly above, from left to right is the chef, constructed only of blends (notice that the blends stick out in various places), next with the contouring masks in place, and then, after being masked. Also shown is the corner with the steaming pot before and after masks were applied.*

Reflective Masks

Super-Realistic Reflection

Advanced Technique

Overview: *Move a copy of a blend area; if you're using type, convert it to outlines; skew and adjust it to the right shape; use filters to make an offset; recolor and remask blends; move blend back into position.*

Two techniques in earlier chapters demonstrated how Thomas•Bradley Illustration & Design (T•BI&D) used Pathfinder filters to generate its basic objects for blending (page 122), and how the blends themselves are formed (page 112). This technique focuses on replicating contouring blends to create reflectivity and surface variation.

A blended area selected and a copy moved off the image area 5" (using Shift-Option and cursor-keys set to .5" increments); and type converted to outlines

1 Replicating an area of your image for placing new details. This process can be used to create color or surface variations, but we'll use the application of type detailing as a demonstration. After you've outlined your image and filled it with contouring blends, choose an area for detailing. With the Shift key down, use Selection and Group-selection tools to select all blends and originating objects for the blends that exist in that area. To move a copy of these blends out of the way, set the Cursor-key distance to .5" in General Preferences (⌘-K). Now hold Shift-Option and press the → key to pull a copy of the selected blends 5" to the right (10 times the cursor-key distance). To move this copy further, use Shift → to move the selected blends in 5" increments, or use → alone to nudge in .5" increments. With the Type tool, place a letter or number on top of the moved blend (see *Chapter 7* for more on type). Click a Selection tool to select the type as an *object* and choose Type: Create Outlines (⌘-Shift-O).

Skewing outlined type, then adjusting and coloring it to fit the blend contour

2 Reshaping type to fit your blended contours and creating an offset. Working from templates, references, or just your artistic eye, use the Rotate, Scale and Shear tools with Direct-selection to adjust various anchor points until the type fits the contour. For the type on the racecar,

Creating reflections for an "outline" by copying the type, then stroking and filtering it using Object: Path: Outline Path and Pathfinder: Unite

T·BI&D skewed the letters (by clicking first in the center of a baseline, grabbing above right, and Shift-dragging to the right). Then they Direct-selected individual points and groups of points, moving them into the visually correct positions.

To create the outlining effect, first copy a solid-filled version, then set the stroke in the desired weight and color. While this object is still selected, choose Object: Path: Outline Path, then Pathfinder: Unite.

3 Pasting the original back on top, designing new colors for copies of the older blends and masking the new versions. First, Paste In Front (⌘-F) the original, unstroked type element. Next, select and Lock blends or objects that won't fall within the detail (Object: Lock or ⌘-2), but that you want to keep for reference. Copy and Paste In Front (⌘-F) each of the source (key) objects for new blends and recolor them for your detailing. To recolor a blend, Direct-select each key object you want to recolor and choose a new color—the blend will automatically update! As necessary, recolor each pair of key objects using the same procedure (bear in mind, blending between *Spot* colors results in *Process* in-between colors). T·BI&D recolored the car blends for the red **3**, then added a tear-shaped blend for more detail. Select and copy (in Artwork mode if necessary) the original **3**, use Paste In Front (⌘-F), press the Shift key and click to add the new grouped blends to the selection, then choose Object: Masks: Make (⌘-7). Group (⌘-G) and Hide (⌘-3) these finished masked objects and repeat the recoloring of copied blends, masked by a top object for any additional highlights and shadows. Choose Object: Show All (⌘-Opt-3) when these masks are complete, group all the masks together and use the cursor-keys to snap this group of reflective details into position. T·BI&D created one more version of the **3** for a dark offset. For areas requiring more reflections, they constructed even more masks upon masks, as well as occasionally applying compound-masks (see page 155). ↩

3

Re-creating blends in new colors and preparing to mask them with a copy of the "3" on top

With the red, reflective blends masked, creating a darker, offset "3"

The dark "3" and the entire group of objects complete, before and after being moved back into position with cursor-keys

Other elements require more stages of blending (see page 155 for compounding multiple objects, like type elements, to apply as a single mask)

Glowing Starshine
Blending Custom Colors to Form a Glow

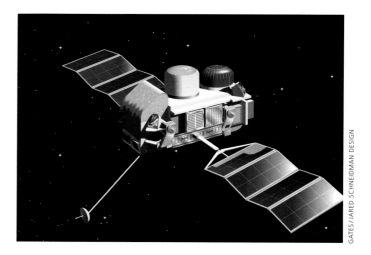

GATES / JARED SCHNEIDMAN DESIGN

Advanced Technique

Overview: *Create a custom color for the background and the basic object; scale a copy of the object; make object adjustments and blend a glow.*

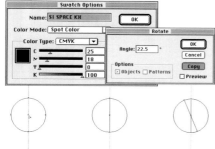

1

The background custom color; dragging a guide to the center of a circle, drawing a center line and rotating a copy of the line

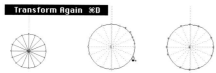

After pressing ⌘-D six times, making guides and adding anchor points at guide intersections

2

After Shift-Option scaling the circle smaller and changing the center to 0% tint; Direct-selecting and moving top, bottom and side points outward

Before and after a 12-step blend

Illumination is the key to creating a realistic nighttime sky. This variation on a technique by Guilbert Gates and Jared Schneidman Design (JSD) will help you create glowing lights, not just stars, simply and directly.

1 **Creating a custom color and the basic object.** Create a background rectangle filled with a dark, custom color (see *Chapter 3*). JSD's background was 25% cyan, 18% magenta and 100% black. In Artwork mode, make a circle, then drag a guide from the ruler until it "snaps" to the circle's center (the arrow turns hollow). With the Pen tool, click on an edge of the circle where the guide intersects, hold Shift and click on the other edge. Select this line, double-click the Rotate tool, specify 22.5° and click Copy. Press ⌘-D to repeat the rotate / copy six times, then select only the lines and ⌘-5 to make them guides. Use the Add-anchor-point tool to add eight points, one on each side of the circle's original points at guide intersections.

2 **Creating the glow.** With the circle selected, use the Scale tool to make a smaller copy of the circle (hold the Shift and Option keys) and specify a 0% tint fill in the Color palette. Direct-select the top point and Shift-drag it outward. Repeat with the bottom and two side points. With the Blend tool, click on corresponding selected points from each circle and specify 12 steps. ◡

Gallery: Bill Snebold

To create this juggling clown, Bill Snebold first traced a scanned sketch (see Chapter 4) *of the left side of the clown with the Pen tool, then made a flipped copy for the right side using the Reflect tool. Snebold traced the apple from a Polaroid photo and carefully created blends throughout (see* Chapter 5). *For the glowing apples, he made a full red apple using blends, then drew subsections of the apple to use as masks. For each color on the apple, he reconfigured the blend colors of the entire apple (see page 162), placed the appropriate subsection path on top and chose Object: Masks: Make. The glows result specifically from blending sections of the apple contour filled with white to the overlapping background color. Where the apple overlapped the face, Snebold had to create approximately 20 blends, many of them masked individually.*

Gallery: John Kanzler

In this illustration for Soccer Jr. *magazine, John Kanzler wanted to create the appearance that his bold characters were outlined by variable-weight black strokes. Beginning with colorfully filled, unstroked objects, he added facial features and dividing lines with unfilled 3-pt black strokes. Kanzler then selected each set of objects that made up a figure to: Group (⌘-G), Copy (⌘-C), Paste In Front (⌘-F) and Object: Lock (⌘-2). Next he selected the group of objects in back and set the fill to Black and Stroke to None. After deselecting the group, Kanzler then used the Direct-selection tool to select individual anchor points and move them outward to create the black "outlines." When necessary he added points with the Add-anchor-point tool. For some of the props, such as the chain links and locks, Kanzler customized unfilled stroked objects by varying the stroke Cap style (see page 49). For the locks he used a 3-pt colored stroke set to the Round-cap, then used Paste In Back to paste a copy behind, which he then set to 8-pt Black. For the chain links, Kanzler drew a few different individual links in color with the Butt-cap and then grouped each link with a thicker black stroke pasted behind. To assemble the chains, he then "mixed and matched" the various outlined links.*

Gallery: Andrea Kelley

For a series of promotional baseball cards produced for Symantec Corporation, Andrea Kelley developed a system to distort the dozens of logos and pictures needing to be placed onto boxes in an identical turned-angle perspective. Kelley first drew a box using the Pen tool, then grouped (⌘-G) and scaled her first logo to a rectangle the size of the angled placeholder on the box (see Chapter 2 *and the Tip "Scaling images to an exact size" in* Chapter 1 *for scaling help). Because the turned face was thinner than a box front, she double-clicked on the Scale tool to specify 85% horizontal (100% vertical) scaling. She dragged the logo from the upper left corner until it snapped to the upper left corner of the turned face. With the Rotate tool, Kelley then clicked on the upper left point again, grabbed the upper right corner and swung it up until it aligned with the top of the box. Next, with the Shear tool, she clicked once more on the upper left corner of the face, grabbed the lower right corner and, holding the Shift key, swung it down until that line aligned with the spine of the box. After moving the logo into alignment with the left corner of the spine and top of the box, she aligned the lower right corner to the box by first clicking Reset and moving the lower right corner up the minimum amount, applying Filter: Free Distort twice. Finally, she held the Option key and chose Filter: Distort: Free Distort again to reset, then slid the right corner to the left a minimal amount.*

Painterly Effects

From Gradient Lighting to Painterly Trees

Advanced Technique

Overview: *Create an illustration in full outline; use filters and manual cut and join tools to separate sections and soften edges containing gradients.*

1

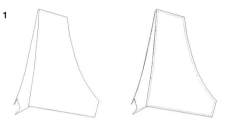

Artwork view of original roof outline and after the Offset Path and Unite filters

2

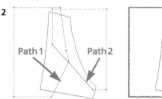

Path 1 and Path 2 objects before and after applying the Roughen filter

A copy of Path 1 selected with Path 2, then after the Minus Front filter

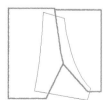 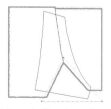

Copies of Path 1 and Path 2, and after the paths have been united, with a third path added

Some circumstances require more than just filling each object with a gradient fill (see *Chapter 5*). Clarke Tate's night rendering of Mann's Chinese Theater for *USA Today* contains many examples of layering gradients upon gradients and of using filters to transform Illustrator's normally hard-edged look into a more painterly effect.

| **Making inset subsections of architectural objects and filling them with different gradients.** With the Pen tool, create detailed outlines of your image, using enlarged templates if necessary (Tate starts with 400% enlarged templates, *Chapter 4*). Since you'll be filling with gradients, make your outlines completely closed paths. Select a simple object, such as a roof, and create an inset copy of it. Choose Object: Path: Offset Path, and specify −6 pt

(if you are working on a smaller scale, you might prefer a smaller inset). With this path still selected, choose Pathfinder: Unite, deselect the inner part of the inset (hold Shift and click it with the Group-selection tool), and then Delete any extraneous objects left by the filter.

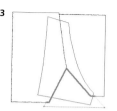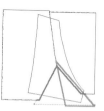

2 Creating roughened divisions to diminish contrast between gradients. Start by selecting the roof inset and hiding everything else (⌘-Shift-Option-3 or hold Option while choosing Object: Hide). You're going to split the roof into four pie-shaped sections so you can vary the gradients within the roof. With the Pen tool, draw closed Path 1, which will surround the entire left side of the roof, bisecting two-thirds of the roof vertically and angling back toward the left so that it forms the left side of a "peace sign." For closed Path 2, surround the entire right side of the roof, creating the right side of the peace sign and overlapping Path 1.

Select both paths, choose Filter: Distort: Roughen and specify a 15% size and 30 segments with the Corner option. Make a new layer (see *Chapter 4*) and place a copy of Path 1 on that layer by selecting Path 1 and Option-dragging its dot in the Layers palette into the new layer. Shift-select Path 2 as well and choose Pathfinder: Minus Front to cut the copy of Path 1 from Path 2.

After the Minus Front filter, and before using Intersect on the last roughened shape

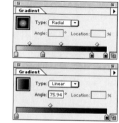

Before and after the Crop filter

3 Creating the bottom of the roof sections. Make a new layer, select Paths 1 and 2 and place copies of these paths in the new layer. With the paths still selected, choose Pathfinder: Unite. Next, on a lower layer, create a triangle that extends beyond the bottom of the roof and overlaps Path 1 and Path 2. Then Shift-select the united path on top, and again choose the Minus Front Pathfinder filter to cut the united path from the triangle.

Draw a last triangle surrounding the right half of the bottom section, choose Filter: Distort: Roughen and use the same settings as before. Now drag a copy of the bottom section to another layer, Shift-select the newest triangle and choose the Pathfinder: Intersect filter.

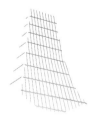

The roof after being cut into sections and filled with custom gradients, and customized with the Gradient tool

Outlining paths to fill them with gradients

The final roof in Artwork and Preview

5

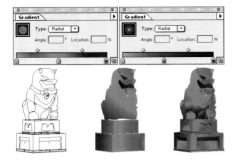

A detail of the tower and a gradient, shown in both the Gradient and Swatches palettes

The main and "recessed" gradients for the lion, shown in Artwork mode, then progressively filled with gradients

Progressive stages of theater detail and the taxi-cab gradient

To fit all these objects within the original roof inset, drag a copy of the roof inset to the top layer. Shift-select all four sections of this copy, set a temporary fill style and choose Pathfinder: Crop.

4 Designing the roof lighting effects. To represent different lighting conditions that affect a roof surface, design some custom gradients (see *Chapter 5*). Tate used two basic color ranges for the roof: a bright, wide-ranging, yellow-to-red radial, and a dark, linear gradient in a range of red-browns. Apply darker gradient to the back objects, with brighter gradients for the front objects. Use the Gradient tool to customize the fill direction in each section (page 108), then group (⌘-G) the roof elements.

Next, with the Pen tool, create stroked lines following the vertical slope of the roof and group them. Using a thicker stroke, create tiling lines that follow the horizontal slope of the roof and group them. Finally, select both the horizontal and vertical lines (with the Selection tool) and choose Object: Path: Outline Path to convert these strokes to filled paths. Now fill each group of "lines" with gradients, unifying them with the Gradient tool.

5 Filling and customizing overlapping objects with multicolored gradients. The more detail you'd like in your image, the more overlapping objects you'll need to create. Again, because you'll be filling these details with gradients, make sure to create closed objects. As you work, group (⌘-G) related objects together for easy reselection.

Design new gradients for different ranges of light and surface in other parts of the theater. Since you've grouped related objects together, Direct-select individual objects to fill each with a gradient. As with the roof, use the Gradient tool to customize each fill (again, see page 108). For his tower wall, Tate created elaborate multicolored gradients. For the lion, he used two radial gradients: the primary gradient covered a wide color and value range, while the shadow gradient remained dark in tone.

6 Creating the front canopy for a painterly tree. Make the basic object for your tree canopy, copy it, and lock it (Object menu, or ⌘-2). Paste In Front (⌘-F) the copied canopy and apply these filters, one after the other: Add Anchor Points, twice (see Tip, page 119); Distort: Roughen (specifying a 5% size, a detail of 10 segments, Corner option); and the default Stylize: Round Corners.

The original canopy and after Add-anchor-points, Roughen and Round Corners filters

7 Creating the back canopy and "holes" for branches. Object: Unlock (⌘-Option-2) the original, undistorted canopy and, while it's selected, apply the Add Anchor Points filter three times (see Tip, page 119), then Distort: Roughen (specifying 5%, 10 segments, Rounded). Fill each shape with different solid colors so you can distinguish them in Preview. Make a new, irregularly shaped object to use as a hole in the front canopy. Select this new object with the front canopy and choose Pathfinder: Minus Front. Then create another object to use as a hole in the back canopy, of roughly the same size and location, but shaped differently enough so you can see parts of the back object while still seeing through to your background. Select this object with the back canopy and again apply Minus Front (⌘-4 applies the last used Pathfinder filter).

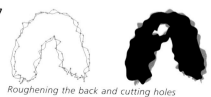

Roughening the back and cutting holes

Adjusting outlined paths for trunk and branches

8 Creating the trunk and branches. Set your palette defaults to a 4-pt stroke weight and no fill (see page 54), and draw a basic trunk with the Pen tool. For branches, create paths of progressively smaller line weights as you move up the tree, then group the branches with the trunk and transform these lines into filled objects with Object: Path: Outline Path. Now taper the objects of the trunk and branches, and fill each portion of the tree with custom radial gradients by using the Gradient tool.

9 Creating the leaves. For the finishing foliage, Lock the tree and create random-sized, light-colored circles with the Oval tool. Select all the circles, group them and apply Filter: Distort: Roughen (specifying 60%, 10 segments, Rounded). Direct-select to refill individual leaves. ◡

Making leaves from filtered circles

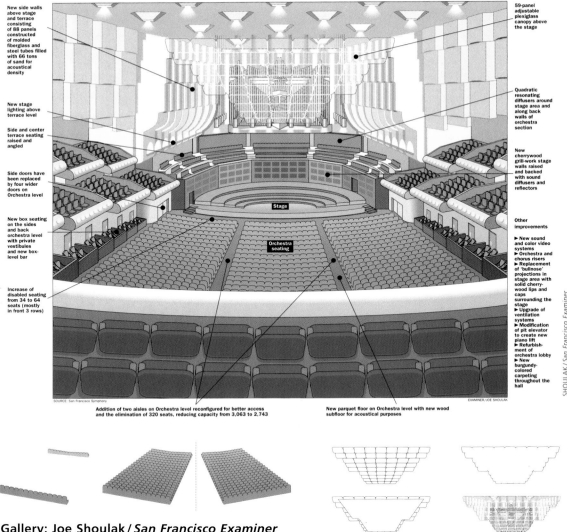

New side walls above stage and terrace consisting of 88 panels constructed of molded fiberglass and steel tubes filled with 66 tons of sand for acoustical density

New stage lighting above terrace level

Side and center terrace seating raised and angled

Side doors have been replaced by four wider doors on Orchestra level

New box seating on the sides and back orchestra level with private vestibules and new box-level bar

Increase of disabled seating from 34 to 64 seats (mostly in front 3 rows)

59-panel adjustable plexiglass canopy above the stage

Quadratic resonating diffusers around stage area and along back walls of orchestra section

New cherrywood grill-work stage walls raised and backed with sound diffusers and reflectors

Other improvements

▶ New sound and color video systems
▶ Orchestra and chorus risers
▶ Replacement of 'bullnose' projections in stage area with solid cherry-wood lips and caps surrounding the stage
▶ Upgrade of ventilation systems
▶ Modification of pit elevator to create new piano lift
▶ Refurbishment of orchestra lobby
▶ New burgundy-colored carpeting throughout the hall

Stage

Orchestra seating

SOURCE: San Francisco Symphony

EXAMINER/JOE SHOULAK

SHOULAK/San Francisco Examiner

Addition of two aisles on Orchestra level reconfigured for better access and the elimination of 320 seats, reducing capacity from 3,063 to 2,743

New parquet floor on Orchestra level with new wood subfloor for acoustical purposes

Gallery: Joe Shoulak / *San Francisco Examiner*

For this illustration detailing the renovation of Davies Symphony Hall, Joe Shoulak drew the first row of seats, then duplicated, moved, darkened, rotated and skewed it. He then blended the two rows using 18 steps. Shoulak next selected and grouped the left seats and, with the Reflect tool, he Option-clicked to the right of the seats to specify a reflection along the vertical axis, and clicked Copy. For the Plexiglass canopy, he skewed, scaled, and reflected rounded rectangles. Shoulak united a copy of the rectangles into one object (by placing an overlapping solid object with the rectangles, and choosing Pathfinder: Unite). He copied the objects that he wished to have appear through the canopy, moved them into a new document (in perfect registration) using Paste In Front, and desaturated the colors (Filter: Colors: Saturate). Shoulak pasted the united canopy on top of the desaturated panels and masked with it. He stroked the rectangles white (no fill) and pasted them on top of the masked panels. Then he grouped and copied the entire Plexiglass section and used Paste In Front to bring it back on top of the main image.

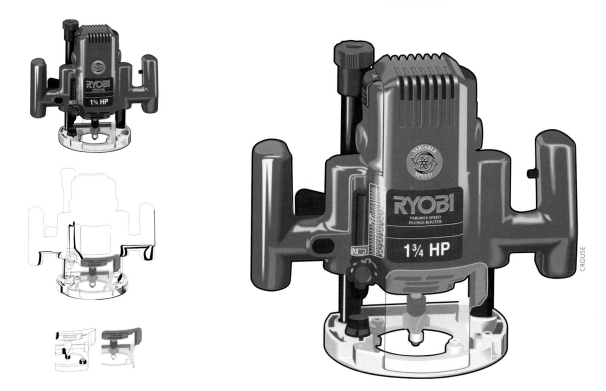

CROUSE

Gallery: Scott Crouse

Scott Crouse finds masked objects cumbersome to work with, so he uses Pathfinder filters to eliminate his masks. After completing the illustration of the router itself, he used the Pen tool to draw an object defining the Plexiglass shield. Then, with the Group selection tool, he selected the lower third of the illustration (encompassing the base and the shield), created a new layer and placed a copy of this selection into the new layer by Option-dragging the colored dot (at the right of the current layer) to the new layer (see page 88). Crouse then locked the original layer, selected and copied the path drawn for the plastic shield, and then applied Paste In Front (⌘-F) and Hide (Object menu, or ⌘-3) to this pasted copy. Next he selected all (⌘-A) and chose Object: Mask: Make to turn the shield object (the topmost object) into the mask for the rest of the selected art. Crouse then grouped the entire selection, hid the selection edges (⌘-H), chose Filter: Colors: Saturate and desaturated the colors. With the objects still selected, he then chose the filter Pathfinder: Crop to use the top object (in this case the mask) to cut away and delete everything outside the mask. Although the Pathfinder filter reduces the number of objects in your illustration (which means smaller file size, easier selections and faster printing), you won't be able to reshape the mask—so make sure the shape of the mask is final and correct. (Also, Crop will delete strokes, so you can only perform this action on unstroked objects.) To finish this illustration, Crouse chose Show All (Object menu or ⌘-Option-3) to reveal the hidden copy of the shield. This object was then cut in two places—the top part was stroked with white, and the bottom part was stroked with a dark gray to depict the lighting along the edges of the Plexiglass shield.

YOCUM

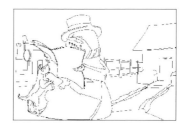

Gallery: Lester Yocum

Lester Yocum created "The Morning Paper" as his first card in his Sno'folks line of greeting cards. In preparation for the composition, Yocum first assembled a poseable model snowman out of foam balls, pushpins, twigs and props for testing expressions, perspective and lighting. Drawing directly from the model, Yocum used the Pencil tool with the Wacom drawing tablet to develop a rough sketch that he then locked on a layer named "Template" (see pages 80–83). In a series of layers on top of this template sketch, he used the Pen tool to draw enclosed objects (white fill, 1-pt black stroke). Once he had blocked out the composition, to ensure predictable color for printing, Yocum used process color reference books to select a palette of colors that reflected the restrained distortions of misty, early morning light. Blended objects were used for the snowman's arms and the dog's back, but the light and shadow in the rest of the image were created with radial and linear gradients that were then customized with the Gradient tool (see Chapter 5 for more on blends, gradients and the Gradient tool).

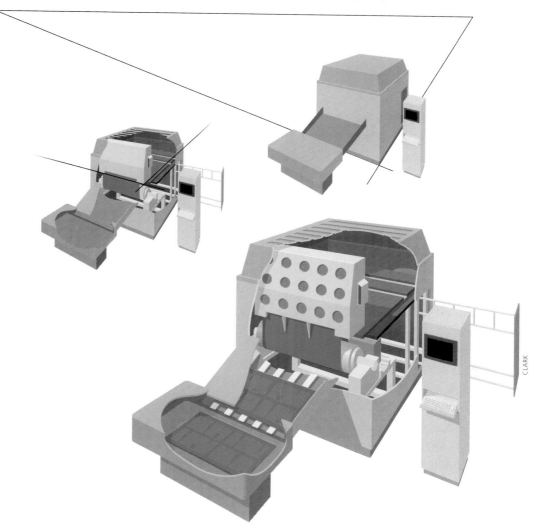

Gallery: K. Daniel Clark

To create this "plate maker" for Publish! *magazine, K. Daniel Clark began with a variation of the perspective guides covered on page 96. With the Pen tool Clark drew three lines: one horizontal line and two vanishing lines (one facing right, one facing left). Instead of converting these lines to guides, Clark kept the lines as paths so he could direct-select a free anchor point (not the vanishing point on the horizon line), and swing that line to a new location. Using these lines as guides, Clark constructed the exterior on an upper layer, and the internal components on the layer below. To create the cut-away illusion, he set the upper "exterior" layer to Artwork mode and locked it (see step 5 on page 83), then cut away the exterior objects with the Scissors tool in order to expose the objects below. For finishing touches, Clark connected the cut objects with the Pen tool, gave the walls "some thickness," created shadows and highlights, and placed additional details within the plate maker and processing tray. He deleted the perspective lines in the versions of the image that he sent to the client.*

WEIMER

Gallery: Alan James Weimer

Alan James Weimer achieved the detailed symmetry in this design by using features of Illustrator's Rotate tool. He began by making a circle divided into sections, with guides (see page 164). Then he created individual elements of the design, such as the leaf, by drawing half of the leaf with the Pen tool and reflecting a copy for the other side with the Reflect tool (see Exercise 9, page 35). Next, with the leaf selected, Weimer selected the Rotate tool and Option-clicked the cursor once on the exact center of the circle. In the dialog box he entered 45° and clicked Copy. To calculate the number of degrees, he simply divided the number of objects needed into 360°. Then Weimer pressed ⌘-D six times to rotate more copies of the leaf around the circle. He repeated these steps to add more elements to his design.

WEIMER

Gallery: Alan James Weimer

To create the diamond-shaped "tile" in the center of this design, Alan Weimer used the techniques shown on the opposite page. He then grouped the primary tile objects and Option-dragged copies of the tile onto a grid of guidelines to ensure proper alignment (shown at right). To complete the design, he used a rectangular layer-mask to "crop" the design (see pages 151–152) on one layer, and on a layer above the mask he added a border of blended, stroked rectangles.

High-density Files
Simplifying Complex Image Creation

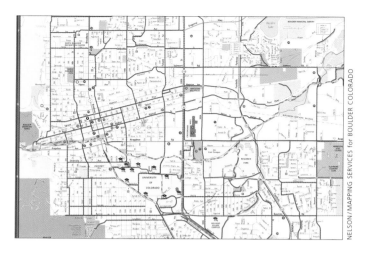

Advanced Technique

Overview: *Use Layers features designed for working with many layers; create multi-colored dashes, tapered lines, self-adjusting scales and graphic databases using brushes.*

Reversing backwards brushes

To change the direction of an open path, click on an end point with the Pen tool to establish the new direction towards that point.
—*David Nelson*

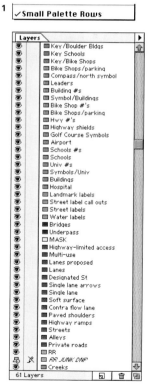

Choosing Small Palette Rows from the Layers pop-up menu to show more layers

From layer functions to brushes that solve many issues, Illustrator now offers professional illustrators and map-makers many tools and features that help streamline the creation and updating of complex images. In creating a large (22" x 28") bicycle and pedestrian map for Boulder, Colorado (a reduced detail of which is shown above), cartographer David Nelson was able to take advantage of dozens of recently added Illustrator features (for more mapping techniques see pages 54–55, 59, 90–91 and 201).

1 Harnessing more Layers features. With documents such as maps that use over 100 layers, the ability to view more layers at a glance with Small Palette Rows (from the Layers pop-up) is essential. When moving or copying objects from one layer to another (see Tip on page 88), you can now drag objects to Hidden layers (as long as they're unlocked). To replicate a customized layer structure in another file, select and copy objects on the layers you wish to duplicate. In the new document, enable Paste Remembers Layers (from the Layers pop-up) and paste, then delete the objects—leaving the new layers!

2 Creating complex colored dashes. Making complex multi-colored dashed lines was impossible using dashes in the Stroke palette—though brushes now make this possible (see pages 54–55 for help with dashed-strokes *and* brushes). Place different colored stroked-lines end-to-end, select and drag them into the Brushes palette, define them as a Pattern Brush and enable "Stretch to fit."

If your dashes are uneven or gapped, select the path and use the Smooth tool (from the Pen pop-up) to "iron out" the problems (see Nelson's Smooth Tip on page 83).

3 Creating tapered brushes. Create elements that taper, like creeks, using brushes. Draw a blue or cyan-filled rectangle, about four inches long and 2–3 pts wide. Select the right pair of anchor points and Average (⌘-Option-J), creating a triangle. Drag this path into the Brushes palette and define it as an Art Brush, using the point-width in the name of the creek. Select the path that you wish to make into a creek and choose your creek brush (see Tip opposite if the creek tapers the wrong way). To create a creek brush that tapers at a different rate, adjust the shape of the triangular object (adding or editing points) and create a new brush with that version.

4 Making a "self-adjusting" scale. Create a map scale, but leave off any text or numbers. Drag it to the Brushes palette and define it as an Art Brush. On your map, draw a horizontal line whose length represents X units of measure in your document (miles, kilometers, etc.) and apply your "scale" brush—which will adjust proportionately to the length of the line. Add numbers for the map units and other necessary text.

5 Using the brushes palette as an "object library."
Illustrator's brushes can be used as an object library. Drag any graphic element (icons, etc.) into the Brushes palette and define it as a Scatter Brush (choose a Colorization if you wish your element to change color or tint—see page 126 for help). To *use* a stored element, either drag it out from the Brushes palette (it expands into an editable object) or, with the Pen tool, click to make a single point and apply the desired brush. To move brushes from one file to another, just paste paths using those brushes. ↻

2

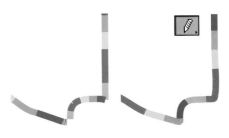

End-to-end strokes (shown enlarged) are made into a Pattern Brush

Pattern brush dashes on a path shown before and after being adjusted with the Smooth tool

3

Two of the objects made into tapered brushes

4

Three "self-adjusting scale" brushes

5

Graphic elements stored as Scatter brushes; Nelson's legend that includes custom brush elements described in steps 2, 3, 4 and 5

Auto-replacing brush objects
Permanently replace all instances of a brush: hold Option and drag one brush over another (you may wish to duplicate the brush being replaced first!). —*David Nelson*

Illustrator & Other Programs

9

Open sesame

Open files created in any program that allows you to save in "raw" PostScript: from the host application, print the file to disk, which saves it as raw PostScript. Then, from within Illustrator, choose File: Open and select the PostScript file, which you can now edit in Illustrator. Be careful: text can get chopped into small text blocks, making editing messy.

Rasterizing in Illustrator

To rasterize selected Illustrator objects, choose Object: Rasterize. You'll then be able to specify the color model (grayscale, RGB or CMYK), and resolution (pixels per inch). Since bitmaps are contained within a rectangular bounding box, you'll also have the option to create a mask outlining the object being rasterized, as well as an option for antialiasing (smooth edges). Be forewarned: you'll need plenty of RAM to do this!

This chapter is an overview, demonstrating Illustrator in concert with other frequently used programs, then introducing you to a range of work in Gallery format. Since so many people use Photoshop, this chapter includes a step-by-step technique for bringing Illustrator images into Photoshop, as demonstrated by renowned artist and author Bert Monroy.

One of the most compelling reasons to use Illustrator's vector-based images (instead of bitmaps, made of pixels) is that you can resize them without sacrificing detail or affecting file size. This makes Illustrator ideal for artwork that needs to be scaled to extremes, from billboards (page 199) to miniatures (page 158). Bear this in mind when you are determining how to integrate your Illustrator image with other programs.

ILLUSTRATOR, PHOTOSHOP & RASTERIZATION

You can easily rasterize objects at any resolution from within Illustrator, though Photoshop is still the preferred way to rasterize high-resolution images. If you need to use Photoshop to rasterize an Illustrator document that includes linked images, you have two choices. The first option is to use the Links palette pop-up menu to embed the linked files, then save this file with a new name and open it with Photoshop to rasterize at the desired resolution. Alternatively, you can export your file to Photoshop 5 format. (See "Exporting Illustrator to Other Programs," later in this introduction.)

ILLUSTRATOR, DIMENSIONS & STREAMLINE

Two other Adobe programs popular with Illustrator users are Dimensions and Streamline. Dimensions allows you to create 3D-looking files that you can edit in Illustrator, or to distort Illustrator files in 3D space (see pages 198–199). Streamline is a program for converting bitmapped images into vector art. Streamline is much more sophisticated at autotracing than Illustrator's Autotrace tool. For example, Streamline can quickly create line art you can use for comps. Beyond its tracing ability, a number of artists are using Streamline creatively to translate scanned drawings or photos into Illustrator art that looks very different from what you might expect (see pages 190–192 for examples).

ILLUSTRATOR PATHS & OTHER PROGRAMS

In addition to being able to bring Illustrator *objects* into other programs, you can import and export Illustrator *paths*. Painter lets you import Illustrator paths as "friskets," stencils, which allow you to isolate regions of your image to apply painting and other effects selectively (see page 194). In Photoshop, paths can define selection areas for isolating areas of your image (pages 184–189), or can be used to define clipping paths (see Tip at right). Photoshop, allows you to create Illustrator-like paths, as well as copy and paste or export paths to Illustrator.

You can import Illustrator paths into 3D programs to use as either outlines or extrusion paths. Once you import the path, you can transform it into a 3D object. Unlike Dimensions, true 3D programs maintain their three-dimensional characteristics until you decide to render an image as an antialiased bitmap. Strata's StudioPro (page 197) and Ray Dream Designer (pages 195–196) are two of the many 3D programs you can use in combination with Illustrator.

COPY & PASTE OR DRAG & DROP

You can copy and paste or drag and drop selected objects between Illustrator and Photoshop 4.0 or later (or any

---

Illustrator for "clipping paths"

Just as you can use masks in Illustrator to define irregularly shaped boundaries for your object or for the entire image (see *Chapter 8*), a number of programs allow you to save in formats that use Illustrator paths to create a clipping path. These paths define the boundary of an image when it's placed in other programs. Shown below is Photoshop's method.

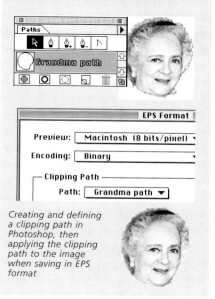

Creating and defining a clipping path in Photoshop, then applying the clipping path to the image when saving in EPS format

Extracting a clipping path

A raster EPS image with a clipping path displays as if it's cropped by the clipping path (see above) as long as it's *linked*. If you *open* the image, or *embed* it (using the Links palette), then the clipping path will convert to a mask (see *Chapter 8*). Be cautious, though—this mask has many more points than it did as a clipping path!

program that supports PostScript drag and drop). Depending on what application you're dragging or pasting Illustrator objects into, you'll either paste in paths or rasterize objects. In the case of Strider Software's TypeStyler3 you can freely drag and drop objects to and from Illustrator and TypeStyler3 (see page 200). With Photoshop, you're given the choice of pasting pixels or paths (pages 184–185).

If you're trying to rasterize in the drag and drop process, be aware that your Illustrator art will automatically be rasterized at the same physical size, or pixel-per-inch ratio you have specified in the program you are dragging to. In addition to dragging and dropping paths from Illustrator to Photoshop, you can also do the reverse.

Note: *Print designers should be aware that dragging and dropping bitmaps from Photoshop to Illustrator results in only 72-ppi RGB files. Instead, save your Photoshop file as a TIFF or EPS and place it into Illustrator to preserve the desired resolution and color mode.*

BITMAPPED IMAGES IN ILLUSTRATOR

You can create image objects, bitmapped images embedded in an Illustrator file, either by rasterizing Illustrator objects, or by placing a bitmapped image such as a TIFF, PICT or JPEG file and deselecting the Link option. In contrast to *linked* bitmapped images, image objects can be permanently altered. There are a number of issues to watch for, concerning both embedded image objects and linked image files. The Links palette keeps track of both types of images in your file (see *Chapter 1* for more).

First, since embedded images become part of your Illustrator file, your file size increases with each image you embed. An embedded bitmapped image takes up almost twice as much disk space as a linked image.

Another argument in favor of linking instead of embedding files is you can make changes to a linked file and resend only that linked file to the service bureau or client. As long as it has the same name it should autoupdate without further editing of the Illustrator image itself.

However, a serious problem does occur when you're transporting or color-separating files containing placed images in anything other than a linked EPS format (grayscale, CMYK, or 1-bit). In case your service bureau or client needs to open your image in a previous version of Illustrator, the image must be in EPS format. To conclude, most experts agree, you should replace embedded image objects with linked EPS files for final printing.

EXPORTING ILLUSTRATOR TO OTHER PROGRAMS

Illustrator has greatly improved the options for saving, importing and exporting to other formats—with dozens of formats supported, so make certain you understand which format is most appropriate for the program you are exporting to. Options for saving an Illustrator file are AI, EPS or PDF file format. However, several other file formats are available for selection through the Export command. In EPS, unlike other formats, saving with the current program version compatibility will not sacrifice any editing capabilities.

To place your Illustrator image into a page layout program such as QuarkXPress, you must save a copy of your image as EPS or export it as TIFF. With Adobe PageMaker you have the unique ability to place raw (or native AI) Illustrator formatted files.

To export an Illustrator file to Photoshop 5 format, choose File: Export, and then Format: Photoshop 5 as the file type. Select the desired color model, resolution, anti-alias or alias and enable the Write Layers option. This exported file will not only rasterize the linked images, it will also maintain the layer structure of the original Illustrator file. Each layer contains the raster version of the objects on a layer that can be used in Photoshop, along with Adobe's ImageReady, AfterEffects and Premiere (see *Chapter 4* for more on layers).

To save your file for use in Adobe Acrobat, simply choose Save As and select PDF format. Though you may not have the full range of editing capabilities, you can open PDF files as editable Illustrator files.

Colorizing 1-bit TIFF images

For details on colorizing 1-bit TIFF images, see Tip on page 80.

CMYK-to-RGB in Illustrator

For Photoshop filters that work only in RGB, use Illustrator's Rasterize command to change an existing image object to RGB. Apply the desired filter, then use the Rasterize command again to convert your image back to CMYK. Be aware that changing color spaces can result in muddy colors (see Tip "Converting RGB to CMYK" in the "Color" section of *Chapter 1* for cautions on this conversion).

So you think it's linked, eh?

If you apply a filter to a *linked image*, Illustrator will *embed* it, meaning your file will increase in size, and you can't update the link any longer. Instead, apply filters to the image in Photoshop *first*, then place it into Illustrator.
—*Robin AF Olson*

The power of Adobe Acrobat

Acrobat's Portable Document Format (PDF) is platform and application independent—which means it allows easy transfer of files between Mac and Windows (for saving in PDF, see text at left).

Sketching Tools

Illustrator as a Primary Drawing Tool

Illustrator with Photoshop

Overview: *Create your details in Illustrator; place Illustrator images into Photoshop at the right size; render and finish in Photoshop.*

1

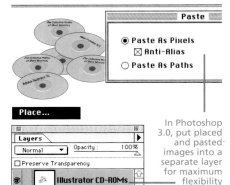

Three ways Illustrator images can be brought into Photoshop: opening, pasting and placing

In Photoshop 3.0, put placed and pasted images into a separate layer for maximum flexibility

With a Powerbook portable Macintosh, Bert Monroy meets with his clients to sketch ideas directly in Adobe Illustrator. Back in his studio, Monroy transforms these sketches into intricately detailed illustrations, which he then scales to the desired size, without sacrificing any of the detail. Monroy constructs his Illustrator images in flat colors and then brings them into Photoshop, where he can rework them into scenes rich in texture, light, shadow and volume.

1 Bringing detailed Illustrator images into Photoshop.
There are a number of ways for you to bring Illustrator images into Photoshop. First, from within Photoshop, choose File: Open and select an Illustrator file. Specify the size and resolution at which you plan to rasterize (turn into a bitmap) the image. Experiment with the results of changing the options. Second, copy the image in

Illustrator, and paste directly into Photoshop, choosing to paste "as pixels." Pasting "as paths" (introduced in Photoshop 3) imports paths to use in defining selections, or to serve as "clipping paths" for saving Photoshop files with nonrectangular boundaries. Third, if you have an open image, you can choose the File: Place command. With the Place command, you can visually resize your Illustrator image before it's rendered. If you have Photoshop 3 or newer, place or paste Illustrator files into separate layers so you can easily alter and move them in relation to the rest of the image.

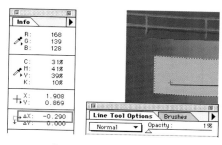

2 Measuring in Photoshop and resizing in Illustrator.

One of the greatest strengths of bringing Illustrator images into Photoshop is that you can render the maximum amount of detail at any resolution. If you resize (smaller or larger) a rendered Illustrator file, you'll sacrifice detail, so the key is to bring Illustrator files into Photoshop at exactly the right size. If simply using the Show Rulers command isn't exacting enough, in Photoshop, first measure the space into which you'll place an Illustrator file. First open the Info Palette, then choose your Line tool, set the minimum opacity (1%) and, with the Shift key down, click and drag from the one side of the space to the other. While doing this, note the value in the Info palette representing the horizontal (ΔX) distance you just measured. In Illustrator, first make certain that "Scale line weight" is enabled in General Preferences ($\mathcal{H}$-K). Then, select the object you want to move into Photoshop and resize it to fit the space you just measured. In the Transform palette, enter the X value as the new width (W), making sure to hold $\mathcal{H}$ as you press Return to maintain proportions (alternatively, you could note the ΔY to enter as the height).

Monroy's preferred method is to prescale and copy his Illustrator file, and from within Photoshop, select the area into which he wants to paste and then choose Edit: Paste Into. He can move the Illustrator image around within that selected area, then deselect it to make it part of the main image or put it into its own layer. 🌑

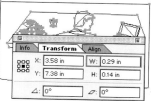

An Illustrator image; next measuring the space for pasting from within Photoshop; then scaling the image to the right size in Illustrator

After selecting an area, using Paste Into to place the copied Illustrator image within the selection

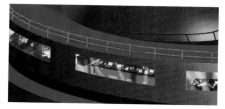

In addition to using Illustrator (to create details) and Photoshop (for retouching), sometimes Monroy brings 3D elements (he doesn't use photos) rendered in RayDream Designer (see pages 195–196) to help him visualize large objects, such as buildings, from different angles

MONROY

Gallery (with Photoshop): Bert Monroy

Bert Monroy constructed this image by placing and retouching Illustrator objects in Photoshop (see pages 184–185). Illustrator enabled Monroy to work with perspective lines (page 96), create microfine lines (such as the bicycle spokes), maintain letter-form details, and make quick, local-color changes.

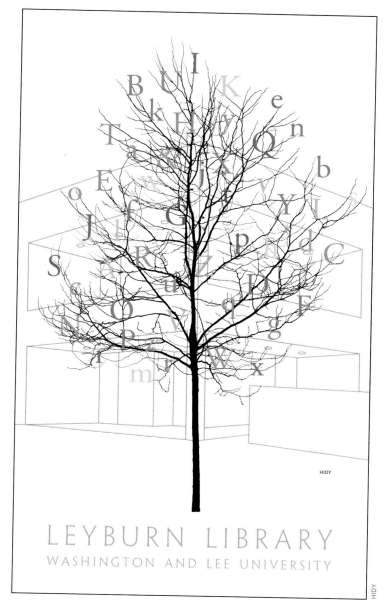

HIDY

Gallery (with Photoshop): Lance Hidy

Lance Hidy began this illustration by scanning a photo of the Leyburn Library into Photoshop. After days of painstakingly isolating the tree from the background, Hidy used Levels to establish a "threshold" determining which pixels would be black and which would be white. He then converted this tree (still technically grayscale) to bitmap and saved it as an EPS using the "Transparent whites" option (page 84). In Illustrator, Hidy traced the building (using a scanned pencil tracing as a template; see page 80 for more on templates) and then placed the EPS tree. Hidy added Point-Type elements (which he distributed randomly,) for the alphabet and used Area Type for the title (see Chapter 7).

Gallery (with Photoshop):
Pamela Drury Wattenmaker

Pamela Drury Wattenmaker initially created the microscope in Illustrator. In Photoshop, she then rasterized a version of the microscope without the type and saved it in EPS format. Drury Wattenmaker then placed the EPS back into Illustrator where she masked it with a rectangle placed on top of it (see Chapter 8 for more on masks). She then cut this masked EPS, selected the type and "frame" and Pasted In Back (⌘-B) the masked EPS to go behind the frame and type, yet in front of everything else.

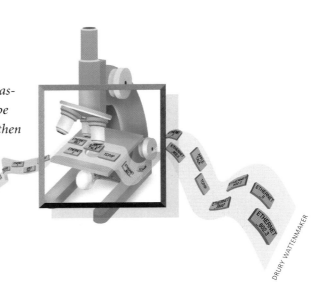

DRURY WATTENMAKER

Gallery (with Photoshop):
Michael Kline / Acme Design

Michael Kline began this image in two separate Illustrator files: one for the background, and another for the "rays." He opened each in Photoshop at the exact same size and resolution so he could use Calculate: Duplicate to load the "rays" as a selection in the background. He then "feathered" the selection 3 pixels and used Brightness / Contrast to "ghost it back." Lastly, Kline saved the composite background as an EPS and placed it back into Illustrator, where he added the airplanes and type.

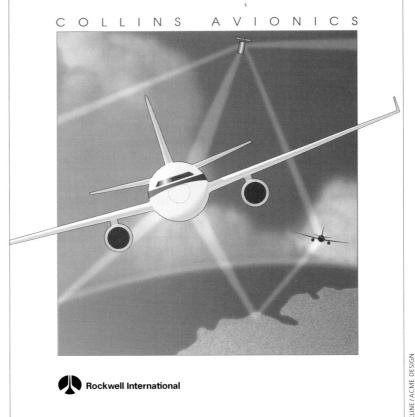

COLLINS AVIONICS

Rockwell International

KLINE / ACME DESIGN

MORRIS (illustration), STOREY (photography) / SAN FRANCISCO EXAMINER

Gallery (with Photoshop): Chris Morris / *San Francisco Examiner*

For an article discussing issues of copyright protection with the advent of digital imaging, Chris Morris created an illustration using black, enclosed, flat-colored objects in Illustrator. Where he wanted eventually to place photographs, Morris created black-stroked, white objects as placeholders. Morris opened the Illustrator image in Photoshop, then from another file, he selected and copied a scanned photo of Peter Gabriel, shot by Examiner *photographer John Storey. In the main rasterized image, he used the Magic-wand tool to select the first placeholder for the photo and chose Edit: Paste Into. While the selection was still active, Morris used Image: Effects (Scale, Skew, Perspective and Distort) to fit the photo properly within the selected space before he "stamped it down." Morris repeated this procedure for each image he wished to place. (**Hint:** In Illustrator, try using colors not used anywhere in your image as placeholders, making it simple to pick up these colors with the Magic-wand within Photoshop.)*

JACKSON / SAN FRANCISCO EXAMINER

Gallery (with Streamline): Lance Jackson / *San Francisco Examiner*

To achieve the hard-edged, yet warm, painterly Illustrator look in this image, Lance Jackson sketched with traditional drawing media, then scanned the drawings into the computer at both high and low resolutions. In Streamline, Jackson translated both resolutions into Illustrator format. Opening the two translated files in Illustrator, Jackson combined them, using primarily the lower-resolution version while copying and pasting details from the higher-resolution version (the face and hands, for example). Finally, Jackson selected and recolored individual objects until he achieved the final effect in this illustration entitled "Doper."

SPOLLEN

Gallery (with Streamline): Christopher Spollen

Although his illustrations have the feel of bitmapped images, Chris Spollen creates them with Illustrator and Streamline. Spollen has developed a way of working with the computer that borrows from his traditional printmaking background. Beginning with scans of old magazines, and sketches of his own, Spollen runs these images through Streamline. Opening the files in Illustrator, he prints them out, and then physically cuts and pastes the printouts, rescans the resulting collages, and reruns the new scans through Streamline. Sometimes Spollen's files go through many "states" before he finally incorporates color into the image; often he reworks a piece using original drawings in Illustrator.

Gallery (with Dimensions, Streamline and Photoshop): Shayne Davidson

Shayne Davidson began this illustration, "Antibiotics: Overuse and Resistance," by arranging a dozen reference photos of children, scanned at 300 pixels per inch (ppi), in a Photoshop layered document. After flattening the layers she chose Image: Adjust: Posterize with 30 levels, then opened this file in Streamline and converted it into vector art with the Color/Grayscale Setup option set to a posterization of 16 colors. She opened the Streamline file in Illustrator, made color adjustments and copied this file. Davidson pasted these vector children "As Pixels" (see page 184) into a new 300 ppi Photoshop document, duplicated this children layer, desaturated the duplicate (Image: Adjust: Desaturate) and moved it below the original children layer (set to "lighten" mode to subdue the overall color). For the medicine bottle with locking snaps and the pills in the foreground, she brought Illustrator-drawn profiles into Dimensions where they were extruded (snap), extruded with a bevel (pills) and revolved (bottle), then the label was mapped onto the bottle (see profiles and label above). For detailing the bottle, Davidson chose Plastic shading, rotated it to look like it was tipped over, and adjusted Window-Show Camera to add perspective. The Dimensions files were rendered in Raster Mode and copied and pasted into the Photoshop file, where she selected and deleted the white background automatically created by Dimensions. She created microbe shapes in Illustrator and Dimensions, pasted them into Photoshop where she applied a variety of filters, then distorted them (Transform: Distort) so they appear to be moving toward the children. Finishing details were created within layers in Photoshop.

Gallery (with modems/QuarkXPress): Dan Cosgrove *(illustration)*, **David Fridberg** *(design)*

For a poster announcing the Smithsonian Institution's 1994 Jazz Orchestra Series, David Fridberg commissioned Dan Cosgrove to create the original illustration. The only problem was this: Fridberg lives in Washington, DC, and Cosgrove lives in Chicago, and the schedule was too tight to allow for even overnight mail deliveries. Illustrator's small file size (compared to Photoshop, for instance) made sending the working versions of the files via modem quick and easy. Cosgrove created rough sketches directly in Illustrator, then "modemed" them to Fridberg to comment on. With immediate

feedback, Cosgrove was able to complete the illustration for the poster in record time. Since he knew that Fridberg would be pulling out individual musicians from the full composition, Cosgrove created each musician in his own layer, making it simple for Fridberg to select and copy any of them by hiding and showing the appropriate layers (see Chapter 4 *for more on layers). With the final illustration received in DC, Fridberg used a combination of Illustrator and QuarkXPress to complete the design for this two-sided, fold-out poster. He created all graphic text (titles and the text on a curve) in Illustrator, although he decided to assemble the full poster from within QuarkXPress. (**Hint:** Since this Wow! book is produced in QuarkXPress, in order to fit the large (14"x20") poster onto this page, I used the File: Save Page as EPS option, then resized the placed page in QuarkXPress.)*

STAHL

Gallery (with Painter / Photoshop): Nancy Stahl

*When Nancy Stahl decided to rework the portrait of the woman from her "Couple in the Field" (page 89), she rasterized and cropped the portrait in Photoshop. Next, Stahl both opened the rasterized image in Painter and imported Illustrator paths as friskets. Using the friskets allowed her to isolate distinct areas of the image for local painting and retouching, and for applying specific effects, such as lighting and texture. (**Hint:** Before importing paths as friskets, Stahl now uses the Pathfinder: Merge filter on a copy of the image to eliminate path overlaps; for more on filters, see Chapter 6.)*

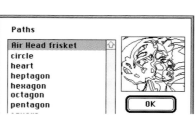

GROSSMAN

Gallery (with RayDream Designer / Photoshop): Wendy Grossman

Wendy Grossman began her illustration "The Bicycle Race" by drawing a tight pencil sketch, which she scanned and saved as a PICT so she could open it as a template in Illustrator (see page 80 for more on templates). Using the template, Grossman created the main composition in Illustrator. She constructed and rendered the flowers and the shrubs in RayDream Designer, giving them the look of a pop-up collage. Then she rasterized the Illustrator file in Photoshop, where she assembled all of the RayDream Designer vegetation and reworked the entire image using the painting and retouching tools.

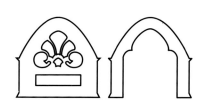

Gallery (with RayDream Designer / Photoshop): Sharon Steuer

*Illustrator was the starting point for this cassette-tape liner (called a "J-card"). The first task I performed in Illustrator was to create separate outlines for each portion of the radio logo (with the Pen tool). Saving each radio outline in Illustrator 3 format, I imported them into RayDream Designer, where I gave each depth and texture, assembled all the radio objects, and rendered them as a PICT file with a mask. Back in Illustrator, relying on source photos for rough visual references, I used the Pen tool to draw the Seattle skyline and the "Space Needle" directly in Illustrator. To establish the overall color scheme, I created gradients and used the Gradient tool to specify their length and direction (see Chapter 5 for more on gradients). I created trim marks by placing an unfilled, unstroked rectangle the size of the final trim and choosing Filter: Create: Trim Marks. I then made the different type objects, rotated the "Goes to Seattle!" line and saved each type object into a separate Illustrator file. In Photoshop, I rasterized, retouched and color-corrected the skyline (see page 184 for more on rasterizing). I then brought each line of type into its own channel, loaded it as a selection and filled it, or, in the case of the drop shadow, offset and darkened it using Levels. Finally, I copied the masked radio and pasted it into place to complete the illustration. (**Hint:** Try pasting type as paths into Photoshop.)*

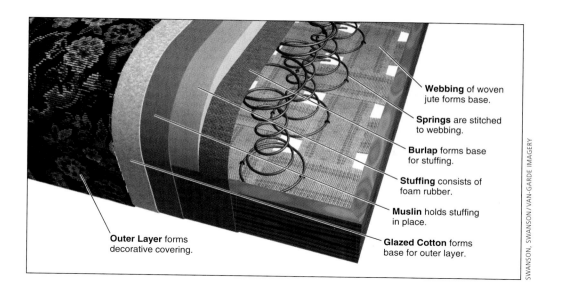

Webbing of woven jute forms base.

Springs are stitched to webbing.

Burlap forms base for stuffing.

Stuffing consists of foam rubber.

Muslin holds stuffing in place.

Glazed Cotton forms base for outer layer.

Outer Layer forms decorative covering.

Layers objects

Weave object

Board object

Gallery (with StudioPro / Photoshop): Dan and Darlene Swanson

For Dan and Darlene Swanson, the first step in constructing realistic 3D renderings is to create accurate profiles of cross-sections in Illustrator. For the upholstery illustration above, the profiles for the various layers of fabric and foam were drawn in exactly the correct positions and sizes in relation to each other. The Swansons imported these profiles into Studio-Pro where they extruded them into the appropriate thicknesses and rotated them into the correct positions. They constructed the interwoven straps by creating a single modular "weave" object, which they replicated and moved to form the "woofs" and "warps." They turned and duplicated the "board" object so the mitered corners would fit together. Texture maps, previously created in Photoshop, were then assigned to each layer, lights were directed into the assembled scene, and the full image was rendered in PICT format. The Swansons lightly retouched the final rendered upholstery image in Photoshop, saved it in EPS format and placed it back into Illustrator, where they added the labels and border. The glass award (above right) required a bit more retouching in Photoshop, namely a few extra highlights painted on the edges, and some reworking of the type.

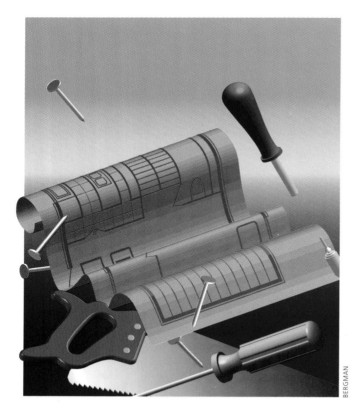

BERGMAN

Screwdriver

Nail

Blueprint profile

Gallery (with Dimensions): Eliot Bergman

Eliot Bergman used a combination of Illustrator and Dimensions to create this "Blueprint for Savings." Bergman began in Illustrator where he drew the flat views of each object, using many filters to help him along; for the handle of the saw, for instance, he chose Pathfinder: Unite to combine basic objects, followed by the Stylize: Round Corners filter. Sometimes Bergman drew only one view of the object; at other times he needed to draw multiple views. For objects such as the saw, Bergman drew one side view only. In Dimensions he extruded the handle using the "Tall-Round" bevel, while giving the

blade no bevel (the extrusion for the blade was much thinner than the handle). For the screwdriver, he drew half of the side view (revolving it around its profile) and the top rounded cap. The nails were also drawn in half-side view and revolved around their profiles. Bergman drew the blueprint full-front and converted the lines to filled objects using Object: Path: Outline Path. (See Chapter 6 for more on filters.) He drew another separate path with the Pen tool to define the profile view of the rolling blueprint. Although he formed and angled all objects independently in Dimensions, in order to avoid the excess objects that Dimensions generates when computing lighting, Bergman designed most of the lighting effects by using gradients as he assembled the separate objects in Illustrator.

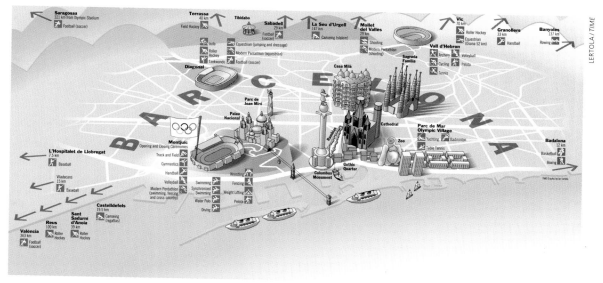

LERTOLA / TIME

Gallery (with Dimensions): Joseph Lertola / *Time*

Joseph Lertola designed this map of the venues at the Barcelona Olympics using Illustrator. He drew an aerial view of only the roads and shoreline, converted the lines to filled objects using Object: Path Outline Path (see Chapter 6 for more on filters), and then brought this aerial view into Dimensions where he angled it back, gave it a small thickness and curved it slightly. Once he achieved this receding perspective, Lertola brought the aerial view back into Illustrator and recombined it with the detailed buildings and assorted icons representing the various events.

MAGLIARI / WORLD WRESTLING FEDERATION

Gallery (with traditional airbrush): Paul Magliari / World Wrestling Federation

Large billboards present unique challenges. Since Illustrator files don't decrease in resolution as they are enlarged, Illustrator could be considered the ideal design environment for the variable size reproduction needs of billboard creation. Paul Magliari began the illustration above by tracing over detailed skyline templates (see Chapter 4 for more on templates) and used custom blends to create subtle changes in color. The World Wrestling Federation then composited the skyline with a traditional airbrush illustration to form the billboard shown above right.

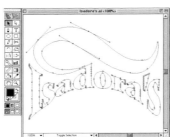

Gallery (with TypeStyler 3): David Stillman

David Stillman needed to create a rich-looking logo for Isadora's Cafe but only had an hour to complete the job. To get the custom shaped look of cast gold, he used the shaping and styling power of TypeStyler 3 combined with the path editing tools in Illustrator. First, he made two text objects in TypeStyler. Using TypeStyler's Shape Library, Stillman selected a double arched shape for Isadora's and a top arched shape for Cafe, so that the two fit together. Next, he dragged the Isadora's object directly from the TypeStyler window into an open Illustrator window This gave him the shaped headline already converted to outlines. He then used Illustrator's path editing tools to draw a simple flourish across the top of the headline and attached it to the top of the letter "d." Stillman then dragged the entire graphic from Illustrator back onto TypeStyler where he finished the logo by choosing Gold from the Style Menu and applying it to both the Isadora's and Cafe objects. The whole process gave just the results he was looking for, yet took less than fifteen minutes to complete, including saving the final Isadora's Cafe logo as a 300 pixel per inch Photoshop document from TypeStyler.

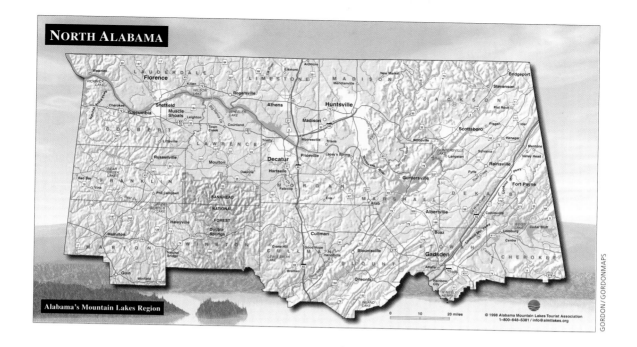

North Alabama

Alabama's Mountain Lakes Region

0   10   20 miles

© 1998 Alabama Mountain Lakes Tourist Association
1–800–648–5381 / info@almtlakes.org

GORDON/GORDONMAPS

Gallery (with Painter, Bryce, MAPublisher, Photoshop and FreeHand): Steven Gordon

For this map of northern Alabama, cartographer Steven Gordon downloaded terrain data from the Internet, processed it in a data reader and imported the resulting PICT image into Painter. He built a color gradation and used the Apply Surface Texture command to create the color relief image. (This process is described in "Building a Terrain Map" in The Painter 5 Wow! Book.*) Gordon searched for an existing photograph to use as a background to "visually convey the sense of mountains and lakes." Since none of the photographs he found contained elements that flowed well around the map, he instead developed the background landscape in Bryce by making an "artificial" terrain and adding surface texture, water and clouds (lower right). Gordon combined the relief and landscape images in Photoshop and then placed this new composite image in Illustrator. Using the MAPublisher suite of filters, he imported map data (roads, rivers, boundaries) into Illustrator, colorized the linework, resized it to fit the relief, and added symbols and type. To register the Photoshop image with the map's Illustrator artwork, he drew a rectangle that matched the image and turned it into cropmarks with the Make Cropmarks command (see Tip on page 147). This enabled him to save the national forest shape (lower left on map) as a separate file, import it into Photoshop and use it as a registered selection for masking and darkening terrain in the forest area. Finally, to prepare the map for this book, Gordon used FreeHand 8's Simplify Xtra to remove unnecessary points from paths, reducing file size from 5.8 to 3.2 MB.)*

Web, Multimedia & Animation

10

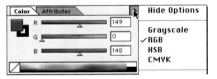

Choosing color modes from the pop-up menu; you can also cycle through color modes by Shift-clicking on the Color Spectrum

Warning: RGB and CMYK

Because Illustrator now allows you to make colors in CMYK and RGB (and HSB) color modes, be cautious: your artwork can now contain objects created in a *combination* of color modes! If you work in print, this could cause all sorts of unpredictable color results. If you're doing print work, *always* work in CMYK (see the "Color in Illustrator" section of *Chapter 1*). Work in RGB exclusively if you're *only* producing for on-screen display. If you intend to use artwork for both print and on-screen, then create the print art first and use Save As to make a copy. You can then change the copy's color mode and export the appropriate file type for your needs.

This chapter focuses on some of the ways you can use Illustrator to prepare artwork for on-screen display. Although everything in this chapter was begun in Illustrator, some of the techniques involve working with Photoshop and rasterization. If you need more help with either, see *Chapter 9: Illustrator & Other Programs.*

The actual assembly of animations and web graphics in this chapter was often produced using a number of other programs, including Macromedia's Director; GoLive's CyberStudio; Adobe's Premier, After Effects and PageMill; Yves Piguet's GIF Builder; Thorsten Lemke's GraphicConverter and Bare Bones Software's BBEdit. Although not all of these are cross-platform, you'll find demos or light versions of some of these programs on the *Wow!* disk. Also check the *Wow!* website for animations and links to related sites (www.peachpit.com/wow.html).

There are a number of other programs, including Photoshop and AfterEffects, that can open "raw" Illustrator files. Artists working with multimedia software, such as Macromedia's Director, can access Illustrator files saved as PICT or BMP. Web designers will find that Illustrator now supports a wealth of file formats that simplify the creation of web artwork.

WORKING IN RGB IN ILLUSTRATOR

Historically, Illustrator art was produced exclusively in CMYK and output to print. Now, Illustrator provides you with the tools to create and output appropriate file types for on-screen images (viewed on a monitor or television), once available only in a raster-based program such as Adobe Photoshop. One of the most important features is the ability to create artwork in RGB. While Illustrator provides a great deal of support for creating on-screen artwork, along with that power comes a few cautions, especially if you're creating artwork for both CMYK and RGB. If you plan to design print *and* on-screen illustrations, please read this chapter thoroughly, starting with the "Warning…" tip on page 202.

To create artwork in RGB, select RGB from the Colors palette pop-up menu (see top of previous page); this sets RGB as the color mode for the next colors you create. You can open an RGB "web-safe" palette of colors (explained later in this section) if you need to create artwork for web use only. You'll find a custom Illustrator Startup file that automatically and exclusively loads this web palette, in the "Custom Prefs" folder on the *Wow!* disk.

A few thoughts on RGB and CMYK color

- **Don't convert the same artwork repeatedly between RGB and CMYK if you intend to print in CMYK.** Converting RGB to CMYK tends to create muddy colors. If you need both CMYK and RGB versions of your artwork, just maintain two versions of your art—one in RGB and one in CMYK.

- **You can work in any color space (mode) if you're doing *screen* resolution graphics.** Remember, though, CMYK files are larger than RGB, and if you're designing for the web, it's particularly important to keep file sizes to a minimum. (Also see "The Web Palette," following.)

- **Create your artwork in CMYK first** if you're going to use it for print, and *then* convert it to RGB. If you create your art in RGB first, you might use "Out of Gamut" colors, which can't print as you see them on the screen (see "Warning…" tip). For *screen*-displayed art, RGB will give you more brilliant colors. For reliable *print* art, work *only* in CMYK. So, watch your color space!

Converting CMYK to RGB

If you already have artwork prepared in CMYK and you need to change color mode for on-screen RGB viewing, make sure you first Save As a copy of your file, then select all (⌘-A) and choose Filter: Colors: Convert CMYK to RGB. Be aware that converting from CMYK to RGB will cause you to lose any association with stored swatches. This means editing swatches will no longer globally update objects filled with those colors.

Rasterizing art for the screen

The process of turning vector art into a bitmap is called *rasterizing*. Anyone creating artwork for the web or for multimedia applications will at some point need to rasterize vector art. There are many ways to rasterize your artwork and many options, including rasterizing at different resolutions, applying Photoshop filters to selected raster images, and either creating a mask or antialiasing your objects—all done while in Illustrator (see pages 178–187 and the remainder of this chapter for more on rasterizing).

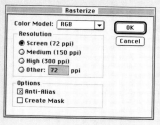

Auto-opening select palettes

You can set the swatch palettes, accessible from Windows: Swatch Libraries, to open automatically when you launch Illustrator. With the selected palette open, choose "Persistent" from that palette's pop-up. Choose it again to reset the palette to close by default.

GIF or JPEG, vector or raster?

Export as GIF89a if your art has large solids and/or is made up of *vector* graphics (such as Illustrator objects). Export as a JPEG if your image includes *raster* images (like photos) with a good balance of colors (or grays), or if your art contains gradients. If your image includes a high-contrast photo or has large areas of solid color, export versions saved in GIF89a *and* in JPEG to see which looks best at the smallest file size.

Adapting to GIF palettes

With GIF format, the goal is to use as few colors as possible while minimizing file size. Use the Adaptive palette option and export your file in different bit depths. Viewing each file in your browser, pick the best-looking one with the lowest bit-depth.
— *Mordy Golding*

The Web Palette

Illustrator includes a noneditable web-safe color palette. Its 216 RGB colors are common to both Mac and Windows platforms and are the most reliable colors for creating web artwork. To access this palette, choose Window: Swatch Libraries: Web or open it directly (see the excerpt from *Coloring Web Graphics.2* on pages 216–217). To create a smaller custom palette from the web-safe palette, simply drag the desired color swatches to the Swatches palette for storage and save the file. (Remember to clear out your palette before you build your custom palette—see "Setting up your palettes" in the *How to use this book* section and pages 216–217.)

Note: *Know your target audience. How they will ultimately view your art should direct how you create your artwork. For example, don't choose a Mac system palette when you export if you are going to a Windows browser. Your art doesn't have to look perfect on every browser, provided you've satisfied the needs of your target audience.*

Welcome JPEGs

An important feature, especially for web designers, is the ability to export files as JPEG (File: Export: JPEG). JPEG (Joint Photographic Experts Group) provides a variable level of compression, but the more compression, the more detail is lost—thus, JPEG is considered "lossy." This is a very useful tool for web designers, who strive to keep their file size as small as possible while keeping quality as high as possible. It's also very helpful to any designer who needs to transfer a layout to a client for approval via the internet (in cases where you might not use a PDF file); smaller files transfer more easily (and sometimes more reliably) and JPEG compression can work very well, often without great sacrifice of detail.

A certain type of JPEG appears all at once in very rough form, then builds up with increasing clarity until the image appears in full. This is called a Progressive JPEG. Web designers already accustomed to Interlaced GIF (Graphics Interchange Format) files can now export the Progressive JPEG counterpart, as well as Baseline and Optimized JPEG, at any resolution. They can also add antialiasing and client or server-side imagemaps, which was not possible in previous versions of Illustrator.

The GIF89a plug-in, and more on JPEGs

This plug-in allows users to open or place GIF files for use on the web. What was once an add-on plug-in is now an Export module. One positive note in exporting both JPEG and GIF89a is that it leaves your original file untouched.

GIF is the most widely used image format on the web. GIF compression works well with vector-based images or files that have large areas of solid color (see the tip, "*GIF or JPEG...*" opposite). GIF files also support transparency and interlacing (JPEGs only support interlacing). To export your artwork as a GIF or JPEG file, choose File: Export and select GIF89a or JPEG from the pop-up on Mac, or from the Save as Type menu on Windows. You'll get a dialog box that lets you select the options you require. Refer to the Tip at right and the *User Guide* for a more complete description of all the options for exporting GIF89a and JPEG, and see pages 212–213.

THE ATTRIBUTES PALETTE & URLS

Illustrator now has a new Attributes Palette that can assign a URL (Uniform Resource Locator) to any object in your artwork. This is another essential tool for web designers—it allows them to create an imagemap, to enable users to link to other web pages by simply clicking on different parts of the image. Illustrator creates a separate text file containing the URL information, which you can then import into an HTML (HyperText Markup Language) editor, such as Adobe PageMill or BareBones Software's BBEdit. To assign a URL to a selection, open the Attributes palette, select an object (Window: Show Attributes), then type in the URL you want to link to in the Attributes palette text field (see pages 212–213 for a technique for applying URLs). Using a web browser, such as Internet

Which palettes are for you?

The GIF89a export module provides many palette options:

- **Exact palette:** Lets you have a minimal number of colors in your image when you don't need to dither (dithering optically mixes pixels, so a few colors can appear as many).

- **System palette:** Creates a palette of either 256 (Mac) or 216 (Windows) colors. The downside of this filter: results may not translate as expected across platforms.

- **Web palette:** Works cross-platform and is most effective when you're using many images and want them to share the same color space. They will display much faster and present a more cohesive look.

- **Adaptive palette:** Can produce varying results. It relies on the web browser to select the most appropriate color palette based on available colors. This may shift the colors in your artwork when it's viewed using different browsers.

- **Custom palette:** Allows you to load a palette you've created in another program.

- **Transparency:** Makes your page/pasteboard color transparent. Choose this option if your artwork has irregular edges—basically, any shape that's not square or rectangular.

Once you've created (or imported and rasterized) the cels of an animation as a stack of Photoshop layers (see pages 208–209), you can use the Layers palette to preview the action before you take the file into an animation system for final preparation. Set the Layers palette's thumbnails to the largest size (choose Palette Options from the palette's pop-up menu) and shorten the palette until only one layer's thumbnail shows. Then press and hold the palette's up or down scrolling arrow to run the movie as a kind of digital flipbook. If your first frame is in the bottom layer of your file and your last frame is in the top layer, scrolling with the up arrow will run the animation forward; using the bottom arrow will run it backward. If the animation runs too fast, control the speed by clicking an arrow rather than pressing and holding, or grab and drag the scroll box at the speed you want.

— *The Photoshop 4 Wow! Book*
(artist Michael Gilmore, CyberFlix)

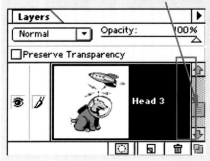

Explorer or Netscape Navigator, you can verify whether your URL is correct by pressing the Launch Browser button on the Attributes palette. Finally, export it using the GIF89a or JPEG Export Module.

A SPECIAL ANNOUNCEMENT FOR WEB DESIGNERS

Many people feel overwhelmed by the enormity of technical details involved in designing for the web. Happily, there's a great wealth of books covering anything from how to write HTML, CGI and Java to designing Cascading Style Sheets and animations. One of the best books about the web is *Designing Web Graphics.2* by Lynda Weinman. An excerpt from one of her newest books, *Coloring Web Graphics.2*, coauthored with Bruce Heavin, concludes this chapter on pages 216–217. For additional resources to help you create web-ready art, check the Adobe website and the *Resources* appendix.

Here's a quick rundown of some of the GIF89a options:

- **Palette options:** See Tip on the preceding page.
- **Transparency:** Areas that objects don't cover become transparent. Choose this for artwork with irregular edges—any outline that's not square or rectangular.
- **Anti-Alias:** Smooths the edges of artwork.
- **Dither:** Blends colors in a limited color palette. Leave it off if for clean-edged vector graphics. Diffusion dither is usually best.
- **Interlacing:** Displays the entire image quickly, in low res, allowing the viewer to see the image as it downloads, until the image is full resolution. A non-interlaced image draws to the screen line by line.
- **Imagemaps & Anchors:** See "Saving and Exporting Artwork" in the *User Guide*, and pages 212–213.

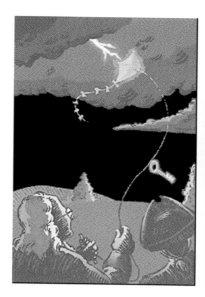 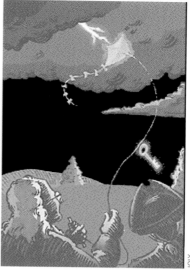

Gallery: Dave Joly

Artist Dave Joly created this two-frame animation for the National Geographic World *website for kids. Joly began this image as a traditional scratchboard illustration, and then scanned the illustration and saved two versions: one scan of the full image, and one cropped detail of the key. Next he then used Adobe Streamline to convert the image to Illustrator objects (see pages 190–192). In Illustrator, Joly placed the converted objects forming the key into position on a layer above (see* Chapter 4 *for layer help). After saving this version as the first frame, he used Rotate on the key object, created some sparkles with the Brush tool, and saved this version as the second frame.*

Gallery: Dave Joly

This moon is one of the Joly's animated holiday greetings characters. Mouth positioning was achieved by adjusting a few anchor points. Whenever possible, Joly uses masks in order to move objects easily— such as the eyeball. Joly made a mask the shape of the outer eye (see Chapter 8 *for more on masking), and was then able to select the blue eyeball and move it into position for additional frames.*

Making Waves

Transforming and Blending for Animation

Advanced Technique

Illustrator with Photoshop

Overview: *Create "key" frames with transformation tools; blend to create steps; transform your steps; bring the steps into Photoshop.*

MONROY

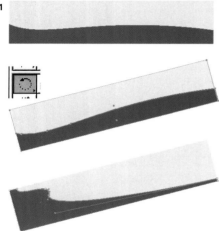

The first key frame; next Rotating a copy; then using the Add-anchor-point and Direct-selection tools to transform the copy into the next frame

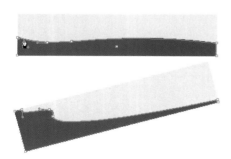

Making certain that the first and last frame have the same number of anchor points in similar alignment for smooth blending (see pages 112-113 for more on preparing objects for smooth blending)

Illustrator's transformation tools, used in combination with the Blend tool, are wonderful animation timesavers. Commissioned by Adobe Systems for a special promotion, Bert Monroy used these techniques to prepare many of the objects within a room for animation.

1 Establishing the "key" frames. To create an animation, you must first establish the "key" character positions. How many key frames you'll need will depend on the character, and how it will be animated. Create a character in a neutral position, and if you'll need help maintaining registration, draw an unstroked, unfilled "bounding rectangle" amply surrounding the character. Select the objects making up the character and the bounding rectangle and Option-drag a copy to the side of the original. On the copy of the character (*not* the bounding box), use the transformation tools and Direct-selection editing to create the next extreme position (for more on transformations, see pages 13–14, and pages 38–41). In Monroy's animation, the characters were: fan, clock second hand, clock pendulum, plant, and the "wave." Monroy first drew the wave in horizontal position using a gray rectangle, and a second object for the blue "liquid." He rotated a copy of these two objects to create the left-tilted position, and then used the Add-anchor-point and Direct-selection tools to adjust the liquid anchor points manually.

2 Using the Blend tool to generate the in-between steps. Also called "tweening," the secret to the illusion of smooth animation is to create the correct number of steps between the key frames. For video animations, smooth illusion of motion is achieved with 24 frames per second (fps) of animation; for film it's 30 fps; for on-screen animation it's simply as many frames as is needed for your animation to run smoothly. To make the steps between your first two key frames, select each pair of like objects and blend between them (for how to blend, see page 103); because you can only apply a blend between two objects, you'll have to apply the blend separately for each pair of like-objects (including your bounding rectangle), making sure that each pair has the same number of anchor points, and that you select the correlating anchor point in each object when blending. For the wave, Monroy first blended in 12 steps from box to box, and then from liquid to liquid. Since the same number of steps was chosen for each transition, the liquid blends were perfectly registered within the box blends.

3 Transforming blends to extend the animation. Rather than continually starting from scratch, sometimes it's easier to rotate, scale, skew or reflect your blends to extend your animation. Monroy selected his box and wave blend objects, and Reflected them vertically as copies (see pages 35 and 172) to create the right-side rocking motion.

4 Pasting into Photoshop. With Illustrator still open, launch Photoshop and create an RGB document larger than your biggest key frame. In Illustrator, copy each character frame and bounding box, and then moving to the Photoshop file, paste "As Pixels" to create a new layer with that step. While that object is still in memory, *also* paste "As Paths" for easy reselection (see pages 184–185). Monroy used his paths to make selections for applying special effects locally—using "Alpha Channels" to create effects such as the darkening on the edges of the liquid, and the bubbles on the surface of the liquid.

2
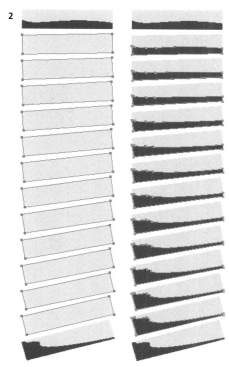

The outer objects after blending (left column), then blending the inner wave (right column)—
Note: Selecting the upper right point on the wave gives the smoothest blend

3

(Reflect dialog box)

4
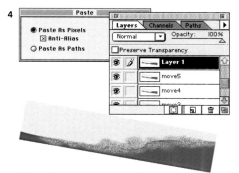

The option to "Paste As Pixels" or "Paste As Paths" when pasting from Illustrator to Photoshop; the frames after pasting into layers; the wave after effects using Alpha Channels

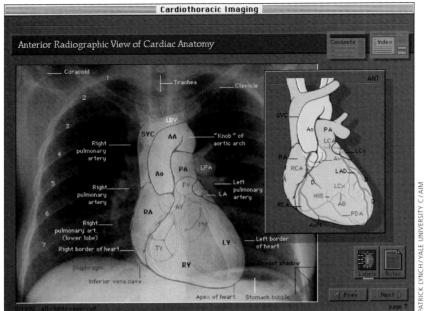

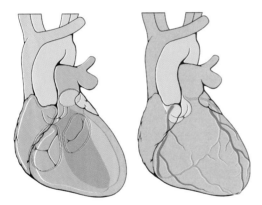

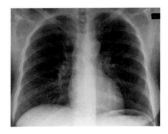

Gallery (with SuperCard / Photoshop): Patrick Lynch / Yale University C / AIM

Patrick Lynch uses Illustrator to create the base illustrations for his interactive CD-ROM development, then uses the Place command from within Photoshop to turn the illustrations into bitmaps. This technique allows him to rasterize fine-lined Illustrator images in much greater detail than would be possible in Photoshop alone (see page 184–186). As a medical illustrator, Lynch uses Illustrator to create detailing in anatomical diagrams, which he can easily adapt by changing colors, adding or subtracting elements, resizing and reshaping, or even overlaying these Illustrator illustrations on top of actual medical films and imaging. For the heart screen above, Lynch rasterized a version of the heart in Photoshop at exactly the correct size and resolution (it had to be scaled slightly horizontally in Illustrator first), and then transparently combined the heart with a scan of an actual chest X-ray. Finally, he brought the individual renderings into SuperCard, where he implemented full interactivity and animation.

 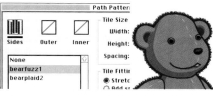 

Gallery: d'JAXN

*Artist d'JAXN doesn't use any high-tech methods when preparing images for multimedia. He began this teddy for the PrintPaks "KidGear" CD by taping his sketch to a Wacom tablet and tracing it with the Pencil tool. After converting those objects into guides (⌘-5, see pages 96–98 and 164), in a new layer (see Chapter 4) he outlined each of the shapes as discrete closed objects with the Pen tool. The floor and the wall were filled with radial gradients (see Chapter 5) and overlaid with objects representing wallpaper pattern and floor texture. d'JAXN then separately rasterized (Object menu) in RGB at 72 ppi, then filtered each with various Gallery Effects filters to create texture. All background objects were then merged using Rasterize again, and then filtered together. Teddy was rasterized, filtered and then masked using a copy of the original paths (see page 140). For detailing, d'JAXN created a plaid pattern for the footpads (which were rotated and scaled individually—see Tip on page 74). To create the teddy's fuzz, he applied a pattern of irregular hatches to copied sections of the outline using Filter: Stylize: Path Pattern to the outline path (see pages 124–128). He then framed all with a solid-filled rectangle before exporting it in GIF "Anti-Alias" format. Using LemkeSoft's GraphicConverter (on the Wow! disk for Mac), he was able to crop it, and converted it to JPEG format at 180 ppi as specified by the client (**Hint:** GraphicConverter can batch Trim too).*

Tabs for the Web

Preparing Navigational Web Maps

Overview: *Design your background tile; Create your tabs; design variations on the tabs for each web page; assign URLs; Export as GIF89a*

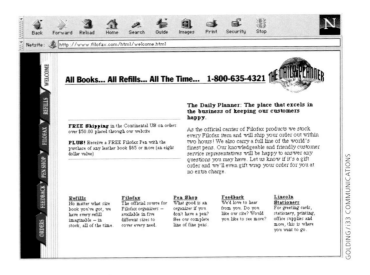

GOLDING/i33 COMMUNICATIONS

1

The background tile (yellow added for contrast)

A detail of the background tile at actual size

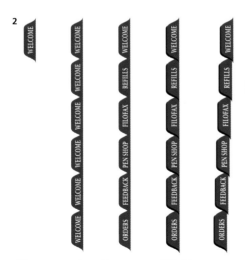

The background tiled to fill the entire screen

2

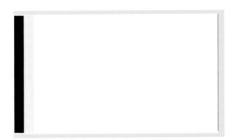

The process of creating one row of tabs

Since Filofax organizers rely heavily on tabs, Mordy Golding of i33 Communications decided to use tabs as a navigation tool for one version of their Filofax product-ordering website. Illustrator's web-related features make it simple to design these web navigation objects.

1 Designing your background tile. To create a website background image, design a tile that will repeat to fill your visible screen. Basically anything that works as a simple pattern tile should work as a web tile (see the *User Guide* for tips on pattern making). To save download time, Golding created the "page edges" in the left part of the screen as part of the background image tile, which is the exact width for their screen design, so it only repeats vertically.

2 Creating your tabs. Design your first tab using the drawing tools (for help with drawing and tracing, see pages 50–51, 80–83), and with the Type tool, label the tab, center-aligned (see *Chapter 7* for help with type). Since his tabs were vertical, Golding rotated his text 90° (specified by double-clicking the Rotate tool). Next, Option-Shift-drag your first tab and label to make a duplicate, and then ⌘-D to repeat the duplication for a total of as many tabs as you have pages in your website. Correct the labels with the Type tool. Golding created six tabs representing the six pages on the website. If you wish, add more detailing to the tabs. Golding added shadow, then staggered the tabs to give the illusion of depth.

3 Creating different versions of the tabs for each web page. To make it easier for viewers to tell which page they are on, create separate versions of your tabs, each highlighting the current page. Golding duplicated his line of tabs six times (one for each web page), then restyled one tab in each group to appear highlighted.

4 Assigning web addresses (URLs) to each tab. When users click on your tabs in the actual website, you want them to be taken to the correct web address, so you'll need to assign web addresses (URLs) to each non-highlighted tab (since highlights indicate your *current* address, these don't need URLs). With your first tab selected, open the Attributes palette, and in the text field labeled "URL," type in the appropriate web address (use the ← and → cursor-keys to scroll), and repeat this for all tabs in this first set. For the next set of tabs, you'll be able to choose the appropriate URL from the pop-up menu to the right of the URL text field.

5 Exporting the files for your web design program. Select, Copy (⌘-C) and Paste (⌘-V) each set of tabs into their own new document. Save each document separately. Next, to save a rasterized version of each file (for placement in your HTML editor) choose File: Export and select "GIF89a" from the format pop-up. Golding set the following GIF89a options: Adaptive Palette (see Tip "Adapting to GIF palettes" on page 204 for Golding's suggested approach to using this option), Interlace (allowing the image to load gradually), Anti-Alias (for smooth, non-jaggy edges), Transparent (to allow the background image to show through where there aren't fills), and since his images had embedded URLs, he chose Imagemap (this created a separate text file that was included in the actual HTML document). 🖱

Creating versions of the tabs for each web page (grey added for contrast)

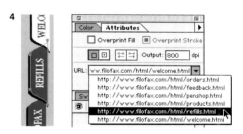

Assigning URLs to each non-highlighted tab

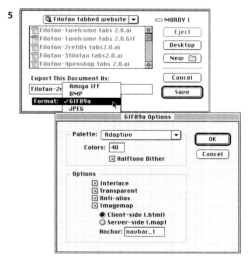

Exporting each set of tabs as GIF89a for use in an HTML editor

Gallery (with Photoshop): Randy Livingston/White Bridge Communications Inc.

Read USA Online Mailorder Bookstore (with virtual bookstores on America Online, CompuServe, and the Web) needed a logo to use in print and online. Randy Livingston designed the logo by moving elements between Photoshop and Illustrator. Beginning in Photoshop, he created the shiny red sphere in RGB using KPT Vector Effects' Glass Lens Bright filter (the sphere will revolve in an animated version). After converting the file to CMYK (for print), he created a circular selection, which he made into a "clipping path" (to mask the ball), saved it in EPS to maintain the mask (see pages 180, 183) and switched to Illustrator where he placed it as a linked file. He added the type, which he then converted into objects (Type: Create Outlines, ⌘-Shift-O). Two rectangles filled with gradients formed the "raised panel" (see Chapter 5 for more on gradients). He then used the Pen tool to create the bevel on the right side of the panel. In the first version that Livingston submitted to the client, he created a recess for the ball by filling a circle behind the ball with a linear gradient. For the final version of the logo, the background was changed to resemble that of an old leather-bound book spine; he scanned a book and leather textures and pieced them together to form the spine in Photoshop where he created a new recess in the spine for the red ball shape. Then using his clipping path to select the ball, he pasted it in place as a part of the Photoshop document. This image was saved as a 300 ppi CMYK TIFF and placed as an embedded image object into the Illustrator page. In Illustrator, he applied Filter: Stylize: Round Corners to a copy of the type shapes and then used Paste In Back to place two copies of the "Read USA" behind (one lighter, one darker) to create the embossed effect. The illustration, directly above left, shows the client-approved RGB version of the logo (rasterized in Photoshop—see Chapter 9) for Read USA's opening screen in America Online's Marketplace.

DRURY WATTENMAKER

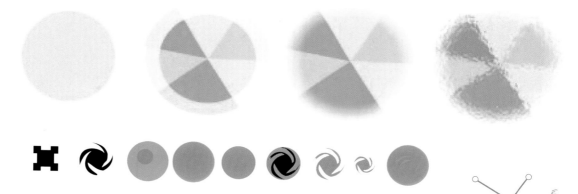

Gallery: Pamela Drury Wattenmaker

In this miniature illustration for an Infoworld *calendar spot Pamela Drury Wattenmaker re-created her initial sketch using the Pen tool to draw separate enclosed objects so they could be filled with different colors. For the background, she created two nested circles with intersecting lines drawn over the circles, and chose Object: Pathfinder: Divide. She recolored and then created blends for each pair of "pie-wedged" objects, selected all the shapes and chose Object: Rasterize at 190 ppi RGB. To this new embedded image object she applied Filter: Gallery Effects, Classic Art 3: GE Glass, with a Distortion of 5, and Smoothness at 3. Although only an RGB image object can be filtered by Photoshop-com-patible filters, Drury Wattenmaker re-applied Object: Rasterize so she could convert the object to CMYK for printing. To create the twirling in the clock face, she created a checkerboard of rectangles, chose Object: Pathfinder: Unite, then experimented on the resulting object with the Twirl tool. Variations of this twirled shape were used as masks over nested sets of blends. The final illustration was saved and sent to the client in EPS format.*

Web-safe Color

Special Supplement by Weinman/Heavin

To load exclusively browser-safe colors into Illustrator, directly open the Web Swatch Library file that ships with the program (and should be in your Illustrator folder). Choose File: Open, then locate the Web file in the "Swatch Libraries" folder (Web.ai for Windows)

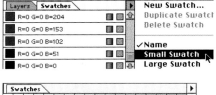

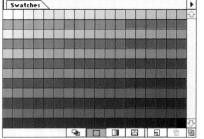

The Web library displayed by name, then shown in an expanded palette viewed by Small Swatch

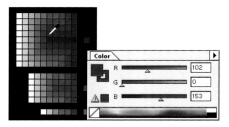

An aesthetically organized GIF format browser-safe palette for color picking, from Lynda Weinman and Bruce Heavin's book and CD-ROM Coloring Web Graphics.2 (see Chapter 3 for help storing colors as Swatches)

This section of *The Illustrator 8 Wow! Book* was written by Lynda Weinman and Bruce Heavin, and was excerpted in part from their book *Coloring Web Graphics.2*. This book and accompanying CD-ROM include invaluable information about screen-based color issues on the web, as well as hundreds of aesthetically organized browser-safe color combinations and palettes for web graphics authoring. Be sure to check out Lynda Weinman's website for more information about web graphics and her book series on this subject: **www.lynda.com/books/**

RGB and web-safe colors

One of the best features of Illustrator for web graphics is its ability to work with RGB color. Like many other computer graphic programs, Illustrator was originally engineered to generate artwork for print projects, and only functioned in CMYK until Illustrator 7. With the popularity of the web, and so many Illustrator customers using this product for web graphics, Illustrator now supports the RGB color space. So, the next question is…how do you use Illustrator with "browser-safe" colors?

Browser-safe colors (also known as "web-safe" colors), for those of you not "in the know," are the 216 colors that will not dither unexpectedly (create unwanted arrangements of colored dots) within web browsers on systems with 8-bit video cards (256 colors). If you think your web audience doesn't have this color limitation, you might be wrong. Since you are a designer and work with graphics, it's likely that you have a high-end system that includes the ability to view graphics in 16-bit or 24-bit color. Most of the rest of the world use their computers for more mundane tasks, such as spreadsheets, word processing and database work. Many web surfers are using Wintel machines in 8-bit mode. If you want to create artwork with colors that will not dither on their machines, you will need to choose web-safe colors.

It would be great if you could load the web-safe colors from Photoshop, but unfortunately, the swatch interface in Illustrator is different, so you can't automatically load

Photoshop palettes into the Illustrator Swatches palette. If you want to make or use custom browser-safe color palettes, the workaround is to create browser-safe artwork in Photoshop and save it as a GIF. You can then Open or Place the GIF inside Illustrator, and use the Eyedropper tool to select any of the browser-safe RGB colors within the image. Once you've picked up a color with the Eyedropper tool, click on the New Swatch icon in the Swatches palette to store that browser-safe color as a swatch. Save the Illustrator document and the new swatch color will be stored permanently with that file. This is a useful technique if you have web artwork you've already made in Photoshop, and you want to create vector artwork that shares the same colors.

CMYK versus RGB color selection

If the values are CMYK, then change them to RGB (choose RGB from the Colors pop-up menu). The color readout will now be from 0–255, instead of in percentages. (To change colors you've already used, see *Chapter 3*.)

The 216 browser-safe colors are constructed from combinations of six red, green, and blue values: 0, 51, 102, 153, 204, 255 ($6^3 = 216$). If you use the Color palette to mix colors yourself, round off each color value to the nearest of these numbers to achieve a browser-safe color.

A few last things to keep in mind:

- You can rasterize your Illustrator images in RGB from within the program; however, the artwork may come out cleaner and crisper if rasterized in Photoshop using Place or Open (see *Chapter 9*).
- Gradients between browser-safe colors *aren't* browser safe.
- If you are using the Eyedropper to pick colors from a GIF file, Illustrator will not let you recolor a stroke. You must transfer the color you've picked into the Illustrator Swatches palette first, using the methods described on this page, and then you can change the stroke color. This seems like a bug, or maybe it's a feature <grin>.

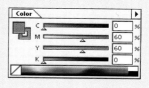

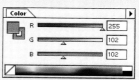

Hint: You can type browser-safe color values into the RGB palette.

Technical Notes

Book Design

Barbara Sudick is the artist behind the *Illustrator Wow!* design and typography. Using Jill Davis's layout of *The Photoshop Wow! Book* as a jumping-off point, she designed the pages in QuarkXPress, using Adobe fonts Frutiger and Minion. Nancy Stahl did the cover illustration; Ivan Torres and Lisa Jackmore allowed us to use their illustrations on the back cover and flap.

Hardware and Software

My primary computer configuration was a PowerMacintosh 8500 180c with 192 MB of RAM, an AppleVision 1710 monitor, APS and Zip drives, SupraFax / Modem, and an APS Archive Python DAT backup using Dantz's Retrospect archiving software. Color proofs were made on a Tektronix Phaser 140 printer. TIFF Export (Vision's Edge) creates thumbnails for the Wow! website.

For software, in addition to Adobe Illustrator I used: Adobe Photoshop, QuarkXPress, QuicKeys (CE Software), Captivate (Mainstay), XPert Tools II (ALAP), Day-to-Day Contacts (Day-to-Day Software) to maintain my database, DropStuff and Stuffit Expander (Aladdin), and Dantz's Retrospect for archiving. I communicated with testers using Claris Emailer, sending pages in Acrobat PDF format.

Pre-press (Color Separations and Proofs)

High Resolution, Inc., based in midcoast Maine, led by Peter Koons and Sandy Soards, produced the color-separated composite film and final color proofs for this book and for its cover. The photos in the book were drum-scanned on an Optronics ColorGetter and imported using Kodak Precision Color Management. Many illustrations were trapped using Island Trapper (Island Graphics Corporation). Screen captures were separated in Photoshop using a GCR with maximum black generation. To track updated placed files and convert spot colors within illustrations, HighRes used PictAttributes (Markware), and Spot (ALAP), respectively. Individual pages were spooled through Helios Ethershare to a Sun Microsystems Sparc Workstation, swapping FPO scans for full resolution images via OPI as served by Kodak Prophecy. Pages were rasterized by Adobe PostScript RIPs and output using Panther imagesetting technology employing ESCOR screening from Prepress Solutions. Color proofs of each page were made using the Kodak Contract proofing system.

How to contact the author...

Sharon Steuer, c/o Peachpit Press, 1249 Eighth Street, Berkeley, CA 94710, or via Internet e-mail: *wowartist@bigfoot.com*, or via the Web: *http://www.peachpit.com/meetus/authors/sharon.steuer.html*

Acknowledgments

My most heartfelt gratitude goes to the more than 100 artists and Illustrator experts who generously allowed me to include their work and divulge their techniques.

Thanks also must go to those folks at Adobe who went out of their way to help me chase down answers to zillions of questions. Special thanks to Jill Nakashima, Teri Pettit, Ian Giblin, Heather Kellum, Susan Gile, Christie Evans, Dave Burkett, Paul Asente and Eric Hess.

This revision required a major team effort, and would not have happened if not for an amazing group of people. Robin Olson was trooper enough to come back for more, and co-authored the text-heavy portions of the Illustrator 8 revisions; Sandy Alves came in as pinch-hitter and tech edited those sections. Diane Hinze Kanzler collected a massive amount of material and organized it for the *Wow!* disk. Peg Maskell Korn did everything I asked of her (and then some) with unsurpassed loyalty and dedication. Elizabeth Rogalin edited cheerfully at all hours. Victor Gavenda mastered the CD. Mordy Golding was the Illustrator 6 revisions co-author, and contributed to the web portions of the book. Richard Cordera edited the information on color-correction. Gary Pfitzer edited the first two editions, and prepared the stylesheet that we all lived by; Elizabeth Rogalin, Karen Unger and Gail Nelson all copyedited sections of this edition. Barbara Sudick expertly designed the layout of this book. As always, thanks also goes to the stellar team of testers and consultants especially Adam Z Lein and Lisa Jackmore. Sandee Cohen's role still defies categorization, though it's certain that there wouldn't have been either a 7 or an 8 *Wow!* book without her.

Thanks to: A.J. Rogers, with Jennifer Jones and Sally Lampe (Tektronix), Aladdin Software and Dantz. Thank you Kathy Arendt of Agfa for proofing the PS3 images. Thanks also to the Adobe Type department, ALAP, Aridi, Avenza, BareBones, BeInfinite, Cartesia, CE Software, Chronchart, Day-to-Day Software, Design Tools Monthly, Dynamic Graphics, Extensis, Hot Door, Ilom, Image Club Graphics, Macromedia, MetaCreations, Photoshpere, Ultimate Symbol, Vertigo Technology and Zaxworks for their special *Wow!* offers.

High Resolution Inc. (Peter Koons, Sandy Soards, Shawna Elwell, Chris Cunningham and John Higgins), a phenomenal prepress facility in midcoast Maine, expertly produced *all* the PostScript color separations for this book. And just for the record, there is no way that a computer separation option would come close to getting the separations that High Resolution got. High Resolution wishes to thank: Island Graphics (Jeff Guns and Mark Alan Cirino), and PrePRESS Solutions (Bob Trenkamp and Irene Schrader).

Thank you Lynda Weinman and Bruce Heavin for adapting the Illustrator section of *Coloring Web Graphics.2*, and for allowing us to include this material.

And of course, thanks to Linnea Dayton (the *Wow!* series editor) and to everyone at Peachpit (especially Corbin Collins, Kate Reber, Cary Norsworthy, Paula Baker, Nancy Ruenzel and Victor Gavenda) for helping pull this book together. And thanks Michael Wyatt for cheering me up!

Artists

Note: *E-mail and Web addresses will be posted on the* Wow! *website:* **www.peachpit.com/wow.html**

Acme Design Company
see also Michael Kline
215 North Saint Francis #4
Witchita, KS 67201
316-267-2263
84–85, **123**, **188** Kline

Erik Adigard, *see* M.A.D.

Adobe Systems, Inc.
345 Park Avenue
San Jose, CA 95110-2704
408-536-6000
see also Laurie Szujewska
141, **145** Laurie Szujewska
140 Min Wang
139, **142–144** James Young

Agnew Moyer Smith, Inc.
503 Martindale Street
Pittsburgh, PA 15212
412-322-6333
56–57, *Wow!* **disk**Kurt Hess
58 Rick Henkel & Kurt Hess
60–61, **100**,*Wow!* **disk**
Rick Henkel

Bjørn Akselsen, *see* Ice House Press

Jen Alspach
jen@bezier.com
70

Jeff Barney
Barney McKay Design
425 E. 1070 S.
Orenn, UT 84058
801-225-9949
67, **94**

Kevin Barrack
3908 Pasadena Drive
San Mateo, CA 94403
415-341-0115
128

Rick Barry
DeskTop Design Studio
1631 West 12th Street
Brooklyn, NY 11223
718-232-2484
82–83, **116**

Kenneth Batelman
407 Buckhorn Drive
Belvidere, NJ 07823
908-475-8124
160

Eliot Bergman
362 West 20th Street
New York, NY 10011
888-COOLPIX
198

BlackDog
Mark Fox
239 Marin Street
San Rafael, CA 94901
415-258-9663
52, **53**

Christopher Burke
4408 Chad Court
Ann Arbor, MI 48103-9478
313-996-1316
64, **92–93**, *Wow!* **disk**

California State Automobile
Association
Cartographic Department
150 Van Ness Ave.
San Francisco, CA 94102
415-565-2468
54–55, **90–91**

Ron Chan
24 Nelson Ave.
Mill Valley, CA 94941
415-389-6549
124–125, **152**

K. Daniel Clark
3218 Steiner Street
San Francisco, CA 94123
415-922-7761
175, *Wow!* **disk**

Sandee Cohen
33 Fifth Avenue, #10B
New York, NY 10003
212-677-7763
12, **71**, **128**, *Wow!* **disk**

Richard Cordero
Digital Graphics Advantage
5460 E. La Palma Avenue
Anaheim, CA 92807
714-701-7160

Dan Cosgrove
203 North Wabash Ave.
Suite 1102
Chicago, IL 60611
312-527-0375
193

Scott Crouse
59 Coleman Road
Winter Haven, FL 33880
941-294-8146
173, *Wow!* **disk**

Michael D'Abrosca, *see* California
State Automobile Association

d'JAXN
Portland, OR 97229-7609
503-526-9573
211

Shayne Davidson
1301 Granger Ave.
Ann Arbor, MI 48104
734-994-6223
192

Rob Day & Virginia Evans
10 State Street, Suite 214
Newburyport, MA 01950
508-465-1386
146–147

Pamela Drury Wattenmaker
17 South Plomar Drive
Redwood City, CA 94062
415-368-7878
188, **215**, *Wow!* **disk**

Linda Eckstein
201 W. 70th St. #6G
New York, NY 10023
212-721-0821
107

Eve Elberg
60 Plaza Street East, Suite 6E
Brooklyn, NY 11238
718-398-0950
120, *Wow!* **disk**

Virginia Evans, *see* Day & Evans

Gary Ferster
756 Marlin Ave., Suite 4
Foster City, CA 94404
415-577-9696
105, **121**

Resources

Note: *E-mail and Web addresses will be posted on the* Wow! *website:* **www.peachpit.com/wow.html**

Adobe Systems, Inc.
345 Park Avenue
San Jose, CA 95110-2704
408-536-6000
www.adobe.com

AGFA
200 Ballardvale Street
MS 200-4-9-B
Willmington, MA 01887
508-658-5600 x5170

Aladdin Systems, Inc.
Stuffit
165 Westridge Drive
Watsonville, CA 95076-4159
408-761-6200

ALAP
XPert Tools
see XChange

Allegiant Technologies
SuperCard
9740 Scranton Road/Suite 300
San Diego, CA 92121
619-587-0500x106

Apple Computer
800-767-2775

APS Technologies
Hardware
6131 Deramus/P.O. Box 4987
Kansas City, MO 64120-0087
800-874-1427

Aridi Computer Graphics
Digital Art
P.O. Box 797702
Dallas, TX 75379
214-404-9171
972-404-9171

Auto F/X
Main Street
Alton, NH 03809
603-875-4400

Avenza
MAPublisher
3385 Harvester Rd, Suite 205
Burlington, Ontario
L7N 3N2 Canada
905-639-3330

Bare Bones Software, Inc.
BBEdit
P.O. Box 1048
Bedford, MA 01730
781-778-3100

Cartesia Software
MapArt Designer
5 South Main Street/P.O. Box 757
Lambertville, NJ 08530
800-334-4291

CE Software, Inc.
QuicKeys
1801 Industrial Circle
P.O. Box 65580
West Des Moines, IA 50265
515-221-1801

Chronchart
4640 Edgewood Ave.
Oakland, CA 94602
510-482-3576

Claris Corp.
Emailer
Santa Clara CA
800-544-8554/408-987-7000

Dantz
Retrospect
4 Orinda Way/Bldg C
Orinda, CA 94563
510-253-3000

Day-to-Day Software
Contacts
244 Westchester Avenue/Suite 310
White Plains, NY 10604
800-329-8632
914-686-1018

Dynamic Graphics Inc.
Clip art, etc.
6000 N. Forest Pk. Drive
Peoria, IL 61614
800-255-8800

Extensis Corporation
Portfolio/ Vector Tools
1800 SW 1st, Suite 500
Portland, OR 97201
800-796-9798/503-274-2020

GifBuilder
Yves Piguet
Av. de la Chabliere 35
Lausanne, CH-1004
piguet@ai.epfl.ch

Graffix Plug-ins
Rick Johnson
(shareware & freeware)
2216 Allen Lane
Waukesha, WI 53186

High Resolution, Inc.
87 Elm Street
Camden, ME 04843-1941
207-236-3777

hot door
CADtools/ Transparency
101 W. McKnight Way, Suite B
Grass Valley, CA 95949
530-274-0626

Illom Development AB
LogoCorrector, Toolbox I
Box 838, Strandgatan 21
Ornskoldsvik, Sweden
S-891 18
+46-660-786-57
info@illom.se

Image Club Graphics
729 24 Ave SE
Galgary, AB T2G5K8

IRIS Graphics, Inc.
Six Crosby Drive
Bedford, MA 01730
617-275-8777

Island Graphics Corp.
IslandTrapper
4000 Civic Center Drive
San Rafael, CA 94903
415-491-1000

LemkeSoft *GraphicConverter*
Erics-Heckel-Ring 8a
31228 Peine, Germany
+495171 72200

Letraset
40 Eisenhower Drive
Paramus, NJ 07653
800-343-8973 x7210

Macromedia
FreeHand, Director, Flash 2
600 Townsend Street
San Francisco, CA 94103
800-989-3762

Publications

Mainstay
Capture
591-A Constitution Ave.
Camarillo, CA 93012
805-484-9400

MetaCreations Corporation
KPT, Painter, RayDream Designer
6303 Carpinteria Ave
Carpinteria, CA 93013
800-846-0111

Microsoft Corp.
Excel, Windows
One Microsoft Way
Redmond, WA 98052
206-882-8080

Pantone, Inc.
590 Commerce Blvd.
Carlstadt, NJ 07072
201-935-5500

PhotoSphere Images Ltd.
Preview Pac
380 West First Avenue, Suite 310
Vancouver, BC V5Y 3T7
800-665-1496

PrePRESS Solutions
Panther
11 Mount Pleasant Avenue
East Hanover, NJ 07936
800-443-6600

Strata, Inc.
StudioPro
2 West St.George Blvd./Suite 2100
St. George, UT 84770
800-787-2823/801-628-9756

Strider Software
Typestyler 3
1605 7th Street
Menominee, MI 49858
906-863-7798

Tektronix Inc
Graphics Printing & Imaging
MS 63-355
P.O. Box 1000
Wilsonville, OR
97070-9980

TruMatch, Inc.
331 Madison Ave.
New York, NY 10017
212-351-2360

Ultimate Symbol
Design Elements
31 Wildertness Drive
Stony Point, NY 10980
914-942-0003

Vertigo Technology
3D Dizzy, 3D Words, 3D HotText
1255 Pender Street
Vancouver, BC V6H3Y8
604-684-2113

Vision's Edge
TIFF Export
3491-11 Thomasville Rd./Ste 177
Tallahassee, FL 32308
800-983-6337
904-386-4573

WACOM
ArtZ Tablet
115 Century Road
Paramus, NJ 07652
800-922-6613

XChange
XTensions for QuarkXPress
800-788-7557

Zaxwerks Inc.
3D Invigorator
5724 Camellia Av.
Temple City, CA 97180
626-309-9102

Design Tools Monthly
400 Kiowa, Suite 100
Boulder, CO 80303-3633
303-543-8400

John Wiley & Sons
26 Berkshire Road
Waltham, MA 02154
Professional Photoshop 5
by Dan Margulis

Hayden Books
Indianapolis IN 46290
317-581-3833
Interactivity By Design: Creating and Communicating with New Media
by Ray Kristof and Amy Satran
teach yourself Illustrator in 24 hours by Mordy Golding
Web Designers Guide to Color
by Mordy Golding and Dave White

New Riders Publishing
Indianapolis IN
Designing Web Graphics.2
Color Web Graphics.2
by Lynda Weinman and Bruce Heavin

Peachpit Press
Berkeley, CA
800-283-9444 / 510-548-4393
Illustrator Illuminated, 2nd ed.
  by Clay Andres
The Painter 5 Wow! Book
  by Cher Threinen-Pendarvis
The Photoshop 4 Wow! Book
  by Linnea Dayton & Jack Davis
The Web Design Wow! Book
  by Jack Davis & Susan Merritt

Step-by-Step Publications
Peoria, IL
800-255-8800 / 309-688-8866
Step-by-Step Electronic Design

Yale University Press
New Haven, CT
203-432-0948
Manual of Ornithology
  by Patrick Lynch & Noble Proctor
The Shape of Time
  by George Kubler

General Index

H

halo effect 70, 165
Hand tool 42
handles *see also* anchor points; Bézier
    curves; direction lines
Hard Pathfinder filter 121, 129
hardware requirements 1
Hart, Steve 102–103
Hastings, Pattie Belle 148
Hatch patterns *see* Ink Pen
Hatches, 117–118, 126–127,
    Wow! disk
Heavin, Bruce 216–217
Help menu 3
Henkel, Rick 58, 60–61, 100
Hess, Eric xvii, 15
Hess, Kurt 56, 58, *Wow!* disk
hidden
    layers 78
    objects 79
Hide (Object menu) 79
Hide Edges (View menu) 18, 54
Hide Page Tiling (View menu) 16, 19
Hidy, Lance 187
highlighting objects 21
highlights *see* lighting effects
hinged curve 6
    defined, *see* Glossary on pull-out
        card
horse illustration 70
How to use this book v
Hue Shift, for colorization 126

I

Ice House Press & Design 148
illustrations *see* images; techniques
Illustrator program
    see also techniques;
            troubleshooting
    Basics (Chapters 1 and 2) 1–46
    Blends (Chapter 5) 99–116
    Colors (Chapter 3) 47–75
    fills (Chapter 3) 47–75
    Paths (Chapter 6) 117–132
    Gradients (Chapter 5) 99–116
    layers (Chapter 4) 76–98
    layout (Chapter 7) 133–150
    lines (Chapter 3) 47–75
    masks & advanced techniques
        (Chapter 8) 151–177
    other programs and (Chapter 9)
        180–201

Web Multimedia (Chapter 10)
    202–215
performance
    see also themes
    controlling file size 25, 26
    deleting layers 88
    gradients vs. blends and masks
        158
    memory 76, 153
    modem use 193
    printing 74
    speed 90
power-key exercises 44–46
program interactions 180
special effects 151–173
templates (Chapter 4) 76–98
training recommendations 4
type (Chapter 7) 133–150
Zen of (Chapter 2) 28–46
Image Formats 23
imagemap 206, 212–213
image objects 119
picking up color from 48
images
    see also EPS; exporting; graphics;
            illustrations; importing;
            PICT images; placing;
            templates; tracing
    bitmapped 180, 181
    continuous-tone, tracing over 82
    crisp, techniques for importing
        80, 82
    embedding 181
    Illustrator, exporting to other
        programs 180–201
    on screen 4
    page, reducing 81
    painterly
        Brush tool 68, 70, 71
        creating 68–71, 171, 174
    placing bitmapped 81
    scaling to an exact size 13
    specifications, documentation
        information 118
    tracing 86
importing
    see also Chapter 9; copying; EPS;
            exporting; formats;
            opening; PICT; placed
            images; templates; tracing;
            embedding; linking;
            rasterizing
    crisp images 80, 82
    graphs *see* pdf on *Wow!* disk

Illustrator images into Photoshop
    186
paths into other programs 180
paths, into Painter as friskets
    gallery: 180, 194
text 142
Info palette
    viewing numeric data with 30
    set measurements 185
Ink Pen filter *see* Pen and Ink
ink pen simulation 68–69, 70, 71
    see also Bézier curves; line caps;
            tools
Inset Path *see* Offset Path
Interlacing 205, 213 *see also* GIF89a
interrupting Preview mode 20
Intersect, Pathfinder filter 120, 125,
    169
Invert Colors (Colors) filter 128, 132
irregularity
    blends, naturalistic effects 107
IslandTrapper program 23
Isadora's Cafe, illustration 200
isometric formulas 56, 57
    views 59
    see also perspective

J

Jackmore, Lisa xviii, xix, 70, *Wow!*
    disk
Jackson, Lance 190
Jared Schneidman Design 104, 164
Javier Romero Design Group 138,
    149, 150
Joined Objects *see* Join, Compounds
joining 9
    see also average; copying; creating;
            deleting; editing; miters;
            transforming
    exercises 31, 34, 35
    Join (Object menu) 9
    miters and bevels 49
    objects 52
Joining & Averaging 9
Joly, Dave 108, 207, *Wow!* disk
JPEG, JPG image, format 24
    importing 181, 204
    exporting 204–205
    gallery 211
justification 133

T

Tab Ruler 135
tabs
  setting up for Area Type 135
Tate, Clarke W. 98, 168–171
Taylor-Palmer, Dorothea 95
Tear-off tools 3
techniques
  actions, *see* Actions; antialiasing;
    applying; assembling;
    contouring; cropping;
    customizing; digitizing;
    drawing; filling; grouping;
    importing; joining;
    layering; lengthening;
    locking; organizing;
    overprinting; posterizing;
    printing; program
    interactions; proofing;
    rasterizing; reducing;
    rendering; reordering;
    resizing; rotating; saving;
    scaling; scanning;
    selecting; sketching;
    tracing; transformations;
    trapping; troubleshooting;
    unlocking
  effects, *see* brush strokes; collages;
    lighting effects; painterly
    images; perspective;
    repeating patterns;
    resolution; special effects
templates 80–83
Template layer xvii, 72
templates xvii, 76–98, 124
  see also techniques
  color images 80, 86
  digitizing logos with 80
  gallery: 52, 187
  layer, 72
  placing artwork 87
  preparing 80–83, 86–88
  reduction of 78, 81
  swatch styling 55
  techniques with 68, 80–83,
    86–88, 89, 98, 124–125
  tracing 80–83, 68, 98
text
  see also type
  filters 136–137
  objects 136
  pick up with Eyedropper 117
texture, creating 126
textures *see* Ink Pen; Path Patterns;
  patterns

Thomas•Bradley Illustration & Design
  112–113, 122, 162–163
TIFF (TIF) images 24
  see also file(s), formats
  bitmapped 182
  coloring 1-bit 80
  supported file formats 180
  see also formats
  template 80–83, 97
  tracing 88
tiles
  retrieve 72
  Transform pattern tiles 74
Time magazine 102, 156
Tinkel, Kathleen 138
tints
  filling objects with 51
  of colors 63
  with Pathfinder Soft/Hard filters
    121
  specifying percentages 63
  tint slider 51
toggles
  see also Glossary on pull-out card;
    tools
Toolbox *see* individual tool names
Tool Tips xv
tools
  see also elements; filters; menus;
    palettes; techniques; also
    under individual tool
    names
  basic, exercises in using 41
tools: *see* individual tools
  Add-anchor-point 6
  Area-Type 133, 134
  Convert-direction point 6
  Direct-selection; Ellipse (Oval);
    Group selection; Knife;
    Paintbrush 68–69; Pen; Polygon;
    Reshape; Rectangle; Rotate;
    Selection; Spiral 117; Twirl 14;
    Type tools 133–135;
    Zoom 17
Torres, Ivan xx, 129, 130–132
Toyo
  CMYK process color models 65
tracing
  see also layers; templates
  scanned art 68
  Streamline use for 181
  as technique for coloring line
    drawings 85, 95
  template 80–83, 86
  true horizontals and verticals 98
tracking 137, 146

training, online help 3
Training folder *Wow!* disk
Transform Again 13
Transform Each 12
Transform palette 14
Transformation tools 13
Transformations 12
  see also copying; creating;
    deleting; editing; moving;
    reflecting; reshape;
    rotating; scaling; skewing;
    twirl; Transform palette
  combining 64, 162, 172
  gradients into masked blends 159
  patterns 74
  perspective lines into guides 97
  reflecting 41, 172
  reshape tool 14
  rotating 117
    lesson 38–39
  scaling
    for placement in other
      programs 83, 182, 185
    lesson 38–39, 41
    line weights 182
    patterns 74
    Scale-line-weight enabling
      106, 182
    smooth blend use 113
  stretching 56
  tools for 117
  views 56
transparencies
  creating shadows 51
  cropping as technique for 125
  cut-away 175
  with filters 51, 122, 124–125
  glowing 165
  GIF options 205
  with value 51
  Web 204, 213
  X-ray 210
transparency 207
transparent whites
  saving EPS images with 85, 95,
    187
trapping manually 55
tree trunks, creating
  with Art brush 127
trees, creating 171
Transform Each (Object menu) 117
Trap, Pathfinder filter 64
trapping 55, gallery 64
  see also printing; techniques
Trim marks 147, 196

W

WACOM
ArtZ tablet use 68, 70, 71, 75,
Wang, Min 138–140
warnings *see* troubleshooting
Watch Your Cursor 4
water effects 127
web exporting 202, 204–206, 212
Web palette 23, 24, 203, 204, 206
Web Ready 204
Web Safe Colors 23, 204, 216
Web Swatch Library 216
weaving
see also techniques
elements, in repeating patterns 73
woof/warp 197
Weimer, Alan 176, 177, *Wow!* disk
Weinman, Lynda 216–217
What's new in Illustrator 8? xv
Whyte, Hugh 66, 111, 120
widening
see also transforming
objects, in a constrained manner
57
Window Controls 18
Window menu
New Window 17
Swatch Libraries 47, 48
Show or Hide 17–18
Attributes 206
Gradient 100, 102
Info 30, 56
Layers 152
Plug-in Tools *see* under tool
name
Toolbox, *see* individual tool
names
windows
finding lost 17–18
Windows commands *see* Chapter 1
and the Finger Dance
Summary on pull-out card
World Wide Web
creating art for, with Illustrator
Chapter 10
Peachpit's address 2
Illustrator *Wow!* Book address iv
Sharon Steuer's address 218
Working Smart 15
working environment
recommendations 30
Working with Palettes 10
Working with PostScript Objects 3
Wow! disk *back pocket of this book*

X Y Z

X-ray transparencies 210
Yale University 50–51, 143, 210
Yocum, Lester 174
Yoga figure 68
Young, James 139, 142–144
Zen of Illustrator 28–46
Lessons on the *Wow!* disk
scaling exercises 35
zero point (origin) 20
Zig Zag filter 118
Zoom tool 17, 19
Zooming In & Out 17

Windows Finger Dance Summary *from "The Zen of Illustrator"*

Object Creation — *Hold down keys until AFTER mouse button is released.*

| ⇧ Shift | Constrains objects horizontally, vertically or proportionally. |

| Alt | Objects will be drawn from centers. |

| Alt click | Opens dialog boxes with transformation tools. |

| [ ] | Spacebar turns into the grabber Hand. |

| Ctrl [ ] | Turns cursor into the Zoom-in tool. Click or marquee around an area to Zoom in. |

| Ctrl Alt [ ] | Turns cursor into the Zoom-out tool. Click to Zoom out. |

| Caps lock | Turns your cursor into a cross-hair. |

Object Selection — *Watch your cursor to see that you've pressed the right keys.*

| Ctrl | The current tool becomes the last chosen Selection tool. |

| Ctrl Alt | Current tool becomes Group-selection to select entire object. Click again to select next level of grouping. To move selection release Alt key, then Grab. |

| Ctrl Tab | Toggles whether Direct-selection or regular Selection tool is accessed by the Ctrl key. |

| ⇧ Shift click | Toggles whether an object, path or point is selected or deselected. |

| ⇧ Shift click ▷ | With Direct-selection tool, click on or marquee around an object, path or point to toggle selection/deselection. **Note:** *Clicking inside a filled object may select the entire object.* |

| ⇧ Shift click ▶ ▶₊ | Clicking on, or marqueeing over objects with Selection or Group-selection, toggles selection/deselection (Group-selection chooses objects within a group). |

Object Transformation — *Hold down keys until AFTER mouse button is released.*

| ⇧ Shift | Constrains transformation proportionally, vertically and horizontally. |

| Alt | Leaves the original object and transforms a copy. |

| Ctrl Z | Undo. Use Shift-Ctrl-Z for Redo (*see page 17 for more on Undo/Redo*) |

To move or transform a selection predictably from within dialog boxes, use this diagram to determine if you need a positive or negative number and which angle is required. (*Diagram from Kurt Hess/Agnew Moyer Smith*)

Windows Wow! Glossary of Terms

⌘
Option / Opt

Use **Ctrl** in place of this symbol.
Use **Alt** in place of this key. This key can be used to modify many of the tools.

← ↑ → ↓

The keyboard Cursor-keys: Left, Up, Right, Down.

Toggle

Menu selection acts as a switch: choosing once turns on, again turns it off.

Marquee

With any Selection tool, click-drag from your page over object(s) to select.

Hinged curve

A Bézier curve that meets a line or another curve at a point.

Direct-selection

Group-selection

Selection

Direct-selection tool selects points and paths.
Group-selection tool. The first click always selects the entire object, subsequent clicks select "next group-up" in the grouping order.
Selection tool (selects the biggest grouping which includes that object— if an object is ungrouped, then only that object is selected).
Note: *See page 9 and Chapters 1 & 2 for help with selection tools.*

Select object (s)

Click on or marquee with Group-selection tool to select entire object.
Click on or marquee with the regular Selection tool to select grouped objects.

Deselect object (s)

To Deselect *one* object, Shift-click (or Shift-marquee) with Group-selection tool.
To Deselect *all* selected objects, with any selection tool, click outside of all objects (but within your document), or press Shift-Ctrl-A.

Select a path

Click on a path with the Direct-selection tool to select it.
Note: *If objects are selected, Deselect first, then click with Direct-selection tool.*

Select anchor points

Click on path with Direct-selection tool to see anchor points. Then, Direct-select marquee around the points you want selected. Or, with Direct-selection tool, Shift-click on points you want selected.
Note: *Clicking on a selected point with Shift key down deselects that point.*

Grab an object or point

After selecting objects or points, use Direct-selection tool to click and hold down mouse button and drag to transform entire selection.
Note: *If you click by mistake (instead of click-and-hold), Undo and try again.*

Delete an object

Group-select the object and press the Delete (or Backspace) key.
To delete grouped objects, use the Selection tool, then Delete.

Delete a path

Direct-select a path and press the Delete (or Backspace) key. If you delete an anchor point, both paths attached to that anchor point will be deleted.
Note: *After deleting part of an object the entire remaining object will become selected; therefore, deleting twice will always delete the entire object!*

Copy or Cut a path

Click on a path with Direct-selection tool, then Copy (Ctrl-C) or Cut (Ctrl-X).
Note: *See the Finger Dance Summary for more ways to copy paths.*

Copy or Cut an object

Click on an object with Group-selection tool, then Copy (Ctrl-C) or Cut (Ctrl-X). For grouped objects, Click on one of the objects with the Selection tool, then Copy (Ctrl-C) or Cut (Ctrl-X).
Note: *See page 19 for more ways to copy objects.*